African American Culture and Heritage in Higher Education Research and Practice

African American Culture and Heritage in Higher Education Research and Practice

Edited by
Kassie Freeman

PRAEGER

Westport, Connecticut
London

Library of Congress Cataloging-in-Publication Data

African American culture and heritage in higher education research and
practice / edited by Kassie Freeman.
    p.   cm.
    Includes bibliographical references and index.
    ISBN 0–275–95844–2 (alk. paper)
    1. Afro-Americans—Education (Higher)—Social aspects. 2. Afro-
Americans—Education (Higher)—Social aspects—Research.
3. Educational anthropology—United States. 4. Educational
anthropology—United States—Research. 5. Higher education and
state—United States. 6. Higher education and state—United States—
Research. I. Freeman, Kassie.
LC2781.A38 1998
378′.00896′073—dc21   98–11130

British Library Cataloguing in Publication Data is available.

Library of Congress Catalog Card Number: 98–11130
ISBN: 0–275–95844–2

First published in 1998

Praeger Publishers, 88 Post Road West, Westport, CT 06881
An imprint of Greenwood Publishing Group, Inc.

Printed in the United States of America

The paper used in this book complies with the
Permanent Paper Standard issued by the National
Information Standards Organization (Z39.48–1984).

10 9 8 7 6 5 4 3 2 1

Copyright Acknowledgment

The author and publisher gratefully acknowledge permission for use of the following material:

Figure 6.1 from the article "Learning in Institutions of Higher Education" by Dr. Lemuel W. Watson,
Illinois State University, published in *Planning & Changing*, Fall/Winter 1996, Volume 27, No. 3/4.

In memory of my great-grandfather, Matthew Freeman;
my grandparents, Estella and Emmitt Wilson
and Missouri and Felix J. Freeman;
and to my parents, Joseph and Lauretta Freeman
for their undying belief in the power of education
and for their passing on to me the importance of the
power of the belief in a Supreme Being

Contents

Tables and Figures   xi

Acknowledgments   xiii

Introduction   *Kassie Freeman*   1

Overview: African American Participation in Higher Education   7
Reginald Wilson

Part I   Considering African American Culture in Higher
Education Research   13

Chapter 1   Black to Africa: Some Research Paradigms Reflecting
a Black World View   15
Raymond A. Winbush

Chapter 2   From Africa to America: The Relationship between
Culture and Experience   23
Mia D. Alexander-Snow

Chapter 3   African American Students and Self-Concept
Development: Integrating Cultural Influences into
Research and Practice   33
Tamela M. Heath

Chapter 4   Historical Origins of Change: Implications for African
Americans in Higher Education   43
Carolyn J. Thompson

Part II   Examining African American Higher Education Research
               Issues and Paradigms   57

Chapter 5   And Who Shall Control Their Minds?: Race
               Consciousness and Collective Commitments among
               African American Students   59
               Walter R. Allen

Chapter 6   The College Experience: A Conceptual Framework to
               Consider for Enhancing Students' Educational Gains   75
               Lemuel W. Watson

Chapter 7   "Am I Black Enuf fo Ya?" Black Student Diversity:
               Issues of Identity and Community   93
               Lori S. White

Chapter 8   Self-Segregation: An Oxymoron in Black and White   121
               Sybril M. Bennett

Chapter 9   Doing What Comes Unnaturally: Increasing African
               American Faculty Presence in Predominantly
               White Colleges and Universities   133
               William B. Harvey

Chapter 10   Cultural Capital and the Role of Historically
               Black Colleges and Universities in Educational
               Reproduction   143
               James Earl Davis

Part III   Addressing Higher Education Policy and Practice
               as They Relate to African American Culture   155

Chapter 11   Policy, Practice, and Performance: Strategies to
               Foster the Meaningful Involvement of African
               Americans in Higher Education Decision-Making
               Processes   157
               Wynetta Y. Lee

Chapter 12   The Relationship between Evaluation Effort and
               Institutional Culture: Mixing Oil and Water?   173
               Bruce Anthony Jones

Chapter 13   African Americans and College Choice: Cultural
               Considerations and Policy Implications   181
               Kassie Freeman

Chapter 14   Higher Education and Teacher Preparation: Meeting
               the Challenges and Demands for Academic
               Success of Urban Youth   195
               Clancie M. Wilson

Chapter 15   Higher Education Policies and Professional Education
               in American Black Colleges   207
               Beverly Lindsay

Concluding Thoughts   *Kassie Freeman*   223

Index   225

About the Editor and Contributors   233

Tables and Figures

TABLES

Table 2.1	North American Shareholders' Occupational Preferences in African Slaves	28
Table 5.1	Time Trends in Student Race Consciousness and Collective Commitment by Sex: 1964, 1970, 1981, 1982, 1983	66
Table 5.2	Comparison of Means Tests, 1981 White Campus Group Versus 1983 Black Campus Group	68
Table 5.3	Comparison of Student Racial Attitudes by Sex, Campus Race, and Family Income, 1981, 1983 Data Sets	69
Table 6.1	Group Comparison of Means and Standard Deviations by Racial Status for the Quality of Effort Factors, Environmental Factors, and Gains Factors	82
Table 6.2	Regression Analyses for Racial Majority and Minority Students' Quality of Effort Factors, Environmental Factors, and Gains Factors	86
Table 7.1	Type of Pre-Western Community and Perspectives of Self and Community Identity for Students Profiled	109
Table 11.1	African Americans in Decision-Making Positions	162
Table 11.2	African American Student Enrollments	162

FIGURES

Figure 3.1	Self-Concept Development in African American Students	39

Figure 6.1   Conceptual Framework for Student Learning, Involvement,
             and Gains   77
Figure 6.2   The Effect of Input   78
Figure 6.3   The Effect of Process   80
Figure 6.4   College Environmental Factors   81
Figure 6.5   Quality of Effort Factors   82
Figure 6.6   The Effect of Output   83
Figure 6.7   Educational Gain Factor   84
Figure 11.1 Policy Process   158
Figure 11.2 Shared Responsibility Model   164

Acknowledgments

This book could not have been completed without the encouragement and support of all the contributing authors. In addition to the incredible amount of work they put into writing their own chapters, they have been friends, mentors, and invaluable resources. I will be forever grateful to each of them for listening to me when I was down-and-out, for sticking with me when I was applying pressure, and for believing in me throughout this process.

I would also like to thank Professor Robert Crowson in my department at Vanderbilt University for his belief in my scholarship and ideas and for encouraging me to pursue this project. Several graduate students at Vanderbilt University worked many hours reading and editing this manuscript. Specifically, I would like to thank Mia Alexander-Snow and Sybril Bennett. In addition to their chapters in this book, they have provided all the extra details that go into completing a manuscript. The support staff in my department also provided invaluable assistance. I would especially like to thank Martha Morrissey for her editorial assistance with this manuscript and with all of my writings and Ida Reale for her continuous support of me in every conceivable way.

To the many students who shared so many of their stories with me about education, I owe so much. It was those countless moving voices from so many African American high school students across many cities that I will carry with me forever and that will always provide the passion for my work.

The task of bringing this manuscript from merely chapters to a book belonged to Debra D. Walters. She spent countless hours thoroughly reviewing each chapter and the manuscript as a whole to ensure that we presented our works editorially sound. I will be forever grateful to her for her passion and caring about her work and the manuscript. We have established a very personal relationship which I hope will last for many years to come. Debra and I both owe much to Deborah Whitford, a production editor for Greenwood Publishing. She provided constant guidance and direction throughout this process.

Finally, I thank Alan Sturmer, editor, for his belief in the possibilities of this book and for all the support he provided me.

Introduction

Kassie Freeman

The inspiration for this book came from two sources: the book *The Mis-Education of the Negro*, written by Carter G. Woodson (1933), and the ideas expressed by Chinua Achebe, African novelist, in an interview with Bill Moyer. In his book, Woodson wrote, "The Negro will never be able to show all of his originality as long as his efforts are directed from without by those who socially proscribe him. Such `friends' will unconsciously keep him in the ghetto" (p. 28). In his interview with Bill Moyer, Achebe recounted how that when he read the novel *The Heart of Darkness,* he was cheering on the hunter until he realized that he was one of the savages being described. Both Woodson and Achebe were describing the importance of each culture telling its own story and/or how the storyteller shapes the imagination and beliefs of those who read or listen. As Achebe discusses, the story can even influence those being negatively written about to subconsciously accept the beliefs of the writer, and, as Woodson indicated, the one who tells the story can unconsciously keep African Americans in the "ghetto."

As an African American storyteller of higher education research, I am amazed at how the educational "story" portrays African Americans—labeling us, for example, as "at-risk," "underachievers," and "unintelligent"—and like Achebe, I recognize that I am one of those individuals being described. I can say with absolute confidence that the African American culture is often inadequately depicted in higher education research, or our cultural perspective is often altogether missing. Although Ogbu (1978), Banks (1988), and other anthropologists and multiculturalists have been writing about culture for some time, not until I began my research study on a group of African American high school students across cities and school types did the research stories that they told about their wants and desires for higher education make me clearly realize the necessity for including culture and heritage in higher education research, for their stories provided an originality, as described by Woodson (1933), that is often not captured by researchers.

Culture and heritage—why are they necessary characteristics to consider in research and policy making? Through culture, individuals' realities are constructed. Ogbu (1988) indicated that people involved in social policy and intervention programs tend to think of culture as what is in a person's immediate environment or family. However, culture, as defined by Ogbu (1988), "is a way of life shared by members of a population. It is the social, technoeconomic, and psychological adaptation worked out in the course of a people's history" (p. 11). As Brown (1963) said, "The simple fact is that people usually think, feel, and act as they do because they were brought up in a culture in which these ways were accepted, not only as good and right, but as natural. It is the sum total and the organization or arrangements of all the group's ways of thinking, feeling and acting" (pp. 2–3). As such, Brown further stated, "In insisting that cultures must be studied as wholes we are really saying that no custom, belief, or behavior can be understood out of its social or cultural context" (p. 15).

Cultural context, then, can be defined as interrelated characteristics that provide a perspective—frame of reference—for understanding individuals' and/or groups' ways of knowing and being. These interrelated characteristics generally include the sum total of the makeup of individuals. By way of example, cultural context is to the individual as conceptual framework is to research. When either is missing, the purpose, clarity of meaning, or sense of direction seems to be unclear or lost. Therefore, when research is absent a cultural context, it is like a missing part of a puzzle. Findings and policies can never be clear because essential parts (the why and how) of the meaning are absent.

For those who argue that all groups in America should be studied under the rubric of the American culture, such an argument underestimates the heritages and frames of reference of different culture groups. For some time, Banks (1988) has indicated that "certain perspectives, points of view, and frames of reference are normative within each culture and microcultural group" (p. 77). While it is not the case that every individual in a group holds a particular view, it does mean that some perspectives occur more frequently within a cultural group than do others (Banks, 1988, p. 78). When research is conducted out of cultural context, findings and applications are often misunderstood or misinterpreted.

Consequently, who conducts research and where and how it is produced have tremendous implications for both the authenticity and the outcomes of research findings and public policy. Programs are developed and instituted, court cases are influenced, and funding patterns for institutions of all types are established based on the outcomes of research, whether from the very basic level of statistics or from full-scaled commissioned studies authorized by different agencies.

Research that has been conducted on African Americans has most often been conducted by individuals unfamiliar with the historical and cultural considerations of African Americans. For example, the most frequently quoted authors writing on African Americans in higher education are non-African Americans. African and

African American researchers such as Ogbu (1988) have indicated that to fully understand the achievement motivation of different cultures, it is necessary to consider differences in historical and structural experiences and the way values are transmitted and acquired. More specifically, researchers often do not begin with a good knowledge and understanding of the conceptual systems of African Americans. Consequently, programs, court cases, and funding patterns often are decided based on assumptions that lack a cultural context and that have been based on deficit models (what African Americans cannot achieve) that have been developed by non-African Americans.

This historical system of knowledge production and dissemination, where non-African Americans have conducted and disseminated information, has severely minimized the capabilities of, underestimated the potential of, and prescribed inappropriate remedies for African American youths at all educational levels.

At the higher educational level, researchers have tended to focus on increasing the motivation and aspiration of African American students in higher education, excluding cultural considerations. The prescription for attracting and retaining African American students, faculty, and administrators has been based on models that have paid little, if any, attention to the heritage and culture of African Americans. Moreover, through their policies and practices, policymakers and educators alike have tended to attach the "at-risk" label to non-Asian minority students due to perceived personal and family factors defined by traditional models. Few studies, however, have examined models that could influence African American students' academic achievement and movement through the educational pipeline based on their cultural characteristics.

Books on race and minority issues in higher education are in abundance. As well, there are books written specifically about different aspects of African Americans in higher education, such as those written by Nettles (1988) on the Black undergraduate experience in America, Gurin and Epps (1975) on a study of students in historically Black colleges and universities (HBCUs), Allen and Epps (1991) on Black students' experiences at White public and historically Black public universities, and Fleming (1984) on the different experiences of Black students at predominantly White institutions (PWIs) and HBCUs. However, this book is a first attempt of some of the most noted African American senior scholars, promising junior scholars, and graduate student researchers to address research and policy issues specific to the culture and heritage of African Americans. In particular, this book provides a cultural context for examining research and addressing policies related to African Americans. It addresses a much neglected area in higher education research literature.

Different from other books, the intent of this book is to suggest the importance of including a cultural context for those who research and write about African Americans. The authors who contributed chapters for this book specifically wrote about some aspect of the African American culture. The book examines such questions as, What is the relationship between African Americans' culture and experiences, and how should their culture be integrated into research and practice?

How do African Americans' intra- and interrelations differ in higher education? How does understanding the African American culture as it relates to higher education research enhance policy making and practice? What role do HBCUs play in African Americans' participation in higher education? What are the policy and practice implications of past and current research on African Americans in higher education?

To address these and other questions, the book has been divided into three parts: Part I—Considering African American Culture in Higher Education Research; Part II—Examining African American Higher Education Research Issues and Paradigms; and Part III—Addressing Higher Education Policy and Practice as They Relate to African American Culture. In order to set the context for this book, Reginald Wilson provides an overview of African Americans' participation in higher education. In Part I, Raymond A. Winbush provides a perspective on research paradigms for reflecting on a Black world view. Mia D. Alexander-Snow more specifically discusses aspects of the African American culture, while Tamela M. Heath examines integrating cultural influences into research and practice as they relate to African American students and their self-concept development. Part I is concluded with Carolyn J. Thompson's writing about the implications of the historical origin of change on African Americans in higher education.

The authors in Part II tackle some of the pressing African American higher education research issues, and in each case, they provide a cultural context. Walter R. Allen asks who shall control the minds of African American students and provides a study to examine the question. Lemuel W. Watson provides a conceptual framework to consider for enhancing students' educational gains. Lori S. White discusses the issue of Black student identity and community. Sybril M. Bennett reviews the issue of self-segregation. To explore the issue of increasing African American faculty presence in PWIs, William B. Harvey reviews it from an "unnatural" perspective. In the last chapter in Part II, James Earl Davis examines a perspective to assess cultural capital and the role of HBCUs in educational reproduction.

Finally, the writers in Part III address higher education policy and practice as they relate to African American culture. Wynetta Y. Lee provides decision-making processes for the meaningful involvement of African Americans in policy, practice, and performance. Related to that same topic, Bruce Anthony Jones asks the question, Is the relationship between evaluation effort and institutional culture like mixing oil and water? In the next two chapters, my research and Clancie M. Wilson's research explore two particularly troublesome areas concerning policy and practice as they relate to African Americans. I examine African Americans and college choice, and Wilson examines higher education and teacher preparation. In the last chapter, Beverly Lindsay addresses the topic of higher education polices and professional education in American Black Colleges. The book ends with my concluding thoughts.

We hope this book will be useful to educators and policymakers as they seek to understand issues related to African Americans in higher education. It has been our intent to provide a book that could particularly be useful in higher education courses, including foundation, research, and policy courses, as it provides a context unique to African Americans. For policymakers, we hope this book will be useful as they think about targeting resources, both financial and service-oriented, for African Americans' pre- and postsecondary educational needs. As more colleges and universities are including multicultural courses, we want this book to be useful as a supplementary text in providing a perspective on topics related to African Americans.

This book has been a family affair from the beginning to the end. It has come about through mutual admiration, respect, and friendship. We hope all of those who read it will find it informative and useful.

REFERENCES

Allen, W., & Epps, E. (1991). *College in Black and White: African American students in predominately White and historically Black public universities.* Albany, NY: SUNY Press.

Banks, J. A. (1988). *Multiethnic education: Theory and practice.* Boston: Allyn & Bacon.

Brown, I. C. (1963). *Understanding other cultures.* Englewood Cliffs, NJ: Prentice-Hall.

Fleming, J. (1984). *Blacks in college.* San Francisco: Jossey-Bass.

Gurin, P., & Epps, E. (1975). *Black consciousness, identity and achievement.* New York: John Wiley & Sons.

Nettles, M. (Ed.). (1988). *Toward Black undergraduate student equality in American higher education.* Westport, CT: Greenwood.

Ogbu, J. U. (1978). *Minority education and caste.* New York: Academic Press.

Ogbu, J. U. (1988). *Cultural diversity and human development.* In D. T. Slaughter (Ed.), *Black children and poverty: A developmental perspective* (n.p.). San Francisco: Jossey-Bass.

Woodson, C. G. (1990). *The mis-education of the negro.* Trenton, NJ: Africa World Press. (Original work published 1933).

Overview:
African American Participation
in Higher Education

Reginald Wilson

The college participation rate for African Americans has fluctuated greatly over the past 10 years. After reaching a low point in enrollment in 1984, African Americans achieved a steady enrollment increase of 34.6% over the past decade. Notwithstanding the progress that African Americans have posted, especially since 1990, they continued to trail Whites in their college participation in 1994. Approximately 43% of White high school graduates ages 18 to 24 attended college compared with 35% for African American. In fact, after demonstrating increases in enrollment over the last decade, in 1994 African Americans posted the smallest percentage gains in undergraduate, graduate, and professional enrollments among the four ethnic minority groups. African Americans also continued to trail Whites in overall graduation rates at Division I institutions. The gap in graduation rates between African Americans and Whites was more than 20 percentage points in 1994. Despite these differences between African Americans and Whites, African Americans experienced growth at the four degree levels in 1993.

In order to better understand the progress that African Americans have made in their participation in, and graduation from, institutions of higher education, it is instructive to reflect the history of African American participation in higher education. It is particularly important for researchers and policymakers to have a context about the African American experience in higher education from which to write and make policy. This overview provides a historical background on African American participation in higher education, discusses the current status of African American participation in higher education, and concludes with thoughts and considerations on the importance of understanding how the past has informed the current predicament of African Americans in their quest for participation in higher education.

HISTORICAL BACKGROUND

Throughout much of the history of America, African American participation in higher education has been in segregated institutions. The majority of African Americans attended historically Black colleges and universities (HBCUs) as recently as two decades ago. Black colleges originated out of a social system that condoned slavery until 1865. From slavery until now, African Americans have had to struggle to have the opportunity to participate in any form of education. Restrictive legislation was passed to prohibit slaves from learning to read and write (Fleming, 1981). Only a few African Americans enrolled at predominantly White institutions (PWIs) in the North before the Civil War. Black colleges were established beginning in the 1850s (Fleming, 1981; Gurin & Epps, 1975). It is understandable, then, that late in the nineteenth and early in the twentieth centuries the great majority of African Americans attended historically Black colleges.

From 1850 to 1856 less than 5% of African Americans out of a population of 4.5 million could read and write. Since that time, African Americans have not only won the right to participate in education but dramatically increased their enrollment in higher education from 600,000 in 1965 to 1.2 million in 1980 (Fleming, 1981). Since the 1980s, however, the change in the participation patterns of African Americans in HBCUs and PWIs is noteworthy.

African American participation in higher education in PWIs is a rather recent phenomenon. This was particularly the case because the majority of African Americans resided in the South, where segregation barriers made it impossible to select PWIs and because admissions barriers at northern PWIs limited access to African Americans (Gurin & Epps, 1975).

However, two revolutions in federal initiatives, Supreme Court actions, and congressional laws dramatically changed both the number of African American participants and their geographic distribution throughout American institutions of higher education. The first initiative was the passage of the GI bill, which increased by the thousands the number of African American veterans able to attend college. The GI bill enabled hundreds of thousands of veterans, including thousands of African American veterans, to attend college independent of scholarship or previous educational achievement. The second initiative was the 1964 Civil Rights Act. As a result of this act, more African Americans had increased opportunities to select PWIs. By 1980, African American enrollment in institutions of higher education had doubled to 1.2 million; but only 20% were attending HBCUs. In spite of this decreased percentage, HBCUs have still continued to play a unique role in American higher education. These institutions have been extraordinary in their achievement of producing an overwhelming percentage of African American leaders "in the face of considerable obstacles, such as discriminatory public funding, hostility of the white power structure, low church support, and minimal response from the white philanthropic community and foundations" (LeMelle & LeMelle, 1969).

Before desegregation, these institutions educated the majority of African American physicians, lawyers and teachers. During their over one-hundred-year history, HBCUs, with their nearly open-door policies, not only were the nearly exclusive avenue of access to higher education for African Americans but took in both the best-prepared African American students and many who would not have been admissible to any college. By disregarding the customary admission criteria, they were able to successfully educate students in defiance of the predictive validity of traditional standardized tests. Additionally, these institutions provided a major source then and now of employment for the educated African American middle class.

The profile of African Americans who select HBCUs has been consistent over time. In the 1970s, approximately 60% of African Americans who attended HBCUs and approximately 45% of African Americans who attended PWIs had fathers who had not graduated from high school (Gurin & Epps, 1975). Since the occupations of many African Americans have been in semiskilled or unskilled jobs, a significant difference between African Americans who selected HBCUs and those in PWIs has been based on patterns of financial support. That is, according to Gurin and Epps, "Only one-third of Black students in Black colleges but one-half of those in White colleges held scholarships or grants that covered most of their college expenses" (p. 29). Therefore, the extent to which financial aid is available to African American students has likely influenced their selection of higher education institutions. Financial considerations have also tended to influence African Americans' consideration of colleges close to home. Therefore, approximately 90% of students attending HBCUs in the South have been southerners.

African Americans who attend HBCUs are generally thought to have lower high school records and lower standardized test scores. In addition, they are generally reported to come from lower socioeconomic status families, and the literature usually indicates that they select colleges close to home (Allen, 1992). However, Allen cautions that the assumption that PWIs provide superior environments for African American educational development is disputable. Additionally, students attending HBCUs, just like students attending PWIs, have to be studied by the type of HBCU institution they select. There are differences in the selectivity of the colleges and the socioeconomic status of students attending different types of HBCUs (i.e., private and public HBCUs). Therefore, caution should be used in making general statements about the background characteristics of all students attending HBCUs.

Studies of African American student experiences at HBCUs and PWIs suggest that many have negative experiences at PWIs and that they suffer lower achievement and higher attrition than do White students (Allen, 1992; Nettles, 1988). In contrast, studies suggest that African American students who attend HBCUs experience higher intellectual gains and have a more favorable psychosocial adjustment, a more positive self-image, stronger racial pride, and higher aspirations (Fleming, 1984; Gurin & Epps, 1975).

Although in the 1980s more African Americans were electing to attend PWIs, in the 1990s many African American students are reconsidering HBCUs because of their interest in embracing history and tradition (Benavides, 1996). While community colleges were significantly increasing access, they did not substantially contribute to increasing baccalaureate degree production because of low transfer rates of African Americans to 4-year schools.

CURRENT STATUS OF AFRICAN AMERICAN PARTICIPATION

The historical overview of African American participation in higher education paints a period of dynamic growth and transition—growth in the numbers of African Americans participating in higher education and transition from attending HBCUs to PWIs. Yet, the picture is mixed. The percentage of African Americans participating in higher education relative to Whites is still not what it could or should be, and the rate of African American graduation from higher education institutions is particularly problematic. In effect, there now exists the paradox of a greater pool of minority high school graduates, better prepared than previously, and a decline in completion of college.

Two recent occurrences have had a significant impact on the progress of African American participation in higher education. First, the higher education desegregation cases, particularly *Ayers v. Fordice* (111 F.3d 1183 [5th Cir. 1997]), have placed more stringent requirements for access to higher education (higher test scores, more academic courses) for African Americans. The imposition of these standards has had a substantially harmful effect on African American participation in higher education.

The second occurrence has been the decline of civil rights and recent legal challenges to affirmative action, which were not accidentally related to the Reagan/Bush administrations. The Reagan and Bush administrations attempted to either dismantle or neglect initiatives intended to empower minorities and women. For example, the Reagan Justice Department considered intervening in 51 affirmative action plans in order to overturn them, even though they had been entered into voluntarily (Orfield, 1989). Also, the Reagan administration attempted to seek tax-exempt status for segregated schools and decreased the amount of student financial aid available in grants while increasing the burden of students.

Certain other socioeconomic factors have also affected the participation of African Americans in higher education: (1) there are more African Americans below the poverty line today than there were 10 years ago; (2) African American unemployment is two and one-half times as high as for Whites; (3) the gap in life expectancy between African Americans and Whites has grown worse for African Americans since 1984; and (4) infant mortality for African Americans has grown worse in the past 10 years.

In spite of these devastating occurrences, African Americans have shown a slight increase at the first professional degree level. In order for African Americans to continue to make progress in their participation in higher education, two factors must be addressed. First, institutions of higher education must demonstrate their commitment to increasing African American access through utilizing variable admission criteria, strong support and retention programs, and counseling students into traditional disciplinary majors. Second, these institutions must work cooperatively with precollegiate schools to significantly enhance the transition process and retention of African Americans into higher education.

Much more has to be done in elementary and secondary schools to increase the quality of education of African American students. For instance, we know that African Americans take fewer high school academic courses in preparation for college than do Whites. Additionally, there is a vast discrepancy between the quality of education in innercity and predominantly minority schools and that in suburban and middle-class schools. Obviously, not only do funding resources need to be more equitably distributed, but teachers' attitudes and expectations about the capabilities of African American students have to significantly improve. Study after study documents that school reform has not made a difference in African American achievement because the reforms have done little to change teachers' beliefs about the potential of these students.

CONCLUSION

African American participation in higher education has been mixed. From the postbellum period to the present, African American participation in higher education has gone through many dramatic changes. Until well past the mid-twentieth century, African Americans attended schools founded specifically to educate African Americans. Over time, with the GI bill of World War II and subsequent wars and after the passing of the civil rights laws, more African Americans are attending PWIs. Yet, with this progress, African American participation in higher education is not what it should be, particularly given the increased need for higher skill levels in the twenty-first century.

What is abundantly clear, however, is that for progress to continue to be made to increase African American participation in higher education the whole picture has to be seen (i.e., past and current conditions affecting their educational experiences have to be taken into consideration). It is difficult to understand the depth of the African American educational experience without a historical and/or cultural context. For example, researchers and policymakers need to better understand such questions as, "What have been the consequences of certain historical periods on African American educational experiences" and "How have these experiences shaped their contemporary experiences?"

This overview has provided a brief historical context and some of the current contemporary conditions affecting African American participation in higher education. Much can be done to increase African American achievement that does not require funding but can be effectuated by changes in teacher attitudes and expectations. It is imperative that those programs that have demonstrated the greatest gains for increasing African Americans' participation in higher education be replicated widely. In order for the progress of African American participation in higher education to continue, researchers and policymakers must insist that there be no reduction in the commitment to improving African American access by institutions of higher education. With that commitment and consideration of the African American educational experience in research and policies, a significant increase in their participation in higher education is likely to be seen.

REFERENCES

Allen, W. (1992). The color of success: African American college student outcomes at predominantly White and historically Black colleges. *Harvard Educational Review, 62,* 26–44.

Ayers v. Fordice, 111 F.3d 1183 (5th Cir. 1997).

Benavides, I. (1996, February 19). Historically Black colleges buying muscle to up enrollment. *The Tennessean,* p. 1A.

Epps, E. G. (1972). Higher education and Black Americans: Implications for the future. In E. G. Epps (Ed.), *Black students in White schools* (pp. 102–111). Worthington, OH: Charles A. Jones.

Fleming, J. (1984). *Blacks in college.* San Francisco: Jossey-Bass.

Fleming, J. H. (1981). Blacks in higher education to 1954: A historical overview. In G. E. Thomas (Ed.), *Black students in higher education: Conditions and experiences in the 1970s* (pp. 11–17). Westport, CT: Greenwood Press.

Gurin, P., & Epps, E. G. (1975). *Black consciousness, identity, and achievement: A study of students in historically Black colleges.* New York: John Wiley & Sons.

LeMelle, T. J., & LeMelle, W. J. (1969). *The Black college: A strategy for achieving relevance.* New York: Frederick A. Praeger.

Nettles, M. (Ed.). (1988). *Toward Black undergraduate student equity in American higher education.* Westport, CT: Greenwood Press.

Orfield, G. (1989, January–February). Reagan's blind eye to civil rights. *Focus,* n.p. (Joint Center for Political Studies).

Part I

Considering African American Culture in Higher Education Research

1

Black to Africa: Some Research Paradigms Reflecting a Black World View

Raymond A. Winbush

During the past few years, the discussion of *Afrocentricity* as a way of viewing the world has been unrelenting. Books, articles and television newsmagazines have been devoted to it. The *Wall Street Journal, New York Times, Time, Newsweek,* and other printed media have devoted several column inches to decrying its presence at universities. Perhaps the most "systematic" critique of Afrocentricity has been voiced by Mary Lefkowitz, a classics professor at Wellesley College who has written several articles and one book (1996) and coedited another book (Lefkowitz & Rogers, 1996) that provide frontal assaults on the paradigm. Lefkowitz argues that she is simply critiquing scholarship, particularly in the area of history. She joins Arthur Schelsinger (1992) and many others in attacking Afrocentricity—her argument being academic while his is supposedly "political." Both of these authors, along with others, would provide several "thumbs down" if asked whether or not Afrocentric paradigms could be used in research design in higher education.

The word "paradigm" is used deliberately since this is exactly what Afrocentricity is. Kuhn's (1962) notion is that scientific advancement *is not* evolutionary, but rather a "series of peaceful interludes punctuated by intellectually violent revolutions," and in those revolutions "one conceptual world view is replaced by another" (n.p.). Science advances with notions of how epistemologies are to be confronted with ideas and discoveries that challenge them. Such is the case with Afrocentricity. The notion of an *African* world view rather than a *European* world view challenges the very foundation of Western intellectual thought.

Elsewhere I have written (1994) about why anxiety is a constant companion to many who criticize Afrocentricity. I am bothered, but not surprised, by how critics of Afrocentricity choose to view it as opposing Eurocentricity and, from this false premise, cite it as just a self-congratulatory way of thinking about history and science. Afrocentricity is "placing African ideals at the center of any analysis that involves African culture and behavior." This definition of Afrocentricity is offered by Asante (1987), whose work is built upon the early work of Maulana Karenga's *Kawaida* theory and even earlier works of Jacob Carruthers of Chicago, Wade Nobles of San Francisco, and Leachim Semaj of Jamaica. Lefkowitz and Schlesinger both bemoan the decline of western intellectual thought via "Afrocentrism" and compare its purveyors to Lamont Cranston-like shadows who pervert the innocent minds of the young. One would think from reading the writings of Afrocentricity's critics that a wave of poor scholarship spewing forth from African-garbed intellectuals has swept the academy and that the barricades against poor scholarship have at last been breached by those seeking to destroy the university.

The attacks on Black scholars who adhere to an African-centered paradigm are reminiscent of the McCarthy era. I believe that advocating African-centered modes of inquiry relative to the study of Black people and science is becoming litmus test not only for tenure but for acceptable scholarship even at the undergraduate level. I have received calls from Black graduate students at the dissertation stage who asked me how to negotiate the political waters of proposing a dissertation that is Afrocentric in its approach. Similarly, I have been asked by scholars seeking tenure whether or not they should make their research less Afrocentric and more "mainstream" and publish their "real feelings" after jumping the tenure hurdle. The chilling effects that bring into question the scholarship of academics seeking to forge new ways of thinking about old ideas are nothing less than McCarthyite in their results. Departments and programs of Black studies are increasingly under attack by those who wish a less disruptive paradigm in the academy when it comes to understanding Black people.

Is there a tolerance for Black scholarship in the academy? Absolutely, as long as the research is confined to fairly traditional methods of inquiry. Universities, despite the image of being bastions of liberalism and tolerant of varied ideas, are conservative when it comes to tolerating truly new forms of inquiry. The image of paradigm-shifting ideas floating out of the academy is more myth than reality. This has been particularly true in the social sciences and humanities. If paradigm shifts can be measured by who receives Nobel Prizes, economists at universities would have a near monopoly in this area. Few true paradigm shifts exist in the social sciences, particularly in the areas of history and the humanities. Even fewer theories in the social sciences have been offered that literally force social scientists to abandon traditional approaches to data.

I believe, as do others, that much of this is because of racist attitudes when it comes to persons of color. While most social scientists consider themselves free of racist world views, Schenrich and Young (1997) argue that "epistemological racism" pervades the academy. They argue that it arises out of the domination of racism in society and that a "White" world view is simply taken for granted by most scientists. The denial that a "White" world view exists among most White scientists manifests itself when journals not accepted "by the mainstream" are viewed with contempt by those who evaluate Black scholars for tenure. This epistemological racism forces Black scholars to adopt strategies for surviving the academy that compromise what they may actually know to be true about Black populations. Publishing the "right stuff" or, as one of my colleagues refers to it, the "White stuff," is a necessary strategy for gaining tenure at most predominantly White institutions (PWIs).

Similar to White scholars, Black scholars also possess world views that can determine the nature of their research. Unlike White scholars, however, theirs is mediated by *race* rather than *racism*. Black scholars have long fought battles to have their voices *heard in an academy* that often holds with utter *contempt research that is* contrary to what is viewed as being what the late Bobby Wright referred to as "victim analysis." Some yield to the demands of the academy's demand for epistemologically racist research. White scholars need not concern themselves with providing research that challenges the evidence that questions the academic status quo insofar as Black populations are concerned. If anything, racist research may actually be rewarded with words such as "courageous" and "challenging" if it provides more rumors of Black inferiority. Hernstein's and Murray's *Bell Curve* and Dinesh D'Souza's *The End of Racism* are good examples of this. Both books have been hailed as challenging existing views of Black intellectual and economic status, even though they were seriously flawed in their analysis. Yet we find that both Murray and D'Souza made the rounds of news shows and other venues with pundits throwing softball questions at hardball racism. The very exposure that such racist scholarship receives from the popular media adds fuel to the fire of what some have referred to as "rumors of inferiority."

NEGROCENTRICITY AND THE ACADEMY

In a 1991 conference at the University of Wisconsin, the future of African American studies was debated. This historic meeting included Henry Louis Gates of Harvard, Molefi Kete Asante of Temple, Deborah King of Dartmouth, and Manning Marable of the University of Colorado. In his paper entitled "African American Studies: The Future of the Discipline," Molefi Asante (1972) began by arguing:

Let me start with a rather broad statement that in a white supremacist environment, you are either for white supremacy or against it. There is no middle ground for the intellectual in an oppressive society. White supremacy is not just a sociological or political theory or ideology, it is also a literary project in the sense of the *Great Books of the Western World* as described by Mortimer J. Adler and William Buckley. One hundred and thirty authors and not one African American is included, not even an African American who sees herself or himself on the margins of the European experience. (p. 21)

Asante's statement reflects the view by many Black and White scholars that knowledge in a White supremacist environment has a political base that furthers the end of White supremacy. He argues further that "a racist political structure will give you racist institutions; a Marxist political structure will give you Marxist institutions, and so forth" (p. 21).

One of the ways White supremacy systems maintain themselves is to produce individuals from the *oppressed* group who further the aims of the system itself. While these individuals are unnecessary in maintaining the basis of supremacists' systems, they are important in confusing oppressed individuals within the system as to the origins of the oppression. In fact, persons of color have institutionalized these persons by referring to them as "Uncle Toms" and "Oreos" in African American culture, "Tio Taco" ("Uncle Taco") among Latinos, "Bananas" among Asian Americans, and "Apples" among American Indians. All of these names advance the idea that there are individuals within a culture who *mimic* the oppressor and advance ideas that White supremacists view as in line with their views.

These individuals are often praised publicly as opposing the more radical views of a group. The classic debate between W.E.B. DuBois and Booker T. Washington illustrates this point. Washington's elevation at the turn of this century as the most powerful African American in this country was achieved by saying things that were pleasing to persons who wished to continue what DuBois referred to as the "nadir of Negro life in America." In contemporary circles, Clarence Thomas among African Americans, Camille Paglia and Phyllis Schaffley among women, and others are touted as "alternative voices" among the shrill opinions from "the Left."

Among persons of African descent, the newest term to refer to these individuals is "Negrocentric," since they reflect a time long past when Black people felt that keeping an eye toward Whites was necessary in all levels of human interactions. The Negrocentric scholar has an eye toward White people and his or her back toward the *Bantustan*, as Adolph Reed (1995) puts in it in his scathing attack against Black public intellectuals. This metaphor, using the notorious "homelands" of the now defunct South African regime under apartheid, implies that some Black intellectuals provide only what I call "executive summaries" to the White community and are fairly disinterested in what is actually going on in Black communities. Their research reflects an eye toward what "mainstream" journals, researchers, and tenure committees might think about research on African Americans.

Negrocentric research is characterized by a limited view of Black people that fails to take into account the victimization of Black people by White supremacy. It is reluctant to place Black people in the context of a wider system of racism that broadens the analysis of research involving White people. If anything, it attempts to sustain the generally held view that something is decidedly wrong with Black people. Negrocentric research in book form usually manages to go through many editions since it reinforces the notion of Black inferiority. I have always been struck at how books that reinforce the notion of gross pathology among Black people remain in print for long periods, despite evidence that may question the credibility of data and/or author. *Soul on Ice* by Eldridge Cleaver, *Black Rage* by Grier and Cobbs, and *An American Dilemma* by Gunnar Myrdal, despite their extremely dated conclusions, have found themselves being relegated to the status of "classics" and are still found on the reading lists of many universities.

Finally, Negrocentric scholarship is usually unwilling to create new ways of looking at data. It is content with the status quo and leaves speculation to more "radical" schools of thought. Challenging existing paradigms that support racist ideas regarding Black people is simply not its purpose. It may nibble around the intellectual edges of more blatant forms of racist ideology such as *The Bell Curve* or *The End of Racism*, but it views such research as predictable aberrations in an otherwise objective method of inquiry. Negrocentric research will remain the generally acceptable way that most White and Black scholars will conduct research involving Black people in the academy, because it is safe.

AFROCENTRIC RESEARCH

It appears that critics of Afrocentricity prefer to offer their own definitions of it rather than citing the originators of the theory itself. Even this is a difficult sentence to write since *Afrocentric* thought has always existed in the writings of diasporic Africans. Alexander Crummell and Martin Delaney, nineteenth-century Black political theorists, both viewed history from the point of view of Africa. More recent examples include authors such as Martin Bernal (1987, 1991), Ivan Van Sertima (1992), Vincent Harding (1981) and Marimba Ani (1994). What these authors have in common is that they force their readers to disengage previously held notions of *history* and social science and present (I hesitate to say "new" and prefer to say "historically suppressed") information that challenges our understanding of antiquity.

But it does not stop there. I believe that if Afrocentricity were limited to revisiting dearly held assumptions about social science and educational research, its critics would rest fairly easy in that it could be dismissed as a basic misunderstanding of the facts. It moves, however, beyond historical analysis into areas that heretofore have gone virtually unchallenged in their assumptions about Africa. Witness, for example, the writings of African American psychologists, such as Akbar (1991), who seek to understand the condition of African American men from a point of view that departs dramatically from the writings of traditional European psychologists. Moreover, his writings, along with the writings of others, have been compiled in the third edition of *Black Psychology* (Jones, 1991), 25 years after the first volume, which contained the beginnings of an Afrocentric psychology. We are also seeing the penetration of Afrocentric thought in economics, the natural sciences, literature, and theology. Indeed, it is not an exaggeration to say that the "Afrocentric idea" is an actual way of reconceptualizing how we view our world. It is in the best tradition of what Elizabeth Minnich (1990) has called the "transformation of knowledge" in that it corrects and allows us to revisit dearly held assumptions about our world that in many cases were wrong and in most cases environmentally and intellectually destructive.

Afrocentric research is an orientation to data that eschews an automatic Eurocentric center to analysis. It places Black people front and center to areas of science that place Black people as objects rather than subjects in their analyses. Years ago a Black scholar, whose name escapes me, distinguished between "Black studies" and the "study of Black people." This simple conceptualization is at the heart of Afrocentric research paradigms. Studying Black people, similar to studying women, has been an indoor sport for many social scientists and educators. Guthrie (1998), through discussing the field of psychology, argued that the social sciences, as a whole, were absolutely racist when it came to persons of color, particularly Black people. Racism, in its extreme form, leads to sterilization of those deemed "feeble-minded" by racist psychologists such as Lewis Terman during and after World War I. While the exact number of those sterilized as a result of low scores on "intelligence" tests is unknown, a conservative figure would be in excess of 10,000. Sterilization of those deemed intellectually inferior has its roots in the nineteenth-century eugenics movement, which sought to achieve superior human beings through breeding. That those thought to be superior were White reflected the overall paradigm of White supremacy pervasive not only in the social sciences but in the natural sciences as well. Critics of Afrocentricity argue that the "natural" sciences are immune to criticisms of racism and androcentricity. They argue that "objectivity" has no color in mathematics, physics, and biology. This is far from true. Harding's (1993) selection of readings proves that, if anything, the so-called natural sciences are deeply embedded with racist ideology that has consistently advocated the exploitation of persons of color through its teachings and use. Likewise, Gould's (1981) thesis is that the history of science during the past 400 years has been built upon a foundation of White male supremacy at the expense of persons of color and women. Afrocentrists move into their investigations with this in mind, and it is intriguing that while there has been a consistent body of White critics of both the social and natural sciences relative to White supremacist thought, the loudest cries against bringing this fact to the academy are directed toward Afrocentrists. Perhaps this says more about the politics of science than anything else, in that there has been a consistent resistance toward Afrocentrists' uncovering and publishing the results of racism in the social sciences. I recall being accused a few years ago by a White colleague of using a "racist book" in one of my psychology courses. The first edition of the book was Robert Guthrie's *Even the Rat Was White* (1998), which provides an examination of the early racist ideology of several sacred icons in the field of psychology such as G. Stanley Hall and Lewis Terman. I asked him why he considered it racist, and he rather reluctantly said that he had never read about the racism of these early founders of psychology and that it was "disturbing" to find out that their research had been conducted with Aryan-like superiority. Such feelings had nothing to do with Guthrie's book being racist, I countered, and, after further discussion, he again rather sheepishly admitted that while the book perhaps might not be racist, it was "extremely disturbing" for the reasons he gave.

I believe that this simple incident captures the reason Afrocentric world views are resisted by many Whites and not a few Blacks in the academy. It is disturbing to read new challenges to old ideology that may not be anchored as firmly in "objective" science as one might think. It is also disturbing to reconsider different ways of looking at Black people in the context of White supremacy ideology. Finally, it is disturbing to both unlearn and learn new authors, books, readings, and opinions about social sciences and education despite claims of an open academy. The academy's door may be open, but only to world views that have an eye toward Europe rather than Africa. Simply put, Afrocentricity rubs many the wrong way because it attempts to bring new authors to the discussion table of ideas.

CONCLUSION

Johnelia Butler refers to women and persons of color as the "increased dialogue of suppressed voices" (Butler, 1989) that we are now hearing in the academy. The Black voices that are talking include Ani, Asante, Van Sertima, and Karenga, among others. To the degree that these voices are heard expands, rather than contracts, the world view of all scholars (Winbush, 1991) regardless of color. Western sciences have tried to avoid the use of the words "ideology" and "science" in the same sentence for fear that it challenges science's supposed "objectivity." Such denial borders on the pathological because of mountains of evidence to the contrary. Writers other than Afrocentrists have said this, and it seems that presenting this fact to students in the classroom can go a long way in promoting more balanced views of Black people.

REFERENCES

Akbar, N. (1991). *Visions of Black men*. Nashville, TN: Winston-Derek Press.

Ani, M. (1994). *Yurugu: An African-centered critique of European cultural thought and behavior*. Trenton, NJ: Africa World Press.

Asante, M. (1987). *The Afrocentric idea*. Philadelphia: Temple University Press.

Asante, M. (1992). African American studies: The future of the disciple. *Black Scholar, 22*(3), 20–29.

Bernal, M. (1987). *Black Athena: The Afro-Asiatic roots of classical civilization, Vol. 1: The fabrication of ancient Greece 1785–1985*. New Brunswick, NJ: Rutgers University Press.

Bernal, M. (1991). *Black Athena: The Afro-Asiatic roots of classical civilization, Vol. 2: The archaeological and documentary evidence*. New Brunswick, NJ: Rutgers University Press.

Butler, J. (personal communication) 1989.

D'Souza, D. (1995). *The end of racism: Principles for a multiracial society*. New York: Free Press.

Gould, Stephen (1981). *The mismeasure of man*. New York: W. W. Norton.

Guthrie, R. (1976). *Even the rat was white*. New York: Harper & Row.

Guthrie, R. (1998). *Even the rat was white* (2nd ed.). Boston: Allyn and Bacon.

Harding, S. (1993). *The "racial" economy of science: Toward a democratic future.*
    Bloomington: Indiana University Press.
Harding, V. (1981). *There is a river. The Black struggle for freedom in America.* New York:
    Vintage Books.
Hernstein, R. J., & Murray, C. (1996). *The bell curve: Intelligence and class structure in
    American life.* New York: Simon & Schuster.
Jones, R. (Ed.). (1991). *Black psychology,* (3rd ed.). Berkeley, CA: Cobb & Henry.
Kuhn, T. (1962). *The structure of scientific revolutions.* Chicago: University of Chicago
    Press.
Lefkowitz, M. (1996). *Not out of Africa.* New York: Basic Books.
Lefkowitz, M., & Rogers, G. M. (1996). *Black Athena revisited.* Chapel Hill: University of
    North Carolina Press.
Minnich, E. K. (1990). *Transforming knowledge.* Philadelphia: Temple University Press.
Reed, A. (1995, April 11). What are the drums saying Booker? *The Village Voice.*
Schenrich, J., & Young, M. (1997). Coloring epistemologies as research methods racially
    biased. *Educational Researchers 26*(4), 4–16.
Schlesinger, A. (1992). *The disuniting of America.* New York: W. W. Norton.
Sertima, I. V. (1992). *Golden age of the Moor.* New Brunswick, NJ: Transaction Publishers.
Winbush, R. A. (1991). Black studies as a liberating force for western scholarship. *Journal
    of Intergroup Relations, 18*(2), 48–53.
Winbush, R. A. (1994, February 23). Afrocentric scholarship and the search for truth. *The
    Chronicle of Higher Education,* B-4.
Winbush, R. A. (1994, May 25). Anxiety and Afrocentricity. *Black Issues in Higher
    Education,* 13–15.

2

From Africa to America: The Relationship between Culture and Experience

Mia D. Alexander-Snow

It is important to keep in mind when learning about "culture," particularly if it is outside your own cultural parameters, that "experience" is culturally defined. Thus "as life circumstances change, and as people attempt to conduct the same sorts of activities under these new circumstances, their cultural understandings will affect the way they both view their circumstances and experiences" (Roseberry, 1994, p. 43). Thus, culture becomes defined in experiential communality—the sharing of particular experiences by a group of people.

The anthropological theories of cultural ecology and historical political economy primarily look at the relationship between culture and experience. Cultural ecology is the study of the relationship of culture to the natural environment. Two distinct phenomena are involved: "the physical environment itself, and the cultural arrangements by which the environment is exploited, including technology and economic organization" (Hatch, 1973, pp. 114–115). Historical political economy adds another dimension to cultural ecology by emphasizing the role that inequality and domination of power have on cultural meanings and expressions (Roseberry, 1994).

Borrowing from the cultural ecology and historical political economy perspectives, I argue that the ecological and geographic factors of preslavery and slavery America encouraged the retention, rather than the destruction, of the traditional African value system or philosophical orientations—"one with nature" and "survival of the people"—and that the value system is embodied in the experiential communality of African Americans in contemporary Black America.

AFRICAN CULTURE: THE PRESLAVERY EXPERIENCE

Being One with Nature

Traditional Africa, from which the vast majority of slaves were taken, was a deeply religious society. The traditional African peoples believed that religion was merely the observable act for the meaningful expression of the African philosophical system (Asante, 1987; Baldwin, 1991; Bennett, 1982, 1993; Herskovits, 1948; Holloway, 1990; Nobles, 1991a, 1991b; Stuckey, 1987). God was viewed as the originator and sustainer of people. He was the source and supreme controller of the force that emanated from the universe. This force, "'a kind of individualized fragment of the Supreme Being itself' continued to exist in man, even after he died. . . . It continued, the African said, in a pure and perfect state which could influence the lives of the living things" (Bennett, 1982, p. 24). Spirits were connected to this force and explained a person's destiny. Everything was functionally connected; to destroy one aspect of the ontological and cosmological phenomenon would cause the destruction of the whole of existence, including the Creator (Baldwin, 1991; Holloway, 1990; Nobles, 1991b; Stuckey, 1987). Once dead, there was neither Heaven to hope for, nor Hell to be feared, essentially reflecting the idea of the vital force (Nobles, 1991a).

The underlying principle, "What people do is motivated by what they believe, and what they believe springs from what they do and experience" (Mbiti, 1970, p. 50), guided the actions of traditional African life. Hence, the African peoples did not separate action from belief, nor did they make concrete distinctions between the spiritual and physical worlds (Asante, 1987; Baldwin, 1991; Bennett, 1982, 1993; Herskovits, 1948; Holloway, 1990; Nobles, 1991b, 1991a; Stuckey, 1987).

For example, the traditional ring dance, which is linked to the most important of all African ceremonies—the burial ceremony—existed mainly as a form of worship directed to the ancestors and intended to achieve union with the spirits and the Creator.

> With the drums sounding [the African people] formed a line of twos, and one couple behind the other danced in the customary counter-clockwise direction about the edges of the cleared space, finally forming a single line in front of the drums, which they faced as they danced vigorously. Retreating in line to their place on the South side, before the ancestral temple they remained there, while one after another of their number danced singly, moving toward the drums and then retreating before circling the dance space. (Stuckey, 1987, p. 12)

This dance is just one of the variations of the ring dances performed by different African ethnic groups; however, it remains the quintessential metaphor for encompassing all aspects of sacred life—rite of passage, death, and rebirth (Stuckey, 1987). The singing and dancing to the tempo of drums, with the tempo and circle ever quickening during the course of the movement, represented togetherness and containment, creating an intensely renewed sense of family and communal unity (Asante, 1987; Bennett, 1982, 1993; Holloway, 1990; Mbiti, 1970).

Survival of the People

Mbiti (1970) contends that all ethnic groups in Africa embraced the African orientation of "the survival of the tribe," and he proclaims that the "tribe" or ethnic group was the integral and indispensable part of nature.

Kinship was the most cohesive device in traditional life, defining all community relationships (which included animals, plants, and inanimate objects), binding together the entire life system of the ethnic group (Holloway, 1990; Mbiti, 1970; Nobles, 1991a). However, the different ethnic groups did not view members of other ethnic groups as a part of their own. The traditional African peoples viewed the "joining" of an ethnic group in the same manner in which they viewed religion—neither was convertible. Therefore, they saw the individual as inextricably a part of an ethnic group (Nobles, 1991a, 1991b). For example, an individual would first identify himself or herself as being a member of an ethnic group, such as an Ashanti or Ibo rather than by birth name. Such exchanges reflected the importance and survival of one's own ethnic group (Herskovits, 1948; Mbiti, 1970).

The kinship system extended beyond the nuclear family to the extended family, where everyone was seen as being related to someone else within his or her ethnic group (i.e., brother or sister, father or mother, grandfather or grandmother, cousin or brother-in-law, uncle or aunt). People held the belief that all individuals owed their very existence not only to those who conceived and nourished them but also to their ancestors and the unborn; it was understood that the individual did not, and could not, exist alone (Nobles, 1991).

Essentially, African people followed the principle "I am because We are, and because We are, therefore, I am," which defined the African view of "self" as embodying a collective, thereby transcending individual identity to include one's self and one's kind (Asante, 1987; Baldwin, 1991; Mbiti, 1970; Nobles, 1991a; Stuckey, 1987).

African Culture: The Slavery Experience

The slave trade, the largest forced migration in history, brought an estimated half-million slaves from Africa to the Americas during the seventeenth century (Holloway, 1990). "In the eighteenth century, the `golden age' of the traffic, some seven million slaves were transported to the Americas" (Van Den Berghe, 1981, p. 125)—this figure does not include those Africans who did not survive the voyage and whose bodies were thrown out to sea. By 1850, one-third of the people of African descent lived outside Africa and had been imported from the west and central coast of Africa to the Americas (Holloway, 1990). The first generation of African Americans consisted of Africans who came from diverse regions (Gold Coast, Ivory Coast, Niger Delta, Gambia, and Senegal) and cultures (Mande, Bantu, Sudanic, and Bakongo) of Africa but particularly from those areas stretching along the coast through West Africa to Central Africa (Bennett, 1982, 1993; Holloway, 1990; Stuckey, 1987). Africans from the Guinea Coast, Sierra Leone, Liberia, the Ivory Coast, the Bight of Benin, the Gold Coast, Dahomey, and the coastal ports of Nigeria had the greatest impact in the cultural formations of African American behavior (Herskovits, 1948). They were not only carriers of the traditional African world view or value system but also extremely knowledgeable about technical and agricultural skills and ideas about complex social organizations (Asante, 1987; Giddings, 1984; Herskovits, 1948; Holloway, 1990; Mbiti, 1970; Stuckey, 1987).

Historical Political Economy

"The study of cultural change—or for that matter, the study of culture as a whole—cannot be attempted without a vivid sense of the historically dynamic nature of the phenomenon" (Herskovits, 1938, p. 25). Roseberry (1994) focuses on the impact that the colonial empires or spheres of capitalist investment (American slavery system) have upon the incorporation of local populations (i.e., West and Central Africa), emphasizing cultural changes in terms of changing circumstances and power. Keeping in mind that enslaved Africans were viewed by European slaveholders as commodity or, more accurately, "chattel," African slaves were without self-dominion and thus were seen as powerless. Africans were bought and sold as one would buy and sell livestock exploited for economic gain (Van Den Berghe, 1981). The economic exploitation of Africans by Europeans affected the Africans' interaction with the Europeans, redefining their cultural meanings. Both European and African were in power struggles for dominion of their respective philosophical orientations or value system. "The European worldview emphasized the individual's `uniqueness,' `distinctiveness,' and `differences.'" This self-concept or "self"-germinated from the axiomatic position "`I think, therefore I am'" (Baldwin, 1991, p. 145). Such an axiomatic position ran counter to the African self-concept "I am because We are, and because We are, therefore, I am." Hence, in terms of self-conception, the African philosophical system did not place heavy emphasis on the "individual" or "individuality" (Nobles, 1991b), and thus the changing political and economic environment forced the traditional African peoples to readapt and then to undergo a process of learning or reconditioning to accommodate their new circumstances (Herskovits, 1948).

With the incorporation of the European slave trade into the life experiences of the African people, the principal African orientation—"survival of the people" or "survival of the tribe"—became modified not only to encompass one's own ethnic group but all African peoples (Bennett, 1982, 1993; Holloway, 1990; Mbiti, 1970). This modification began with the "middle passage" (Bennett, 1982, 1993; Holloway, 1990; Stuckey, 1987).

All African ethnic groups on slave ships to America experienced a common horror. "As such, slave ships were the first real incubators of slave unity across cultural lines, cruelly revealing the irreducible links from one ethnic group to the other, fostering resistance thousands of miles before the shores of the new land appeared on the horizon" (Stuckey, 1987, p. 3). The African had begun to define "self" in direct oppositional relation to the European (i.e., the African [Black] and the European [White]).

Prior to the middle passage, traditional Africans viewed "survival of the people" as encompassing only one's own ethnic group. Once on land and thrust into an environment and alien culture that denied the enslaved Africans any social, political, and economic power, "survival of the people" had become a universal axiom, "We" (African/Black people) and "They" (European/White people), in which all African ethnic groups were seen as one. Thus, there was the formation of a collective consciousness of resistance by Africans. The slaveholders made conscious efforts to separate members of the same ethnic groups in the hopes of breaking down the collective reinforcement that had begun to take hold during the middle passage (Bennett, 1993; Nobles, 1991a, 1991b; Stuckey, 1987).

Cultural Ecology and the Physical Environment

Cultural ecologists view the environment as having the greatest impact on culture (Hatch, 1973). "The interaction of communal man with his unique environment will result in a set of guiding beliefs which dictate the values and customs the people adopt; ultimately, this set (or sets) of values determine man's social behavior" (Nobles, 1991a, p. 56).

Referring to Table 2.1, Holloway (1990) outlines the North American slaveholders' occupational preferences in African slaves. It is significant to note that the importation of African people based on their skills and regional "job fitness" was a significant factor in the development of North American regions. As southern planters became more aware of the different agricultural/technical skills cultivated in certain geographic regions of Africa, they specifically imported ethnic groups from those areas that would be of use to their industry (Herskovits, 1948; Holloway, 1990). For example, South Carolina primarily imported slaves who had strong agricultural skills. "Plantation tasks in North America did not place any new technological demands on African labor, and the Africans' familiarity with the cultivation of rice, corn, yams, and millet in the Senegambian hinterlands prepared them for the kind of labor that was required in the Mississippi Valley" (Holloway, 1990, p. 14).

While the slaveholders were developing their resources in North America, the regions of West and Central Africa were losing their human capital—a most valued resource. So, instead of continuing to "divide and conquer" and keep the Africans divided, slaveholders were actually binding similar cultures and ethnic groups together. For example, the Senegambians, noted first to arrive in South Carolina, became an integral part of the development of agrarian culture of the American plantation. The Wolofs were primarily imported for house servants and artisans, and thus elements of their culture were retained within the developing culture of America (Holloway, 1990). Many "Americanisms" can be traced back to Wolofs, including such words as OK, bogus, boogie woogie, and phony (Holloway, 1990).

Table 2.1
North American Shareholders' Occupational Preferences in African Slaves

Occupation	African Ethnicity Preferred	Culture
House Servant	Mandingo	Mande
	Yoruba (Nagoes)	Cross River
	Dahomean (Fon)	Akan
	Fanti	Akan
Artisan	Bambara	Mande
	Melinke	Mande
Rice Cultivator	Temne	Mande
	Sherbo	Mande
	Mend Kishe	Mande
Field Slave	Calabar	Niger Delta
	Ebo	Niger Delta
	Ibibio	Niger Delta

Source: Adapted from Holloway (1990).

The rigidly enforced isolation of African slaves from participation in European social institutions enabled "New World Africans" to retain the African orientations of "survival of the people" and "one with nature." Africanized Americans imposed their cultural rituals and customs on such European institutions as religion (Bennett, 1993; Holloway, 1990; Mbiti, 1970; Stuckey, 1987). The Africans adapted the Christian religious customs to fit their needs and circumstances by defying all rules, standards, and structures established by the European sects (Holloway, 1990), and it became an expression of a thrust toward liberation. "The adoption of some religious form was necessary, not only because religion is a focal point of African culture but also because it is generally a focal point of resistance and survival" (Bennett, 1993, p. 162).

The adaptation of the ring dance, known in North America as the "shout," allowed for Africanized Americans to stay in accordance with the African orientations "one with nature" and "survival of the people." It was the main context in which Africans recognized common values.

> The shouters formed in a ring, men and women alternating, their bodies close together, moved round and round on shuffling feet that never left the ground. With the heel of the left foot they pounded out the fundamental beat of the dance and with their hands clapped out the varying rhythmical accents of the chant for the music was an African chant and the strut an African dance . . . adapted to Christian worship. Round and round the ring would go. One, two, three, four, five hours, the very monotony of sound and motion inducing ecstatic frenzy. (Holloway, 1990, p. 108)

The gathering together for celebration of life and spirit through the movement of the bodies in direct rhythm to the beat and force of nature allowed the Africans to have expression with nature, God, and their ancestral spirits (Bennett, 1982, 1993; Holloway, 1990; Stuckey, 1987). The act of rhythmically moving in unison created both a physical and psychological oneness of being—neither inseparable, both experiential and communal.

The concepts of kinship and the "survival of the people" were incorporated into the life experience of the plantation. The "in-breeding" of slaves across the different ethnic groups developed new blood lineages (Bennett, 1982, 1993; Holloway, 1990; Mbiti, 1970; Nobles, 1991a; Stuckey, 1987). There developed the feeling of "one big happy family" (Bennett, 1982, 1993; Giddings, 1984). The slaves had a feeling of community, a recognition of special obligations, and an "us" perspective that they never had prior to being taken from their homelands. The experiential communality reinforced the value for unity, cooperative effort, and collective responsibility (Baldwin, 1991).

The extended network provided a sense of continuity and life stability in a world that was often anything but secure (Bennett, 1982, 1993). These "organic" family structures allowed African traditions (i.e., high moral codes of behavior and respect of self) and the rituals for rite-of-passage ceremonies to continue to be transmitted from generation to generation. By other individuals, each learned his or her duties and responsibilities toward oneself and the collective self of the tribe or people (Mbiti, 1970).

It was not uncommon for the traditions to be carried by the adoption of a storyteller or songstress (Bennett, 1982, 1993; Mbiti, 1970; Stuckey, 1987). For example, "one slave woman explained that if a woman wasn't acting as she should, her neighbors would adopt an African custom, and play the banjo on her: make her the subject of a public sing that warned her that she `better change'" (Giddings, 1984, p. 45). In whatever means accessible to the slaves, music was always made an integral part of their expression.

> The dawning sense of peoplehood was stimulated by external exigencies, by segregation on the plantations and in the towns, but it was stimulated also by internal exigencies, by the need to be together, by the need to express a different worldview, by the need to see beyond the blocked horizon. Working together in the fields, playing together on holidays, and suffering together on good days and bad days, the pioneer African Americans began to think of themselves as a common people with common aspirations and a common enemy. (Bennett, 1993, p. 155)

CONTEMPORARY BLACK AMERICA

America is an African as well as European invention (Bennett, 1982). Culture has been "reinterpreted" and "borrowed," having acquired different meanings and functions than it had in the culture of origin (Van Den Berghe, 1981). African

Americans in contemporary Black America have emerged out of the institution of slavery embodying the synthesis of the African value system with the European natural rights philosophy and the Bible; this synthesis was a practical philosophy "forged in the heat of battle as a tool of survival" (Bennett, 1993).

Some scholars have proclaimed there is little in African American culture that can be traced to African past, while other scholars such as Herskovits (1948) suggest that "culture is dynamic; that only completely static cultures are dead ones" (p. 20).

Remove the contemporary trappings of socioeconomic, political orientations that define most African Americans today, allow them to come together, and watch closely for the natural rhythm in their step, the spiritual yearnings in their song, the trials and triumphs in their stories, and one will see that traditional African culture is very much alive in the power and soul of African American people. One will also begin to see the collective consciousness of traditional and contemporary African peoples—"a collective orientation stemming partly from the African past and partly from the experiences of the situation" (Bennett, 1993, p. 155). The experiential communality embraced the value for unity, cooperative effort, collective responsibility, and concern for the community among Black people (Baldwin, 1991).

The experiential communality permeates into the Black consciousness and largely defines cultural meanings embodied by African American music (i.e., rap, gospel, and spirituals), religion (stylized manner in which the minister conducts the sermon, "dancing in the aisles"), art (graffiti, poetry, literature), community (reference to one another as "brother" or "sister," and "family reunion" when all are a part of the family and invited to join in the musical celebration (the Million Man March, the Urban League). To define African American culture without these "expressions" is to understand that Blackness is more than a biological fact; it functions as a commitment to a historical project that places the African person back on center, and as such the African self-consciousness—communal phenomenology—will manifest itself in a wide variety of self-affirming, positive (pro-Black) beliefs, attitudes, and behavior among African Americans (Asante, 1987; Baldwin, 1991).

CONCLUSION

The first generation of African Americans came from various regions of the world and Africa, spoke different languages and dialects, and reflected different aspects of the African value system (Bennett, 1982, 1993; Holloway, 1990; Mbiti, 1970; Nobles, 1991a; Stuckey, 1987). However different the expressions of African world view may have seemed, all encompassed a core of cultural and philosophical meanings that placed the emphasis on the "understanding of all things—i.e., the individual, the tribe (community), and the universe" (Nobles, 1991a, p. 51). The traditional African peoples essentially shared one over-arching philosophical system and did not place heavy emphasis on the "individual," believing that only in terms of other people does the individual become conscious of his or her own being (Bennett, 1982, 1993; Holloway, 1990; Mbiti, 1970; Nobles, 1991a, 1991b; Stuckey, 1987).

This philosophical system, commonly referred to as African philosophy, can be defined as "understanding, attitude of mind, logic and perception behind the manner in which African peoples think, act, or speak in different situations of life" (Mbiti, 1970, p. 5). Nobles (1991a) relates Mbiti's definition of African philosophy to the spiritual disposition of a people or "collective consciousness" in which "the decisions and judgments made, values adopted, culture practiced, and the aesthetic forms created are all under the control of the human brain" (Holloway, 1987, p. 108). Mbiti (1970) argues that the collective consciousness ultimately "defines the social behavior a people will express in *common*—their cultural configuration (Nobles, 1991a, p. 56). Therefore, the set of guiding beliefs common to the African philosophical orientations (i.e., "unity," "one with nature," and "survival of the people") must be understood in relationship to the African peoples and their environment (Hatch, 1973; Herskovits, 1948; Nobles, 1991a).

African American culture cannot simply be defined by retained cultural artifacts but must also be defined by the philosophical-psychological linkages between Africans and Africanized Americans (Asante, 1987; Baldwin, 1991; Bennett, 1982, 1993; Holloway, 1990; Mbiti, 1970; Nobles, 1991a, 1991b; Stuckey, 1987). In other words, "culture is at once both socially constituted (it is a product of present and past activity) and socially constitutive (it is part of the meaningful context in which activity takes place)" (Roseberry, 1994, p. 42).

REFERENCES

Asante, M. K. (1987). *The Afrocentric idea.* Philadelphia: Temple University Press.

Baldwin, J. (1991). The Black self-hatred paradigm revisited: An Afrocentric analysis. In R. Jones (Ed.), *Black psychology* (n.p.). Berkeley, CA: Cobb & Henry.

Bennett, L., Jr. (1982). *Before the Mayflower: A history of Black America.* New York: Penguin Books.

Bennett, L. (1993). *The shaping of Black America.* New York: Penguin Books.

Giddings, P. (1984). *When and where I enter: The impact of Black women on race and sex in America.* New York: Bantam Books.

Hatch, E. (1973). *Theories of man and culture.* New York: Columbia University Press.

Herskovits, M. J. (1938). *Acculturation the study of culture contact.* New York: J. J. Augustine.

Herskovits, M. J. (1948). *Man and his works: The science of cultural anthropology.* New York: Alfred A. Knopf.

Holloway, J. E. (1990). *Africanisms in American culture.* Bloomington: Indiana University Press.

Mbiti, J. S. (1970). *African religions and philosophies.* Garden City, NY: Anchor Books.

Nobles, W. W. (1991a). African philosophy: Foundations for Black psychology. In R. Jones (Ed.), *Black psychology* (pp. 47–57). Berkeley, CA: Cobb & Henry.

Nobles, W. W. (1991b). Extended self: Rethinking the so-called negro self-concept. In R. Jones (Ed.), *Black psychology* (pp. 295–304). Berkeley, CA: Cobb & Henry.

Roseberry, W. (1994). *Anthropologists and histories: Essays in culture, history, and political economy.* New Brunswick, NJ: Rutgers University Press.

Stuckey, S. (1987). *Slave culture: Nationalist theory and the foundations of Black America.* New York: Oxford University Press.

Van Den Berghe, P. (1981). *The ethnic phenomenon.* New York: Praeger.

3

African American Students and Self-Concept Development: Integrating Cultural Influences into Research and Practice

Tamela M. Heath

Ways of being, feeling, and knowing are shaped by many things, not the least of which is one's social and cultural experiences. For African American youth, the educational setting, be it the classroom, the college campus, or the schooling structure as a whole, is often incongruent with the culture in which their styles of being and knowing are embedded. This mismatch has proven to be detrimental to the development of both cognitive and affective outcomes for African American students. Probably one of the most talked-about outcomes that Black students are known to suffer is that of their self-concept. Self-concept development is a central part of psychosocial development in college students. A positive self-concept has been linked to being one of the most important college outcomes.

Self-concept is a reflection of students' feelings about their group and the importance of that group in the environment where they happen to be learning. Simply stated, if students do not feel loved and supported as a group, they will not display a positive self-concept or feelings of self-worth. Since self-concept is found in the research literature to be an important factor in academic and social success in college, it is important for researchers and practitioners to be aware of how to promote a positive self-concept in students. For African American students, promoting a positive self-concept may be very closely linked to promoting and empowering African American students as a whole in the college community.

This chapter outlines the nature of self-concept development for African Americans. It also describes some of the barriers to the growth of African American students' academic and social self-concept and the college environmental influences that have been found to stimulate their self–concept development. The chapter concludes with recommendations for both scholars and practitioners concerned with enhancing psychosocial development in Black students.

THE NATURE OF AFRICAN AMERICAN SELF-CONCEPT

African American psychological development is best understood through the sociohistorical factors that make-up the African American's experience. First, one must consider the historical structure in which American schooling takes place. The structure has its roots in segregation and separation, where certain groups of people were not entitled to the same type of education as other groups. Historically, African American students never had the same educational opportunities as White students and, therefore, started out at a different place altogether. African Americans began with a system that banned their participation altogether and that later provided limited access, but only as a matter of law, not as a commonly-accepted practice. Although, presently, legal restrictions on access to schooling and higher education have been lifted, the remnants of racism still exist at the very core of the schooling structure (Morgan, 1995).

Second, one must understand the sociological environment in which the present-day schooling of African Americans takes place. African American students are faced with adversity at every level of their schooling careers. Those who are resilient enough to make it through to the postsecondary schooling system in this country do so wearing battle scars on their psychological being. What is it like to be an unwanted stranger in a strange land? One might say that African Americans live in a system in which, if they are to succeed, they must mold themselves and their thoughts in order to "fit in." Thus, it might be said that the resilient ones are able to fit their actions and thinking into the expectations and acceptances of the dominant culture. However, research is now showing that there are positive pieces of African American culture that contribute to the success of those students who make it through the pipeline.

African American culture is very rich in social tradition. Family relationships, group social interaction, support, and achievement have historically been a part of African American culture. African American families have been found to be rooted in support structures and extended relationships (McAdoo, 1988). The culture is one in which social interactions and connectedness with the group are very important aspects to identity development. Black identity development has been linked to the extent to which young people associate with the cultural context of being Black (Cross, 1991). Research has demonstrated that the more that African Americans relate to their own Blackness, the more that they feel a responsibility and an affinity to the group.

Community and interconnectedness are the foundation of identity development within the Black community. In many cases, individualism and competitiveness are contrary to the African American way of being. Jagers and Mock (1995) have talked about Afro-cultural communalism. This communalism is the tendency of African Americans toward collectivist orientation or the preference for interdependence among people. Students who are driven by this communalistic orientation cannot describe themselves in individualistic terms. In fact, much of their self-identity is grounded in their social concern for, and need to be with, others. Gilligan (1984) talked about this when she looked at the moral development of women. Women base their moral decisions on how much they feel others might approve of their actions. Yet, communalism goes far beyond being affected by the thoughts of others.

Upon reflecting on these observations, I have adopted the assumption that African American self-concept is built upon how the individual relates to, and feels about, the group with which he or she identifies. I am reminded of myself as a young elementary school student attending an all-White school. Although I was very proud of being of African descent (my mother was very involved in the Black power movement), I felt very self-conscious about how my peers felt about my being Black. I did not know if they thought I could do the work. Although I was a high achiever in school, I always doubted my abilities and talents. In fact, I was consistently told that I was "smart for a Black girl." This type of communication is enough to weigh heavily upon a student's self-concept. Students build and establish views about themselves based on how they feel about their group. By "their group," I mean their race, their family, their school and schooling experiences, their gender. When Black students think about themselves, they automatically think about themselves in relation to the group with which they identify.

This has to be taken into account in the research that is done concerning self-concept. When researchers operationalize self-concept, they must realize that this view is based in the very mainstream, dominant group notions of how students describe themselves. In order for students to "buy into" this notion of the self, they have to think of themselves very independently. It is possible that students who are communalistic and who are not able to separate themselves from their community would respond in a very different way than would those students who are independent-minded.

When asked to rate their academic abilities in comparison to people their own age, African American students might draw upon their own group orientation in their responses. If African American students have been programmed that they are less academically prepared than other groups, then individual students are likely to take this into account as a group orientation. Thus, academic abilities are rated lower comparatively for Blacks for the very reason that they are not likely to compare themselves individually but, instead, compare themselves as a member of a larger reference group. In actuality students are understanding the question to read, How would you rate your group compared to other groups on academic abilities? Therefore, there might be Black students who are very successful academically but who actually rate themselves lower on this trait.

Academic self-concept and the way it is measured in most survey research are not a measure of individual self-concept of ability for African American students. Students are constantly compared to other groups on the basis of constructs that do not apply to them in an environment that is incompatible with their way of being. In order to get a true measure of their feelings about their academic abilities, you must ask questions that speak to their orientation, such as How would you rate your individual academic abilities compared to other students in your school or students your age? Studies on self-concept suggest that African Americans' socially oriented culture influences development of African American students.

STUDIES ON AFRICAN AMERICAN SELF-CONCEPT

Banks (1972) writes in the prologue to *Black Self-Concept,* "The ideal self in America has been made synonymous with Caucasians, and particularly middle-class whites" (p. 7). In effect, the previous models for self-concept development have been those of the White male. What this has meant for other groups, particularly for African Americans, is that their self-concept is seen as less adequate in comparison to that of White males (Banks, 1972; Gurin & Epps, 1975; Powell, 1973).

Several studies have looked at self-concept in African American college students. Some studies have been comparative in nature, while others look at correlates of growth. Still others look into the issue of how culture and environment influence differences in self-concept. Self-concept notably has an empirical basis, being a psychological phenomenon. However, relatively no studies look at how African Americans make meaning of their so-called self-concept, and, as such, no instruments or measures, to date, operationalize self-concept as a social or communalistic construct. Therefore, all of the studies presented in this chapter have as a basis for their results the underlying assumption that self-concept is inherently independent. This could explain some of the mixed results found within literature on the subject.

A major study by Gurin and Epps (1975) revealed that self-concept in African American students is related to their racial identity. Gurin and Epps found that students who attended historically Black colleges and universities (HBCUs) actually tended to have higher self-concepts than those who did not. Students who were grounded in Black pride had higher scores on self-concept than those who were not. Powell (1973) studied the impact of desegregation on the self-concepts of Black children in the South. She found that children who attended school with a predominantly Black student body actually had higher self-concepts than those who were integrated into White schools. This is probably because the students in Black schools were in an environment that valued their way of being and actually encouraged it.

On the other hand, Astin (1990) found differences among Black and White students in their self-ratings on various personality characteristics. Blacks tended to rate themselves higher on the more social characteristics (like popularity, social self-confidence, and leadership ability), while Whites rated themselves higher on the more academic traits (like mathematical ability and writing ability). Differences in the development of self-concept between Blacks and Whites have been attributed to a number of things. Some theorists believe that self-concept in Blacks is related to their level of racial self-identification (see, e.g., Banks, 1984; Parham & Helms, 1985). Others attribute these differences to changes in the sociocultural environments of students. For instance, Madhere (1991) found that self-esteem for

African American preadolescents is related to the amount of significant-other closeness they perceive or receive, suggesting an interpersonal dimension to the structure of self-concept for Black youth. Powell (1985) found that Black students in southern schools scored higher on self-concept when they were in an environment where they were with other students like themselves, where they felt supported and welcomed rather than alienated and isolated.

Other research examines different college environments that contribute to the development of self-concept for African American students compared to Whites. For example, the racial makeup of an institution has been found to be a significant influence on self-concept in Blacks. HBCUs have been found to be related to success for Black students along a number of dimensions. Cross and Astin (1981) found that attending an HBCU was "the most significant predictor of full-time persistence" (p. 84) for Black students. Other studies have found HBCUs to be significantly related to academic achievement (Allen, 1981; Smith, 1991); degree attainment (Thomas, Mingle, & McPartland, 1981); and graduate school enrollment (Brazziel, 1983; Heath, 1992). Much of the success of HBCUs has been attributed to at least two things—first, the presence of a supportive peer network and the absence of racial alienation which may be present at predominantly White institutions (PWIs) (Allen, 1981; Davis, 1990; Jackson & Swan, 1990); second, more supportive student and faculty relations at HBCUs for Black students who attend these institutions compared to those who attend PWIs (Allen, 1981; Jackson & Swan, 1990).

SELF-CONCEPT AND ACADEMIC ACHIEVEMENT IN COLLEGE

Research is clear that students with high academic achievement in college also have high academic self-concept. This also tends to be the case for African American students. However, studies have also shown that Black students have lower academic self-concept regardless of their achievement levels compared to other groups. There is no doubt that the more positively a person feels about his or her academic abilities, the more likely that person will achieve. Yet, why is it that Black students have lower academic self-concept scores as a group than do other groups? One answer to this question can be found in the schooling environment. It has been found that a person's environment (particularly the quality of his or her relationships) is of extreme importance in maintaining a positive self-concept (Burns, 1979). In an educational setting, "feedback in the form of verbal and non-verbal communication provides reinforcement (both positive and negative) for behavior and information about oneself, both of which influence self conception, and the expectations others hold of one, and which one holds about oneself" (p. 286).

Teacher feedback and environmental empowerment of students are the keys to the enhancement of students' feelings about their academic worth. As described earlier, the structure of American schooling and how it alienates African American students create an environment of feeling unwanted. Not only is it important to empower students' individual feelings about their abilities, but students must also receive positive cues about the capabilities of members of their reference group. The schooling environment must make students feel that their group is not only capable but important to those who hold the power. Why do students who attend HBCUs have a higher self-concept than those in PWI environments? It is the result of the cues that they get from administrators, teachers, parents, and other students about the importance and abilities of Black students to these players.

Erikson (1968, p. 57) believes that institutions cannot help but develop students' sense of self:

> If higher education induces major changes in students' cognitive style, it is likely to induce change in other aspects of personality as well. According to Piaget's notion of *horizontal décalage,* a change in one dimension requires assimilation and "filling in" across other aspects of functioning. If the changes are significantly widespread and irreversible, a new stage of development may be reached. This potential impact of learning on personality may be one reason why the process of education and its intended result, learning, are almost inevitably accompanied by anxiety. It is also the reason that most educational institutions can be said to be in the business of promoting ego development, even if they merely conceive of themselves as providing students with opportunities to gain intellectual skills and mastery of a discipline or profession.

If institutions of higher education are in the business of promoting ego development, then it stands to reason that students are influenced by how important and supported they feel in the environment in which they participate.

In my most recent research (Heath, 1994), I posed a model for the development of academic and social self-concept in African American students (see Figure 3.1). In the model, students' precollege SES grades, as well as aspirations, are controlled for first. These variables are related to their incoming (or pretested) self-concept scores. Their self-concept is shown to dictate which type of institution they chose, i.e., private or public. The type of institution is related directly to the environmental factors such as faculty support and academic and social integrations. The environmental factors are then related to their self-concept on post-test four years later.

As it turns out, the environment at institutions of higher education plays an important role in the development of self-concept for Black students. Which aspect of the environment plays the most important role in self-concept development? According to this research, the answer lies in the faculty as well as the peer environment. The study identified a model using causal modeling techniques that included elements of the students' background or precollege experiences, precollege self-concept scores, institutional structural characteristics, the faculty environment, the peer environment, and integration as temporal determinants of self-concept development. In this study, for both Black men and Black women, the

Figure 3.1
Self-Concept Development in African American Students

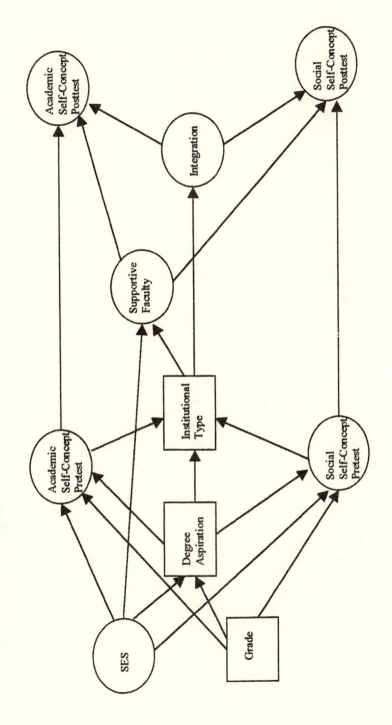

most powerful determinant of academic and social self-concept was integration. The more African American students participated in activities that immersed them in their academic and social environment in college, the higher were their scores on academic and social self-concept. Interestingly, important indicators of integration were the peer and faculty environments. The peer environment refers, in more specific terms, to the likelihood students were to network with peers and study with them. The faculty environment refers to the commitment among the faculty to the emotional and academic problems of students, as well as to the concerns of minority students. Quite interestingly, the peer and faculty environments were directly related not only to integration, but also to self-concept development.

The importance of peer environment and faculty support can be useful in understanding how to be effective with African American students. This research suggests that it is through peer and faculty environments that educators can have the biggest impact on African American students' self-concept.

PRACTICAL AND SCHOLARLY IMPLICATIONS

What are some of the implications of the information presented in this chapter? I would like to explore this question in two ways. There are implications for scholars who are looking to do research on African American student psychosocial development, and there are practical implications for professionals in the business of helping African American students.

Scholars must understand the assumptions that underlie the research that they are undertaking. These assumptions reflect not only those of the researcher himself or herself but also the larger societal assumption that holds them to the instruments and operational definitions which they employ. The instruments that researchers have used are very much formulated upon their individual and societal assumptions. Nobles (1987) reminds social science researchers of the detriment to African American students when the African American culture is ignored within the field of psychometrics. The items used to examine the self-concept of students are taken from instruments that do not take into consideration a cooperative orientation among students. Research would be far advanced if it looked at how African American students view their definition of self-concept. Do students relate themselves to a particular reference group when describing their individual traits? If so, does this have an impact on the way they rate their traits or not? Until researchers have an answer to these questions, they cannot possibly know whether the self-concept scores of African American students are truly reflective of the students' feelings about themselves or whether these scores provide a statement about the feelings these students have concerning how their institution values their group.

It is no coincidence that students who attend HBCUs score higher on self-concept measures than do those at PWIs. These very institutions have been known for their support of African American students, as well as their heightened expectations of the success of African American students. This speaks to the amount of support and empowerment that is required at the institutional level in order to produce positive results in students.

It is imperative that practitioners look into breaking down those structures that create isolation and competitiveness among students. The education of current professors and the hiring of minority faculty who have proven to be effective mentors to minority students are a beginning. Empowerment of specialized curricula such as African American studies departments is another effective means of empowerment of students. Finally, supporting student organizations, encouraging students to network, and taking part in group collaboration both on a social level as well as on an academic level are of great importance.

REFERENCES

Allen, W. R. (1981). Correlates of Black student adjustment, achievement, and aspirations at a predominantly White southern university. In G. E. Thomas (Ed.), *Black students in higher education: Conditions and experiences in the 1970s* (pp. 127–141). Westport, CT: Greenwood Press.

Astin, A. W. (1990). *The Black undergraduate: Current status and trends in the characteristics of freshmen.* Los Angeles, CA: Higher Education Research Institute.

Banks, J. A. (1972). Racial prejudice and the Black self-concept. In J. A. Banks & J. D. Grambs (Eds.), *Black self-concept,* (pp. 5–36). New York: McGraw-Hill.

Banks, J. A. (1984). Black youths in predominantly White suburbs: An exploratory study of their attitudes for higher education. *Journal of Higher Education, 53*(1), 3–17.

Brazziel, W. (1983). Baccalaureate college of origin of Black doctorate recipients. *Journal of Negro Education, 32,* 102–109.

Burns, R. B. (1979). *The self-concept in theory, measurement, development and behavior.* New York: Longman.

Chickering, A. W. (1969). *Education and identity.* San Francisco: Jossey-Bass.

Cross, P. H., & Astin, H. S. (1981). Black students in Black and White institutions. In G. E. Thomas (Ed.), *Black students in higher education: Conditions and experiences in the 1970s* (pp. 76–90). Westport, CT: Greenwood Press.

Cross, W. E. (1991). *Shades of Black: Diversity in African American identity.* Philadelphia: Temple University Press.

Davis, R. B. (1990). Social support networks and undergraduate student academic success-related outcomes: A comparison of Black students on Black and White campuses. In W. R. Allen, E. G. Epps, & N. Z. Haniff (Eds.), *College in Black and White: African American students in predominantly White and in historically Black public universities* (pp. 143–160). Albany: SUNY Press.

Erikson, E. H. (1968). *Identity, youth, and crisis.* New York: W. W. Norton.

Gilligan, C. (1984). *In a different voice: Psychological theory and women's development.* Cambridge: Harvard University Press.

Grambs, J. D. (1919). African American students in predominantly White and in historically Black public universities. In W. R. Allen, E. G. Epps, & N. Z. Haniff (Eds.), *College in Black and White: African American students in predominantly White and in historically Black public universities* (pp. 285–204). Albany: SUNY Press.

Gurin, P., & Epps, E. (1975). *Black consciousness, identity, and achievement.* New York: John Wiley & Sons.

Heath, T. M. (1992). *Educational aspirations and graduate enrollment among African American college students: Turning dreams into realities.* Paper presented at the Association for the Study of Higher Education 1992 Annual Convention, Minneapolis, MN.

Heath, T. M. (1994). *The development of self-concept among African American and White college students and its relationship to retention and educational aspirations.* Unpublished doctoral dissertation. University of California, Los Angeles.

Jackson, K. W., & Swan, L. A. (1990). Institutional and individual factors affecting Black undergraduate student performance: Campus race and student gender. In W. R. Allen, E. G. Epps, & N. Z. Haniff (Eds.), *College in Black and White: African American students in predominantly White and in historically Black public universities* (pp. 127–142). Albany: SUNY Press.

Jagers, R. J., & Mock, L. O. (May 1995). The communalism scale and collectivistic-individualistic tendencies: Some preliminary findings. *Journal of Black Psychology, 21*(2), 153–167.

Madhere, S. (1991). Self-esteem of African American preadolescents: Theoretical and practical considerations. *Journal of Negro Education, 60*(1), 47–61.

McAdoo, H. P. (1988). *Black families.* Newbury Park, CA: Sage.

Morgan, H. (1995). *Historical perspectives on the education of Black children.* Westport, CT: Praeger.

Nobles, W. W. (1987). Psychometrics and African-American reality: A cultural antimony. *Negro Educational Review, 38*(2), 45–55.

Parham, T. A., & Helms, J. E. (1985). Relation of racial identity attitudes to self-actualization and affective states of Black students. *Journal of Counseling Psychology, 32*(3), 431–440.

Powell, G. J. (1973). *Black Monday's children: A study of the effects of school desegregation on self-concept of southern children.* New York: Appleton-Century-Crofts.

Powell, G. J. (1985). Self-concept among Afro-American students in racially isolated minority schools: Some regional differences. *Journal of the American Academy of Child Psychiatry, 24*(2), 142–149.

Smith, A. W. (1991). Personal traits, institutional prestige, racial attitudes, and Black students' academic performance in college. In W. R. Allen, E. G. Epps, & N. Z. Haniff (Eds.), *College in Black and White: African American students in predominantly White and in historically Black public universities* (pp. 111–126). Albany: SUNY Press.

Thomas, G. E., Mingle, J. R., & McPartland, J. M. (1981). Recent trends in racial enrollment, segregation, and degree attainment in higher education. In G. E. Thomas (Ed.), *Black students in higher education: Conditions and experiences in the 1970s* (pp. 107–125). Westport, CT: Greenwood Press.

4

Historical Origins of Change: Implications for African Americans in Higher Education

Carolyn J. Thompson

INTRODUCTION

As the twenty-first century approaches, the collective efforts that brought about the educational progress of African Americans during the past century are threatened. Recent legislation in several states is almost certain to reduce the numbers of African American students admitted for both undergraduate and graduate study in public higher education (Jaschik, 1995). Programs and financial resources once available in colleges and universities to correct historical racial inequities at the student and faculty levels have been challenged (Healy, 1996b, 1996c). Departments and programs established in colleges and universities for the study of African peoples and the amelioration of educational and social conditions of African Americans in several states (i.e., Alabama, Mississippi, and Ohio) are in jeopardy as policy efforts are directed at their futures (Guernsey, 1996; Healy, 1996a, 1996c; Jaschik, 1995). Public higher education institutions that have historically provided opportunities specifically for the individual and race uplift of African Americans are being threatened as federal and state legislation attempts to bring conditions about through policies that have always been challenged in practice. These escalating circumstances are leaving limited college options available to African Americans. African American youths today are no more responsible for the commitment (or lack) of elected officials to provide resources for their educational development, or the curricula available in their schools, than African American youths at any other time throughout this century. As the twentieth century closes, the educational and social warfare initiated over a century ago to sustain the overall social status of African Americans and protect the self-anointed privilege of others continues.

The accomplishments of this century and initiatives directed at improving educational outcomes for African Americans in the next century must first revisit the context that shaped the limits of what has been achieved so far and examine the present educational conditions of African Americans. This is the goal of this chapter.

Civil rights legislation of the antebellum and Reconstruction era was developed using the premise that people of African descent were not equal to those of European descent, regardless of their status as free or slave. One of Abraham Lincoln's presidential debates provides evidence of this sentiment when he stated, "I am not, nor have ever been in favor of bringing about in any way the social and political equality of the white and black races . . . there is a physical difference between the white and black races which I believe will forever forbid the races living together on terms of social and political equality" (Maltz, 1990, p. 2). Lincoln's view was among the more liberal for that time since he was promoting the freedom of slaves. Years later in the case of *Plessy v. Ferguson* (163 U.S. 537, 16 S.Ct. 1138, 41 L.Ed. 256 [1896]), the Louisiana statute that required railway companies to provide separate but equal "accommodations for the white and colored races" (*Id.*), it was determined that the Fourteenth Amendment was not "intended to abolish distinctions based upon color, or to enforce social, as distinguished from political equality, or a commingling of the two races upon terms unsatisfactory to either" (*Id.*, 163 U.S. at 544, 16 S.Ct. at 1140; 41 L.Ed. at 258). Because of these sentiments Maltz (1990) describes the attempt of the Thirty-ninth Congress of 1865 as unsuccessful, stating that their "first effort to protect the civil rights of blacks ended in failure. Moreover, the circumstances of the failure demonstrated that only those civil rights measures which could appeal to the most conservative of mainstream . . . were likely to become law" (p. 49). Consequently, the successive struggles of each decade of the twentieth century have sought to legally redefine the freedom, rights, and equality of African Americans, while also attempting to level the playing fields in various education and employment arenas. Though we would like to believe that common beliefs differ greatly today from those during the antebellum and Reconstruction era of the nineteenth century, the same holds true today for race-related, civil rights legislation (i.e., affirmative action), that it must appeal to the most conservative of mainstream beliefs to become law. Many supportive views attempted to shape civil rights discussions during the antebellum and Reconstruction periods to develop the Thirteenth, Fourteenth, and Fifteenth Amendments to the Constitution (Maltz, 1990). The more common beliefs of that time period, however, are the basis of institutional racism operating today.

Education has long been a means to upward mobility for the underclass and working class in the United States. The sustained disparity in college and university access, participation, and educational attainment among racial groups and the controversy that accompanies discussions that shape policies in educational systems and workplaces are indicators of the resilience of racism and the political dominance of the privileged. Watkins (1996) contends that politics is the realm through which racism is best understood, indicating that "U.S. racial politics is the product of a desire for free and cheap labor spanning nearly 400 years. Racism and exclusion belong within the category of power, hegemony, and the economic arrangements of U.S. society" (p. 6). Accordingly, as Smith (1995) suggests, evidence of contemporary institutional racism is apparent by the existence of an African American underclass in our society and educational systems.

College Access

The disparity in the college preparation of African Americans serves to restrict access to college by limiting precollege academic and nonacademic programs. These school resources are inequitably distributed based on the wealth of school districts rather than needs of our nation's students. It is evidenced by the distribution of various populations to certain types of programs and schools. Almost half of all high school seniors in 1992 were enrolled in college preparatory programs rather than vocational/technical or general programs (National Center for Education Statistics [NCES], 1995d). However, research indicates that "African Americans tended to be concentrated in schools that are academically inadequate, since those schools with a majority of African American students tended to be vocational or technical, special education, or alternative schools rather than regular schools" (Nettles & Perna, 1997a, p. 59). Enrollment in college preparatory courses, however, is closely related to parent education and socioeconomic status (SES), which is also associated with race. Forty-three percent of African American high school seniors in 1992 were in the lowest SES[1] quartile, while fewer than 20% of the Whites were in this SES group (NCES, 1995d). Thus, the types of high schools enrolling African Americans and the larger representation of African Americans in the lowest SES quartile further reinforce the historical disparity in college preparation made available to them.

Further confounding the problems related to inadequate college preparation are current elementary and secondary school resources and practices. The next generation of children to enter grade school will do so at a time when the majority of African American youths are concentrated in schools that rank in the bottom one-third of the nation's schools on educational achievement tests (Nettles & Perna, 1997b). These schools should be allocated greater resources to address student achievement needs. However, when considering one of the schools' most crucial resources (teachers), these schools are not supported in the same way as those attended by other students. Schools attended mainly by African Americans rely heavily on long- and short-term substitutes to fill vacancies. Whereas the teachers selected for employment in these schools have taken fewer undergraduate courses in their major teaching areas and consequently are not as well prepared as teachers in schools enrolling predominantly White populations, these schools are also not as likely to support the efforts of their teachers to acquire additional preparation through in-service training. When these teachers attend in-service programs, they are not as likely to be included in curriculum decisions. Teachers as school resources, including their preparation, experiences, and job stability directly influence the educational experiences of African American students. These experiences are related to the lower achievement levels of African American children, which are the lowest in mathematics, reading, and history of any of the reported racial or ethnic groups, such as White, Asian American, Pacific Islander, Latino American, and Native American (Nettles & Perna, 1997b).

Mathematics achievement scores reported by the National Assessment of Educational Progress (NAEP) reveal that three out of every four African American 4th and 8th graders score below the basic level in the NAEP mathematics tests. The results are only slightly better for the 12th graders, where two-thirds score below the basic level. These results are most unfavorable, especially when compared to their White counterparts where the converse is true—three of every four score at or above the basic level in these three grade levels (Nettles & Perna, 1997b). A critical "gatekeeper" course is geometry—a course associated with a greater likelihood of admission to and persistence in college—where proficiency is defined by four levels of mastery (NCES, 1994). While only slightly more than one-third of African Americans completed at least one year of geometry as 10th graders, roughly half of the White students completed a year of geometry. African American 10th graders are only one-fifth as likely to fall into the advanced mathematics proficiency group when compared to their White counterparts. Mathematics achievement is critical because it provides students with greater access to career and college options. These results suggest difficulty in store for African Americans seeking to move from the United States underclass unless progress can be made in this area.

NAEP reading achievement scores reveal that African Americans scoring below basic levels represent more than two-thirds of 4th graders (69%), more than half of 8th graders (56%), and nearly half of all 12th graders (48%) (Nettles & Perna, 1997b). Moreover, "when schools are ranked by the average score on the reading assessment, African Americans represent a higher percentage of students in the bottom one-third . . . of all schools" (pp. 108–109).

The results of NAEP history achievement scores are equally distressing. Nearly two-thirds of African American 4th and 8th graders score below basic levels (64% and 67%, respectively). Greater than four out of five 12th graders score below basic levels (83%). In fact, among all oppressed groups in the United States, more than two-thirds of all students score below the basic level in history—78% of Latino Americans, 67% of Pacific Islanders, and 70% of Native Americans (Nettles & Perna, 1997b). These results suggest a need to rethink both the content and approach to teaching history at elementary and secondary levels. Among the questions raised by researchers at the Frederick D. Patterson Research Institute[2] is, "What actions are needed to ensure that the levels of enthusiasm for school that are exhibited by African American preschoolers are maintained through later years rather than dissipate into absenteeism, tardiness, and opting-out of school activities?" (p. 362). NAEP results may be the result of history being taught as a series of facts rather than conclusions drawn from inconclusive evidence (Loewen, 1995), most of which represents the perspectives of descendants of colonists. Perhaps a more inclusive and challenging approach would be to train history teachers to teach history the way historians discover it: critically examining and challenging historical facts while raising insightful questions about the nature of specific events. Such methods and the questions raised could serve to introduce students to the role of archaeologists, anthropologists, historians, and others in how history is constructed from knowledge acquired from the archival documents, individuals, the earth, and the universe. Who knows what career and educational aspirations might result from intellectually engaging students in this manner, rather than requiring that they regurgitate purported facts. Thus, the role of K-12 schooling in preparing students for college through their teachers, programs, and other resources becomes increasingly critical.

Postsecondary Participation

African American student participation and subsequent attainment are both affected by their precollege educational experiences. Of students continuing their education beyond high school, African Americans are more likely than White students to aspire to a degree lower than a baccalaureate. African American undergraduates enrolled in historically Black colleges and universities (HBCUs), however, are more likely to aspire to advanced degrees (NCES, 1995c). Students enrolled in HBCUs, on the average, have lower academic profiles than other students, yet they are still more likely to graduate. Moreover, while HBCUs enroll fewer than half of all African Americans who attend college, they award approximately one-third of the baccalaureate degrees earned by African Americans each year (Roebuck & Murty, 1993). Thus, threatening the livelihood of institutions that have historically and successfully provided African Americans entree into the workforce and professional life, preparation for graduate and professional studies, and movement from society's underclass cannot be viewed as a viable alternative for equalizing opportunities and conditions between races. Participation cannot increase while opportunities are eliminated, and the inadequacy of public education resource distribution initially excludes African Americans.

When examining college enrollment trends for African Americans for the 15-year period from 1976 to 1991 (NCES, 1993), data reveal only marginal gains overall, along with a decline for African American men (3.9% in 1991, down from 4.6% at the undergraduate level in 1976). This is not encouraging, given that fewer than 4% of African American males are enrolling in college at any level. Concerns are further raised when considering the nonacademic factors that disadvantage African Americans. Their parents are three times as likely as those of White students to earn less than $20,000 annually, and they are more than twice as likely to have one or both parents deceased (10.1% and 4.4%, respectively) (Astin, 1990). As we begin the twenty-first century, postsecondary enrollments are expected to increase by over 13%, adding nearly 2 million more students to the 14.2 million enrolled a decade earlier (NCES, 1993). It is expected that more than three-quarters will enroll in public colleges and universities, increasing public enrollments by over 30% for traditional college-age students alone (recent high school graduates).

One-quarter of these students are expected to be from presently underrepresented groups, of which African Americans are the largest group (U.S. Bureau of the Census, 1992). African Americans traditionally have not been the principal market for college recruitment. Yet, in order to sustain their enrollments, twenty-first-century colleges and universities will be looking to nontraditional populations, and African Americans should be among them.

Postsecondary Attainment

In the NCES (1993) report on the levels of educational attainment for students six years after their senior year of high school, African Americans were the least likely of any racial group to progress beyond high school, with only 69% having only a high school diploma, while 19% had either a two-year license or degree. African Americans were only half as likely as Whites to have acquired at least a four-year or graduate degree in that time period (10% and 21%, respectively). When considering levels of educational attainment by socioeconomic status, African Americans in the upper SES level lag behind their White counterparts in attainment of baccalaureate degrees by roughly 13% (NCES, 1993). For African Americans in the middle-income levels, their comparable attainment with Whites at the baccalaureate level trails by 5%. Considering the lower degree attainment levels of African Americans overall, greater attention needs to be given to policies and practices of inclusion, rather than the current trend toward equitably worded, exclusionary legislation.

Along with the disparity in college participation and attainment today are the inevitable economic challenges for African American families that are character-istic of the lack of commitment of political officials to the U.S. under- and working classes. The underclass represents the socioeconomic class of people whose incomes are below subsistence levels. At nearly 13% of the overall U.S. population and 16% of school-age children, African Americans represent the largest minority group and the largest underclass, with 44% of African American households having preschool-age children subsisting on annual incomes below $10,000. This is 4 1/2 times greater than White families with preschool-age children (Nettles & Perna, 1997b). Of the households that have children who will be of college age by the year 2000, African American youths are three times as likely as White youths to come from single-parent households (nearly 52% compared with roughly 18%, respectively), most of which are female-headed households. This poses serious college affordability concerns when we consider the inequitable earning power of women compared to men. These findings further emphasize the necessity of increasing the earning power of African Americans by improving the quality of education in general and providing access for their greater participation in postsecondary education.

At nearly one-half century beyond the landmark *Brown v. Board of Education* (347 U.S. 483, 74 S.Ct. 686, 98 L.Ed. 873 [1954]) case, which represented one of the nation's greatest challenges to provide quality public education for all races and better prepare citizens for the nation's workforce (Thompson, 1996), it is a time to reevaluate and improve policies and practices directed at correcting historical and present injustices.

THE PLIGHT OF HBCUs

As the twenty-first century closes, the distinctiveness that defined historically Black colleges and universities (HBCUs) now threatens their demise. While the first HBCU was founded in the mid-1800s, most were established after the Civil War for the purposes of educating former slaves. Although HBCUs welcomed all who applied without regard to race, legal mandate mainly in southern states prohibited the education of people of African descent with Whites and dictated the establishment of separate but equal educational systems (Garibaldi, 1984). In northern states that did not have dual systems of education, discriminatory admissions practices limited the access of African Americans to many public and private colleges and universities. Thus, with the prevailing social ethos, without separate systems and institutions for African Americans, racial uplift through education during the last century would not have been possible.

Presently, HBCUs number just over 100 and represent approximately 3% of the colleges and universities in this country. Roughly 85% are four-year institutions, with three universities; and roughly 41% are public institutions (Garibaldi, 1984). The public institutions are the result of the Second Morrill Act of 1890 (Butts, 1939). The First Morrill Act of 1862 provided land in each state for the establishment of land-grant colleges to study agriculture, industry, and mechanical arts. With the provision of the Second Morrill Act of 1890, a number of southern and southern-border states established separate institutions for people of African descent, where they could also study agriculture, industry, and mechanical arts.

With the passage of the Civil Rights Act of 1964 (U.S. Bureau of National Affairs, 1964), states supporting dual systems of higher education were required to dismantle them. Several decades later, with sustained evidence of the established dual systems, some state-supported HBCUs are threatened with closure because the representation of a White student population has not reached the previously established numerical quotas (see Thompson, 1996). In the state of Alabama a federal district judge determined that, in the case of the HBCUs only, their pride in their African American heritage had a segregative effect on student choice (Healy, 1996a; Jaschik, 1995). The attorney for the HBCUs argued that "(i)t was hypocritical for the government to expect black colleges to change while black students at predominantly white institutions are expected to subdue their heritage and amalgamate with the people there and the symbols that we abhor" (Healy, 1996a, p. A21).

States with established dual systems of education developed unequal educational institutions for African Americans. Economic arrangements of U.S. society have long demanded free and cheap labor (Watkins, 1996). Accordingly, racial politics in this country is based on the premise of constitutional equality with social inequality, with *Plessy* arguing, "If the civil and political rights of both races be equal one cannot be inferior to the other civilly or politically. If one race be inferior to the other socially, the Constitution of the United States cannot put them upon the same plane" (163 U.S. at 551–552, 16 S.Ct. at 1143, 41 L.Ed. at 261). Based on the belief by many Whites that people of African descent were unequal, not only were dual educational systems for African Americans established to be unequal by providing programs that led to lower-status jobs, but also, in the 30 years since the passage of the Civil Rights Act, states like Alabama have not made, or are only recently making, provisions for improvements in academic programs (Healy, 1996c; Jaschik, 1995). Some, like Alabama, are still rejecting HBCU requests for greater land-grant responsibilities, a greater share of more popular academic programs, and increasing course offerings in African American studies at the PWIs (Jaschik, 1995). If such requests were honored, they would bring the responsibilities of the two types of institutions within the state closer to equality. States are grappling with questions posed by Williams (1984) over a decade earlier: "Is it ethically and politically correct for the U.S. government to promote the existence and growth of ethnically identifiable black institutions on the one hand, and at the same time to pressure for desegregation or full participation for blacks in all other U.S. public institutions?" and "Do black colleges offer public benefits nowhere else available and therefore transcend incremental attempts to achieve equity?" (p. 179).

Williams (1984) proposed the development of unique research agendas for HBCUs, recommending the initiation of "a policy to assist selected states to develop at least one major black research university . . . which would rest firmly on the conviction that ethnic identity is an aspect of institutional diversity in U.S. higher education that should be preserved" (p. 186), as in the case of tribally controlled community colleges. A similar approach had previously been recommended by the Carnegie Commission in 1970 (Williams, 1984). Such an agenda is in keeping with arguments posed by Carter Woodson (1933) 51 years earlier. In *The Mis-Education of the Negro,* Woodson asserts that "(t)he unusual gifts of the race have not been developed." (p. 7). "The thought that the Negro is one thing and the white man another is the stock-in-trade argument of the Caucasian to justify segregation . . . . The differences of the races, moreover, is no evidence of superiority or of infirmity. This merely indicates that each race has certain gifts which the others do not possess" (p. 8). However, the belief by Whites that differences indicated the inferiority of African Americans is what W.E.B. DuBois argued was "responsible for the segregated, underfunded, and inferior schooling of African Americans" based on "the unholy alliance of the white North, and the reactionary South" (Watkins, 1996, p. 14). The system was merely a product of the politics of controlling the plight of African Americans. DuBois firmly believed that HBCUs "should teach about social problems" and "should mercilessly critique every manifestation of injustice" (p. 14).

Nevertheless, beliefs about African inferiority, along with the nation's need to maintain a class of citizens functioning at the lowest spheres of the social order

(Watkins, 1996; Woodson, 1933), resulted in the federal government's never making "a forthright attempt to enhance the development of black colleges" (Williams, 1984, p. 187). Arguments against expenditures for their development reflect the incorrect judgment that HBCUs failed to achieve expected results with public funds allocated for this purpose (Williams, 1984). In the name of justice, laws now dictate that federal and state dollars can no longer support segregated institutions with majority African American student populations. Ironically, the same discriminatory admissions practices in historically PWIs not only sustain, but are being strengthened to sustain, majority White student populations.

Lessons Learned from K-12 Desegregation

Examination of desegregation attempts in K-12 public education offers insights for HBCUs. The past 40 years of U.S. educational history have demonstrated that court orders do not make desegregation work. African Americans were, and are still, seeking equality of education based on quality school facilities and academic program offerings and equal representation of the contributions of all peoples to the development of this country and the world, along with equal treatment of African American children in schools. Tate, Ladson-Billings, and Grant (1996) argue that the intended outcome of landmark decisions from "*Plessy* to *Brown* to the over 500 pending" (p. 35) related cases was to apply mathematical solutions to legal issues to address social realities. They argue that "(b)ecause equality is a mathematical construct, it must conform to the logic of the discipline" (p. 37). Therefore, the "model must have `certain verbal interpretations' that describe the phenomenon to be observed" (p. 38). However, in *Brown* and other desegregation legislation, no verbal interpretation of observed equality has been given. Rather, responsibility has been entrusted to school authorities and to states to transform segregated systems to integrated realities of education. In addition to the failure of legislation to specify desired observed equality, the educational gains African Americans were seeking have been lost because White self-interest had not been accounted for; "white parents would not send their children to all-black schools, nor would they allow blacks to attend their schools" (p. 37).

White self-interest has been served in the 1990s when states have resisted requests to equalize responsibilities for desired academic programs and land-grant responsibilities in public HBCUs, limiting their desirability to other state residents (Healy, 1996c, Jaschik, 1995). It has also been served when states have failed to provide public HBCUs with resources to develop unique research and curricular agendas to serve pressing public needs (Watkins, 1996; Williams, 1984). Inhibiting the desirability of HBCUs, while not strengthening them academically, can only facilitate their inability to meet the demands of state desegregation mandates.

AFFIRMATIVE ACTION

The last decade of this century is plagued with challenges to affirmative action in college admissions and hiring, with legislation supporting some challenges but not others. The result is certain to lead to a reduction in the number of African Americans admitted to both undergraduate and graduate programs. Affirmative action allows the use of race-based classifications in college and university admissions and hiring practices for the purposes of correcting historical inequities from past discrimination practices and to promote racial diversity on campuses (Michaelson, 1995a).

Today's affirmative action policies have their origins in outcomes of civil rights efforts and college and university student revolts of the 1960s (Cahn, 1969; Hare, 1969; Harper, 1969; Orrick, 1969; President's Commission on Campus Unrest, 1970; Smith, Axen, & Pentony, 1970). The civil rights protests of the 1960s often drew hundreds of protesters (Smith et al., 1970) and even thousands, as in the 1963 march in Washington led by Rev. Martin Luther King, Jr. While mass protest efforts were accompanied by spokespersons of small groups or legal representatives, the masses represented the collective, articulated, desired outcomes to be achieved. Kelley (1994) notes that one of the benefits of mass protests, such as those in the 1960s, is that collective action makes for anonymity, making it difficult to single out and punish individuals involved. While many paid dearly through their arrests, beatings, and lynchings, masses were able to return to their daily activities with few consequences.

Today's affirmative action efforts are often articulated through thoughtful essays explaining their commitment to diversity by presidents of universities (i.e., Harvard, Princeton, and Stanford), statements by national organizations like the American Council on Education, and lengthy legal battles (Michaelson, 1995b). At other times the responsibility rests on the commitment of small groups or individuals among college and university administration and faculty members (Michaelson, 1995b). Too often the visible gains experienced from affirmative action policy has resulted in these individuals being the "first" or "only" African American or person of color hired in specific roles. Thus, anonymity is lost in these struggles, and the consequences of articulated commitment or protest often result in martyrdom. Many know the consequences of martyrdom, where others see their actions as either inadequate or senseless or contrary to the prevailing views. As a result, the desired outcomes that moved masses of African Americans and others during the civil rights movement may not become a reality until the masses are once again moved to speak collectively on these ameliorative issues.

Legislation that has emerged challenging affirmative action programs and practices is considerable and national. In 1995, the University of California Board of Regents voted to bar the administration from using racial and gender preferences in admissions, hiring, or contracting (Schmidt, 1996). In 1995, the U.S. Court of Appeals for the Fifth Circuit determined that the University of Texas at Austin Law School could not use diversity as a basis for race-based policies in admissions (Lederman, 1996). Segregation in law school admissions had apparently occurred too long ago to warrant a remedy based on race (Healy, 1996b); and the university was, therefore, forced to eliminate certain scholarship and retention programs directed at African American and Mexican-American applicants. At the same time,

Louisiana's race-based aid programs are not in jeopardy because discrimination against African Americans was determined to be as recent as 1988, nor are Alabama's $20 million grants for White students to attend the state's HBCUs in jeopardy since the programs were created in 1995 (Healy, 1996b). These are only a few examples of the challenges to affirmative action in recent years. Yet their outcomes set a precedent for future initiatives. Michaelson (1996b) suggests that "educators must make the case for affirmative action themselves; the courts are unlikely to do it for them" (p. A48).

CONCLUSION

African American educational reform ideology today (Afrocentrism, multiculturalism, and others) has its "roots in the protest ideology that first emerged in the early 19th century" (Watkins, 1996, p. 6). These ideologies must be revisited and taught to the masses, and their outcomes must be studied in order to accomplish a more comprehensive political participation of African Americans. Woodson observed the depoliticizing and silencing of African Americans that result directly from the process of schooling with inadequate curricula (Watkins, 1996). The results of depoliticizing are apparent in the inferior academic achievements of schoolchildren, as demonstrated in reading, history, and mathematics scores; the disparity in college participation and completion among African Americans; and the large, sustained African American underclass. Depoliticization is also apparent in the protest of youth drug and gang culture. Yet, political reenergization must be accomplished not only among those in the African American educational community, but through the informed protests of the African American communities at large. As with protests throughout this century, they are informed by the collective, reflective experiences of those within the larger communities. Recent attacks to affirmative action, challenges to HBCUs, and efforts to bring about educational equality and social mobility should not dismantle the accomplishments of this century. Rather, they should serve as springboards for social, political, educational, and spiritual reform efforts into the next century.

NOTES

1. An NCES composite measure of parental education, family income, father's occupation, and household characteristics.

2. The Frederick D. Patterson Research Institute was recently established by The College Fund/UNCF "to design, conduct, and disseminate research to policymakers, educators, and the public with the goal of improving educational opportunities and outcomes for African Americans" (Nettles & Perna, 1997b).

REFERENCES

Astin, A. W. (1990). *The Black undergraduate: Current status and trends in the characteristics of freshmen.* Los Angeles, CA: UCLA, Higher Education Research Institute.

Brown v. Board of Education, 347 U.S. 483, 74 S.Ct. 686, 98 L.Ed.2d 873 (1954).

Butts, R. F. (1939). *The college charts its course: Historical conceptions and current proposals.* New York: Arno Press.

Cahn, M. M. (1969). The 1968–1969 San Francisco State College crisis: A minority report. *Phi Delta Kappan, 51*(1), 21–25.

Garibaldi, A. (1984). Black colleges: An overview (pp. 3–9). In Antoine Garibaldi (Ed.), *Black colleges and universities: Challenges for the future.* New York: Praeger.

Guernsey, L. (1996). Lecturing presidents, Ala. judge demands progress in desegregation. *The Chronicle of Higher Education, 43*(4).

Hare, N. (1969). Black invisibility of White campuses: The positiveness of separation. *Negro Digest, 18*(5), 39–43, 91–94.

Harper, F. D. (1969). Black student revolt on the White campus. *Journal of College Student Personnel, 10*(5), 291–95.

Healy, P. (1996a). Black college struggles with court order that it recruit Whites. *The Chronicle of Higher Education, 42*(22), A28.

Healy, P. (1996b). Desegregation programs in many states may be vulnerable to legal challenges. *The Chronicle of Higher Education, 43*(5), A40–A41.

Healy, P. (1996c). Georgia may face lawsuit for keeping public Black colleges. *The Chronicle of Higher Education, 43*(38).

Healy, P. (1996d). A myriad of problems for public Black colleges. *The Chronicle of Higher Education, 42*(36), A30–A31.

Healy, P. (1996e). Ohio lawmakers debate why their state's public Black college fell into disarray, and whether it can make a comeback. *The Chronicle of Higher Education, 43*(4), A36.

Jaschik, S. (1995). Alabama desegregation: Federal judge says the state's two public Black universities must become less so. *The Chronicle of Higher Education, 41*(48), A21 A22.

Kelley, R.D.G. (1994). *Race rebels: Culture, politics, and the Black working class.* New York: The Free Press.

Lederman, D. (1996). Justice department urges high court to uphold affirmative action. *The Chronicle of Higher Education, 42*(39), A26.

Loewen, J. W. (1995). *Lies my teacher told me: Everything your American history textbook got wrong.* New York: New Press.

Maltz, E. M. (1990). *Civil rights, the constitution, and congress, 1863–1869.* Lawrence: University Press of Kansas.

Michaelson, M. (1995a). Building a comprehensive defense of affirmative-action programs. *The Chronicle of Higher Education, 41*(46), A56.

Michaelson, M. (1995b). A time to increase public understanding of affirmative action. *The Chronicle of Higher Education, 42*(45), A48.

National Center for Education Statistics. (1993). *Projections of education statistics to 2003.* Washington, DC: U.S. Department of Education, Office of Educational Research and Improvement.

National Center for Education Statistics. (1994). *National education longitudinal study of 1988, second follow-up: Student component data file user's manual.* Washington, DC: U.S. Department of Education, Office of Educational Research and Improvement.

National Center for Education Statistics. (1995a). *Enrollment in higher education: Fall 1984 through fall 1993.* Washington, DC: U.S. Department of Education, Office of Educational Research and Improvement.

National Center for Education Statistics. (1995b). *Making the cut: Who meets highly selective college entrance criteria?* Washington, DC: U.S. Department of Education, Office of Educational Research and Improvement.

National Center for Education Statistics. (1995c). *Minority undergraduate participation in postsecondary education.* Washington, DC: U.S. Department of Education, Office of Educational Research and Improvement.

National Center for Education Statistics. (1995d). *A profile of the American high school senior in 1992.* Washington, DC: U.S. Department of Education, Office of Educational Research and Improvement.

National Center for Education Statistics. (1995e). *A profile of the American high school sophomore in 1990.* Washington, DC: U.S. Department of Education, Office of Educational Research and Improvement.

Nettles, M. T., & Perna, L. W. (1997a). *The African American education data book, Vol. I: Higher and adult education.* Fairfax: Frederick D. Patterson Research Institute of the College Fund/UNCF.

Nettles, M. T., & Perna, L. W. (1997b). *The African American education data book, volume II: Preschool through high school education.* Fairfax: Frederick D. Patterson Research Institute of the College Fund/UNCF.

Orrick, W. H., Jr. (1969). *Shut it down! A college in crisis, San Francisco State College, October, 1968 to April, 1969. A staff report to the national commission on the causes and prevention of violence.* San Francisco: San Francisco State College. (ERIC Document Reproduction Service No. ED084943).

Plessy v. Ferguson. 163 U.S. 537, 165 S.Ct. 1138, 41 L.Ed.2d 256 (1896).

President's Commission on Campus Unrest. (1970). *The report of the president's commission on campus unrest.* Washington, DC: Superintendent of Documents, U.S. Government Printing Office. (ERIC Document Reproduction Service No. ED083899).

Roebuck, J. B., & Murty, K. S. (1993). *Historically Black colleges and universities: Their place in American higher education.* Westport, CT: Praeger.

Schmidt, P. (1996). Professors' group condemns U. of California ban on affirmative action. *The Chronicle of Higher Education, 42*(39), A29.

Smith, R., Axen, R., & Pentony, D. (1970). *By any means necessary: The revolutionary struggle at San Francisco State.* San Francisco: Jossey-Bass.

Smith, R. C. (1995). *Racism in the post-civil rights era: Now you see it, Now you don't.* Albany: State University of New York Press.

Takagi, D. Y. (1992). *The retreat from race: Asian American admissions and racial politics.* New Brunswick, NJ: Rutgers University Press.

Tate, W. F., Ladson-Billings, G., & Grant, C. A. (1996). The *Brown* decision revisited: Mathematizing a social problem. In Mwalimu J. Shujaa (Ed.), *Beyond desegregation: The policies of quality in African American schooling* (p. 77–85). Thousand Oaks, CA: Corwin Press.

Thompson, C. J. (1996). African American student leadership: Implications for quality in college achievement in the 21st century. In Mwalimu J. Shujaa (Ed.), *Beyond desegregation: The policies of quality in African American schooling* (pp. 185–205). Thousand Oaks, CA: Corwin Press.

U.S. Bureau of National Affairs. (1964). *Civil Rights Act of 1964, with explanation as passed by the Congress and sent to the president.* Chicago: Commerce Clearing House.

U.S. Department of Education. (1997). *Minorities in higher education, No. 9.* Washington, DC: Office of Educational Research and Improvement.

Watkins, W. H. (1996). Reclaiming historical visions of quality schooling: The legacy of early 20th-century Black intellectuals. In Mwalimu J. Shujaa (Ed.), *Beyond desegregation: The policies of quality in African American schooling* (pp. 5–28). Thousand Oaks, CA: Corwin Press.

Williams, J. B. (1984). Public policy and Black college development: An agenda for research. In Antoine Garibaldi (Ed.), *Black colleges and universities: Challenges for the future* (pp. 178–198). New York: Praeger.
Woodson, C. G. (1933). *The mis-education of the negro.* Trenton, NJ: Africa World Press.

Part II

Examining African American Higher Education Research Issues and Paradigms

5

And Who Shall Control Their Minds?: Race Consciousness and Collective Commitments among African American Students

Walter R. Allen

Education has always played a central role in the determination of the circumstances of Black life in America. One cannot validly study the economic status, residential patterns, or future prospects of African Americans without making reference to the relationships between Blacks and the educational system of this country. Educational access, or the lack of it, has been and continues to be a powerful determinant of the unequal economic, cultural, political, and social status of Blacks in America (Allen & Jewell, 1995). For this reason, Black Americans have historically struggled to gain equal access to the nation's schools and have expressed the desire to exert some control over the content of the schooling process as it relates to them (Franklin, 1984). These motives were most succinctly stated during the 1960s social movements in New York City to gain community control of schools. The rallying motto was, "We are engaged in a struggle over the control of minds (and futures) of our children" (Hare & Castenell, 1985, p. 24).

This chapter looks at collective consciousness and commitments among African American students in institutions of higher education in the United States for answers to the question of who controls the minds of college-educated Blacks. Do these students emerge from the schooling process with strong race consciousness and collective commitments that equip and motivate them to serve as effective advocates for the development of African American communities? Data are used from a national study of 1,500 African American undergraduates attending

This research was completed as part of the National Study of Black College Students. Funding was provided by the Ford and Charles S. Mott Foundations for data collection and by the Joyce Foundation for data analysis. Funding from the UCLA Academic Senate paid for paper preparation costs. Please address inquiries to the author at: Department of Sociology, 210 Haines Hall, University of California–Los Angeles, Los Angeles, CA 90095–1551; email, WALLEN@UCLA.EDU.

historically Black colleges and universities (HBCUs) and predominantly White institutions (PWIs). Specifically, race consciousness and collective commitments are considered as related to student family background, personal characteristics, and campus experiences.

In his cross-cultural study of minority education, Ogbu (1978) confirms the link between poor minority performance in school and the continuation of a castelike status for selected minority groups. Using data from Israel, the United States, Britain, India, Japan, and New Zealand, Ogbu convincingly outlines the procedures by which the dominant group of a country exercises control over that country's educational system as a means to protect the dominant status in the society. Ogbu (1978, pp. 349–354) finds the following general features to be true across the six societies studied:

1. Economic inequality between the minority and dominant groups was usually attributed to group differences in educational attainments.
2. Historically, there were marked differences in the educational access of minority and dominant groups. In the past, minority groups were either first denied formal education and later given inferior education or given inferior education from the beginning.
3. There was a wide gap in educational attainment between the minority and dominant groups in each of the six societies.
4. Minority group members explained this wide discrepancy in educational attainment by referring to inequalities of the prevailing castelike stratification system and in the legal or extralegal discriminatory policies/practices of the dominant group. Dominant group members explained these same discrepancies in educational attainment by linking educational problems to personal, familial, cultural, or biological inadequacies of the minority group members.
5. To the extent that efforts were taken to close the education gap between minority and dominant group members, these efforts generally revolved around changing or rehabilitating minority group members (e.g., correcting certain "deficits" minority group children supposedly take with them to school owing to their cultural, biological or family heritage). Rarely was attention given to breaking down the institutional or socioeconomic barriers that these children and their families are required to face.
6. None of the societies studied had a history of rewarding minority group members equally for equivalent training and ability.

Ogbu's formal and scientific model states that universally dominant groups rely upon the educational system for assistance in the difficult task of asserting and maintaining control over minority groups. Ogbu's meticulous discussion of the role played by the educational system in the maintenance of superordinate-subordinate relationships between dominant and minority group members is not necessarily a new one; many scholars have made similar points in the past.

BACKGROUND

"I think this anthropology is just another way to call me a nigger" (Gwaltney, 1980, p. xix). This quote from John Gwaltney's *Drylongso* (1980) personifies a system of belief in Black American communities about the duplicity of educational institutions in America in the oppression of Blacks. *Drylongso* relates the everyday culture of African Americans as seen through the eyes of common, everyday people. In simplest form, Gwaltney presents a view of schooling in America as largely detrimental to the interests of Blacks because of the stress placed upon maintaining the status quo—a status quo that finds Blacks at the bottom of the social hierarchy.

As early as 1903, W.E.B. DuBois discussed the critical need among Black Americans for college-educated leaders who would be able to assist the economic, social, and cultural uplift of their people. This "talented tenth" was to provide the guidance and expertise necessary for the development of the Black masses on all fronts. DuBois (1903) argued that "the Negro race, like all races, is going to be saved by its exceptional men. The problem of education, then, among Negroes must first of all deal with the talented tenth; it is the problem of developing the Best of this race" (p. 33). Beyond questions of improved educational access, DuBois was also concerned with the content of schooling received. For it was DuBois' contention that "the boy who does enter the white school and gets on reasonably well does not always become a useful member of our group. Negro children in integrated schools and northern colleges often know nothing of Negro history[,] . . . of Negro leadership and doubt if there ever have been leaders in Africa, the West Indies, and the United States who equal white folk. Some are ashamed of themselves and their folk" (DuBois, 1973, p. 151).

Carter G. Woodson (1933) presents an even more radical statement of the concerns articulated by DuBois when he concludes that African Americans have been "miseducated" to the extent that they have been raised to be a people apart from their roots and community. Such "educated" Blacks pursue their studies in schools largely controlled by Whites: "The education of the Negroes, then, the most import thing in the uplift of the Negroes, is almost entirely in the hands of those who have enslaved them and now segregate them" (Woodson, 1933, p. 22). As a result, Woodson (1933) argues, "the Negro's mind has been all but perfectly enslaved in that he has been trained to think what is desired of him" (p. 24). Woodson goes on to say that such miseducated Blacks will rarely challenge the status quo. Indeed, they go so far as to resist identification and involvement with other Blacks: "These educated people . . . decry any such thing as race conscious-ness. . . . They do not like to hear such expressions as `Negro literature,' `Negro poetry,' `African art,' or `thinking Black'" (Woodson, 1933, p. 7).

It seems that African Americans have long been concerned with what manner Black people are graduated by the nation's colleges and universities. Most recently, a furor has been created by debates over the supposed gulf between middle-class and so-called underclass Blacks in this country. Wilson (1978) concludes, for example, that class cleavages have begun to emerge and solidify among African Americans. These changes reflect shifts in the relationship between class and race in the post-industrial United States. The effect has been to create a privileged elite whose identifications and loyalties are determined more by economic factors than racial ones. In that respect, this group of elite Blacks is more closely allied with middle-class Whites than with lower-class Blacks. Echoing Wilson's analysis, Sowell (1980) suggests that, in many instances, the interests of lower-class and middle-income African Americans are diametrically opposed. In his assessment, policies and programs meant to aid all Blacks instead often disproportionately assist the Black elite. This privileged group thus becomes increasingly invested in protecting its advantages to the detriment of the larger masses of Blacks.

While many reject such interpretations (Farley & Allen, 1989; Willie, 1979), there is a need to evaluate empirically the validity of such contentions. Are members of the Black elite alienated from their less fortunate brethren? If so, what are some factors associated with such disaffection? These and similar questions are the focus of this chapter. Black students attending PWIs are appropriate subjects for such an inquiry because: (1) they are tomorrow's Black leadership, and (2) many of them are also children of today's Black elite. In both capacities, these students enable us to draw inferences about the attitudes and commitments of the Black elite toward the larger community of Black people.

Since the historic *Brown v. Board of Education of Topeka* Supreme Court decision outlawing segregated public education, significant shifts have occurred in Black student patterns of college attendance. In 1950 the majority of Black college students attended HBCUs; by 1970 three-quarters of all Black college students were attending PWIs (Abramowitz, 1976). Similarly, as estimated, 57% of all baccalaureate degrees conferred on Black students during 1978–1979 were granted by PWIs (Deskins, 1983). From the point of view of school desegregation, the observed shift in Black student enrollments from Black to White campuses is cause for celebration. However, when we consider the implications of these shifts in college enrollments for other aspects of African American life, conclusions are slightly more ominous (Allen & Jewell, 1995). Most notable are questions surrounding the potentially negative effects of education at PWIs. Will such educational experiences weaken race consciousness and collective commitments of this generation of Black college students? Will they be less effective community leaders in the future than their peers educated at HBCUs?

PROBLEM, DATA, AND METHODS

This chapter investigates race consciousness and collective commitment among Black community leadership, examining their current identification with, and commitments to, African Americans. When they move into the middle and upper class, will these students be assets or liabilities to the quest of African Americans for development and advancement?

Race consciousness can be defined as an awareness of, and identification with, one's racial heritage. Implicit in this definition is the assumption that racially conscious Blacks will be better informed about their people's history and structural relationships in this society. Further, it is assumed they will be concerned with, and convinced of, the need to improve the life circumstances of African Americans. To the extent they would feel personal responsibility and dedication to improving the lives of the masses of African Americans, Blacks can be said to exhibit collective commitment. Collectively committed Blacks expect themselves (and others) to invest skills and resources in the uplifting of the larger Black community.

Research on race consciousness and collective commitment among Blacks has been limited and, in many cases, misdirected (Cross, 1991). A common interpretation assumes these orientations to be "anti-White," when they are, in fact, "pro-Black." The example of the society's response to the Black power movement offers a classic case in point (Carmichael & Hamilton, 1967). This strategy, with its emphasis on self-pride, self-definition, and empowerment for Blacks, was incorrectly evaluated as a campaign of hatred toward Whites. More recently, studies of Black attitudes have labeled pro-Black positions as *a priori* anti-White. Blacks who refer to the social realities of race discrimination, racial disparities in economic status, and inferior schooling opportunities are described as exhibiting "a fairly high degree of hostility towards Whites" (Wojniusz, 1979, p. 57). Likewise, racial attitude research on Blacks skirts the gut issue of Black oppression, preferring instead to focus on whether or not Blacks *think* racial discrimination is inevitable (Schumann & Hatchett, 1974), despite the historic, concrete, and overwhelming evidence of persistent race discrimination in the United States.

This investigation is patterned after Gurin and Epps' (1975) study of Black students attending HBCUs which examines the interface between Black consciousness, collective commitments, personal identity, and individual achievement. Findings from this study refute the accepted view that high individual achievement is incompatible with strong ethnic identification and/or strong commitment to the collective body. Many Black students in their sample were classified as "committed achievers." These students managed to combine successfully high individual achievement and aspirations with strong group identification and commitments to collective action aimed at improving the circumstances of African Americans. Gurin and Epps (1975) find that "traditional academic achievement and individual goals were not necessarily in conflict with strong commitments to the group and collective action" (p. 386). In a related study of African American students at a PWI, Pitts (1975) examines the processes by which they became politicized. He begins by asking whether Black graduates of PWIs "serve consciously or not to legitimize 'the system,' to insulate White institutions from Black discontent" (Pitts, 1975, p. 281). Over their college careers, Black students in Pitts' study became politicized in order to cope with the oppressive, alienating PWI environment. Racial communion (Black fraternization) and racial consciousness (efforts to reduce Black disadvantage) were two manifestations of Black student political activity. Pitts (1975) concludes that, although racial communion and race consciousness orientations would likely persist beyond graduation, the percentage of "Black college graduates who are likely to dedicate their daily activities to promoting racial uplift and liberation from oppressive structures are a minority, even among those who have participated in an aggressive student movement" (p. 313).

Two contrasting views of Black college student race consciousness and collective commitments emerged from these studies. On HBCU campuses, Black students tended to be high on both race consciousness and collective commitment. On PWI campuses, Black students scored high on race consciousness, but questions were raised about their subsequent collective commitments.

The major purpose of this chapter is to examine how well African American college students manage to integrate individual and collective aspects of identity and achievement at a PWI versus an HBCU. However, several related questions will also be addressed. Findings from the research just surveyed helped lead to the following hypotheses:

1. Race consciousness and collective commitment levels will be comparable for African American students on Black and White campuses.
2. Student race consciousness, collective commitments, and achievement will be related to student personal characteristics, specifically:
    a. There will be significant differences by student sex and campus race in student background characteristics.
    b. There will be no significant differences in student racial attitudes by sex, campus race, or family socioeconomic status.
    c. There will be no significant differences in student collective commitments by sex, campus race, or family socioeconomic status.

Data were collected from African American undergraduates attending public PWIs and HBCUs. Data were collected as part of the National Study of Black College Students, which used self-completed questionnaires to gather information on student achievements, attitudes, and backgrounds. Participating students were randomly selected from registrars' lists of currently enrolled Black students for 1981 (PWI campuses) and 1983 (HBCU campuses).

Institutions participating in the 1981, 1982, and 1983 studies were chosen on the basis of regional diversity and accessibility. The 1981 study gathered data on six public PWI campuses (University of Michigan–Ann Arbor; University of North Carolina–Chapel Hill; Memphis State University; State University of New York–Stony Brook; University of California–Los Angeles; Arizona State University). The final response rate for the 1981 study was 27%, representing 695 undergraduate students. The 1982 study gathered data from the six campuses of the 1981 study and from the University of Wisconsin–Madison and Eastern Michigan University. The final response rate for 1982 was 35%, including 902 Black undergraduates. Since 1982 was the first year of a longitudinal data collection, the sample was disproportionately composed of freshman (57%).

The indicators of student race consciousness and collective commitment are taken from the Gurin and Epps study (1975, pp. 193–233). The dimensions tapped by these measures are Black nationalist ideology, self versus system blame, beliefs about the modifiability of discrimination, and stress on collective action as a vehicle for social change. Also used is a set of racial attitude items that tap attitudes toward the expressed need for a Black political party, interracial dating, the importance of the Black church, and the degree of unity among Blacks on the campus. College grade point average is self-reported. The key test factors used are student sex, campus race, and family income. The major variables of college grade point average, racial attitudes, and student background are examined in relation to these test factors.

FINDINGS

Gurin and Epps' investigation of trends in Black student activism and ideology reveals striking shifts in response patterns from 1964 to 1970 (see Table 5.1). Over this period, both sexes drastically increased their tendency to attribute system blame; to express pessimism about the eventual elimination of discrimination; to call for collective social action by Blacks; and to see the control of African Americans' fate as being externally located. Other less pronounced changes are also apparent in Black student ideology from the 1970s to the 1980s. Overall, the pattern of student responses in the 1980s was more restrained than in the 1970s, thus rejecting the hypothesis of stable attitudes. It should be pointed out, however, that by no means were the responses in the 1980s conservative. A majority of respondents opted for the system blame response, saw race discrimination as unlikely to change, and believed that external factors often determined individual outcomes.

In an interesting reversal of the 1970 pattern, more students subscribed to the view that many Blacks bore individual responsibility for not doing better in life. Males were significantly more likely than females to adopt this position ($X^2 = 6.3$; $p = .01$). Excepting this item, the data supported Gurin and Epps' findings of no significant sex differences. The most consistent items from the 1970s to the 1980s were control ideology and advocacy of collective action. In both decades and on both types of campuses, students split more or less evenly on their acceptance of collective action and were strongly accepting of the idea that some people are externally disadvantaged.

Comparison of African American students on PWI and HBCU campuses, in terms of background characteristics, reveals several important differences (Table 5.2). Looking at the differences by race of campus, Black students on PWI and HBCU campuses differed significantly by all the measures of background examined. The majority of African American students on PWI campuses reported higher grades in high school than in college. These students attending PWIs also came from higher-status families, their fathers worked in higher-prestige occupations, and their families earned more annually. Black students on PWI campuses expected to move into occupations that were much higher in power and prestige than did their peers who attended HBCUs.

Turning our attention to sex differences in student background characteristics, we again find pronounced differences. Perhaps most significant is the observed shift in grades from high school to college. Females lost ground in the transition. In high school, their grades were higher than those for males. By college this

Table 5.1
Time Trends in Student Race Consciousness and Collective Commitment by Sex: 1964, 1970, 1981, 1982, 1983

	1964[1]		1970[1]		1981[2]		1982[2]		1983[2,4]	
	Men	Women	Men	Women	Men	Women	Men	Women	Men	Women
Self-Blame-System Blame										
1. a) The attempt to "fit in" and do what's proper hasn't paid off for Blacks. (System Blame)	56%	52%	84%	86%	63%	67%	59%	57%	80%	74%
b) The problem for many Blacks is that they really aren't acceptable by American standards. (Individual Blame)	44% 100%	48% 100%	16% 100%	14% 100%	37% 100%	33% 100%	41% 100%	43% 100%		
2. a) Many Blacks have only themselves to blame for not doing better in life. (Individual Blame)	61%	67%	41%	44%	68%	57%	73%	70%		
b) When two qualified people one Black and one White, are considered for the same job the Black won't get the job no matter how hard s/he tries. (System Blame)	39% 100%	33% 100%	59% 100%	56% 100%	32% 100%	43% 100%	27% 100%	30% 100%	34%	31%
Modifiability of Discrimination[3]										
3. a) The so-called "White backlash" shows once again that Whites are so opposed to Blacks getting their rights that it is practically impossible to end discrimination in America.	23%	26%	64%	65%	74%	78%	63%	70%	69%	65%

b) The so-called "White backlash" has been exaggerated.	77% 74% 100% 100%	36% 35% 100% 100%	26% 22% 100% 100%	37% 30% 100% 100%	71% 56%
Individual Mobility-Collective Action					
4. a) The best way to overcome discrimination is through pressure and action. (Collective Action)	21% 13%	56% 51%	51% 47%	40% 37%	
b) The best way to overcome discrimination is for each individual Black to be even better qualified than the most qualified White person. (Individual Action)	79% 87% 100% 100%	56% 51% 100% 100%	51% 47% 100% 100%	60% 63% 100% 100%	
Control Ideology					
5. a) People who don't do well in life often work hard. (External)	34% 33%	69% 65%	63% 66%	57% 62%	39% 32%
b) Some people just don't use the breaks that come their way. (Interval)	66% 67% 100% 100%	31% 35% 100% 100%	37% 34% 100% 100%	43% 38% 100% 100%	
			(188) (132)	(279) (522)	(378) (475)

---

[1] From Gurin and Epps (1975) study of Black students attending historically Black colleges and universities: 1965–70.

[2] Gurin and Epps items replicated for Black students attending predominantly white universities: 1981, 1982. Replicated for Black students attending historically Black institutions: 1983.

[3] The 1981 wording differed slightly from that in 1964 and 1970. Please see Appendix for comparison.

[4] Questions were revised and some were dropped from 1982. The percentages represent the proportion of respondents who agreed with the statement. Blanks indicate excluded questions.

pattern had been reversed. A possible explanation for this drastic shift is provided in the fact that males in our sample came from higher-status families, as judged by their fathers' occupations and family income. It should also be noted that males in this sample reported occupational aspirations that far exceeded those of their female peers.

Table 5.2
Comparison of Means Tests, 1981 White Campus Group Versus
1983 Black Campus Group

		White	Black
A.	College Race		
	Undergrad GPA	2.60	2.74*
	High School GPA	3.32	2.95*
	Father's Occupation	43.03	33.50*
	Family Income	6.01	5.75*
	Occupational Aspirations	71.82	69.65*
		Male	Female
B.	Student Sex		
	Undergrad GPA	2.72	2.64*
	High School GPA	3.02	3.19*
	Father's Occupation	37.98	36.47*
	Family's Income	6.12	5.69*
	Occupational	72.37	69.44*

*=significant at .05 or beyond

Student racial attitudes were found to vary in important ways by sex, campus race, and family income (Table 5.3). Females were significantly more likely, for example, to agree that a national Black political party was needed. More striking, however, is the fact that fully three-quarters of both sexes agreed with this rather radical proposition for the redefinition of African American participation in the country's political process. It was also surprising to note the sizable proportions of both males and females who agreed that interracial dating and marriage are acceptable. However, males were much more liberal on this score. This, no doubt, reflects the stereotypic realities of courtship in our society, for men as initiators are more likely to benefit from the relaxation of norms allowing for cross-race dating and marriage. Males and females concurred in their belief that the Black church had helped to improve the conditions of Black people in this country. The two sexes differed, however, in their estimations of the amount of unity and sharing to be found among Blacks. Males judged there to be significantly more unity on campus than did females.

Our comparison of racial attitudes across HBCU and PWI campuses reveals a most striking paradox: African American students on PWI campuses were more radical on the point of whether or not a Black political party was needed (Table 5.3). By a large majority, Blacks on PWI campuses agreed that African Americans should form an independent political party. Students on the different

Table 5.3

Comparison of Student Racial Attitudes by Sex, Campus Race, and Family Income, 1981, 1983 Data Sets

	Sex		Campus Race		Family Income			
	Male	Female	Black	White	≤$15K	≤$25K	≤$50K	>$$50K
1. There is a need for a national Black political party. Agree	76.3%	77.6% (N=1534)	72.3%	81.0%* (N=1536)	81.0%	77.6%	75.2% (N=1424)	72.2%*
2. Interracial dating and marriage are equally as acceptable as within race dating and marriage. Agree	46.2%	37.7%* (N=1541)	40.9%	41.3% (N=1542)	37.8%	41.7%	41.7% (N=1427)	47.2%
3. In general, the church has helped the conditions of Black people in this country. Agree	71.3%	69.3% (N=1541)	79.3%	62.7%* (N=1542)	71.2%	68.5%	74.6% (N=1426)	65.1%
4. There is a great deal of unity and sharing among Black students at this university. Agree	57.3%	51.9%* (N=1543)	44.1%	61.9% (N=1544)	55.3%	56.5%	53.7% (N=1427)	50.0%

race campuses found interracial dating and marriage to be equally acceptable. However, African American students on HBCU campuses were significantly more likely to believe that the Black church had made important contributions to the improvements of Black life. They were significantly less likely to believe that their campuses were characterized by great unity and sharing among students. It may well be that these two findings are explained by the more limited contacts of Blacks on PWI campuses with Black churches (i.e., usually these schools are removed from Black communities with active Black churches) and by the greater reliance of Blacks at PWIs on their racial peers for support (i.e., because of their scarce numbers). In any case, the pattern of responses suggests a greater politization around race for African American students on PWI campuses—probably because of their greater sense of racial awareness resulting from being a small minority.

The comparison of racial attitudes across income levels provides a nearly direct test of questions surrounding the race consciousness and collective commitments of elite Blacks (Table 5.3). Interestingly enough, only one of our measures of racial attitudes shows a clear and unequivocal relationship with economic status. Lower-income African American students were significantly more likely than high-income African Americans to agree that a national Black political party is needed. In fact, the relationship is linear: the higher the family income, the more likely a student opposed this notion. A similar, though not significant, trend is also apparent for Black student attitudes toward interracial dating and marriage. Students whose families earned less tended to be less accepting of this idea than those from higher-income families. While no clear income trends are apparent in student attitudes toward the Black church, there seems to be a general tendency for feelings of unity among Blacks to decline as family income levels increase. In this sense, higher-status African American students seemed to feel slightly less a part of their respective Black university communities (at the very least, they tended to see these communities as being less unified than did lower-income students).

SUMMARY, DISCUSSION, AND CONCLUSIONS

The question raised in this chapter sprang from an interest in the implications for Black community welfare of a leadership increasingly trained outside the spheres of Black community influence and control. Motivated by raging debates over the supposed class cleavages among African Americans, this chapter has sought to address the issue of whether or not contemporary Black students in institutions of higher education represent an elite group trained for leadership but doomed to be estranged from their potential constituencies. The findings are convincing that this is not the case. Today's Black students seem to retain high levels of race consciousness and collective commitment. It should be pointed out, however, that their levels of commitment and consciousness are perhaps not as high as Black communities might prefer. For example, compared to Gurin and Epps' 1970 sample of African American students attending HBCUs, the Black students in the sample used in this study were decidedly more moderate. These differences are attributable, in part, to institutional context effects. HBCUs are, by their very nature, more closely connected and aligned with Black communities. Consequently, they provide settings more conducive to the development (and maintenance) of high race consciousness and collective commitment.

The observed differences in students attending HBCUs in the Gurin and Epps sample and those in our sample are due, in part, to important period effects that differentiate the two student cohorts. From 1970 to 1981 profound shifts occurred in Black student race consciousness and collective commitments. Responses became generally more conservative. Undoubtedly the civil rights movement (late 1950s and early 1960s) registered societal-wide impacts (Morris, 1984). The cohort of Black students responding in 1970 had, during their formative years, experienced these historic events through acquaintances, the media, and sometimes firsthand. The result was to differentiate them sharply from earlier cohorts of African American college students. Unlike their predecessors, Black students in the 1970s were a generation versed in the rhetoric of Black power and sensitized to the dynamics and history of Black oppression. Our findings reveal that these students were also more radical than their counterparts of the 1980s whether on HBCU or PWI campuses.

Rather than maintain the high race consciousness and collective commitments of the 1970s as expected, Black students in 1981, 1982, and 1983 showed a clear moderation in the pattern. We are reminded that the formative years of these students occurred during a time of relative Black affluence. The economy was expanding, jobs were plentiful, and equal employment or affirmative action programs were paying off in new opportunities for African Americans in high-status positions. On the surface, it seemed that battles for collective advancement had been won—doors were opening throughout the society. This generation therefore shifted its focus from the collective to the individual level. The appropriate quest, or so it seemed, was for personal excellence. African American students were advised to prepare themselves to compete successfully for the newly created opportunities.

In sum, it can be argued that the respective cohorts of Black students in higher education each responded appropriately to the expectations (implicit and explicit) of its historical era. In one case, young adults were expected to join (and, at points, lead) the push for equal opportunity for Blacks in education, employment, housing, and the society at large. In the other case, young adults were expected to develop their minds and talents in anticipation of a vast wave of educational and employment opportunities for African Americans. The burning question at hand is, How will the current generation of Black students respond to the contemporary scene? Economic stagnation, inflation, government reductions in spending, and an increasingly conservative political tilt have combined to sharply decrease Black opportunities for economic, political, and social advancement. In many instances, Blacks have actually lost ground (Reid, 1982). The bright economic prospects for which the 1980s cohorts of Black students were groomed have dimmed sharply. Will they respond by joining forces with the larger Black community to again pressure for expanded collective opportunities, or will they opt to pursue an independent course, secure in the knowledge that their degrees will ensure at least some modicum of personal financial well-being?

As this chapter concludes, we have come full circle, bringing us again to the point of questioning the strength of bonds between Black students in higher education, as potential members of an expanding Black elite, and the larger Black community. Obviously, where these bonds are weak, the leadership potential of these students will be limited, if not nonexistent.

Class cleavages and differences have always existed among African Americans. House slaves were differentiated from field slaves, artisans from laborers, and physicians from teachers. What is new, however, is the possibility (however slim) of subordinating one's racial identity to one's class identity. This option was largely nonexistent for Black Americans previously, when race was more castelike in its definition (Lincoln, 1979; Wilson, 1978). History proves that for Blacks, such options are ultimately more facade than reality. In times of economic stringency, race tends to be reasserted as a criterion for deciding how to allocate scarce resources. At the very least, economic downturns tend to damage most those groups with historic economic disadvantages (i.e., Blacks and women more so than Whites and men). Increased unemployment among African American professionals, persistent educational inequities for their children, and the chronic precariousness of their personal financial situation make this point forcefully. Be that as it may, the social rhetoric continues to offer (as if it were a real possibility) Black college students the option of disassociating from their racial heritage as a route to upward social mobility.

If these findings can be trusted, African Americans in higher education today are resisting this offer. They continue to identify with, and be committed to, the collective good. Reported attitudes aside, the next few years will tell the tale. As these students graduate and enter the competitive marketplace, will their actions mirror their expressed ideologies? Will these students prove themselves capable and dedicated enough to provide the necessary leadership for African American communities in what are surely to be desperate times? To be successful leaders, they must repress strong temptations to "go for themselves," for "the rules have been changed. The lines of division have been laid between the few and the many, and the challenge to the few is to prove themselves worthy to be a people apart from their roots. In short, there are signs that America is prepared to write off the Black masses in exchange for accepting the Black elite" (Lincoln, 1979, p. 30).

APPENDIX: VARIABLE MEASUREMENT

Black students' race consciousness/collective commitment was measured by a battery of items:

Self-Blame versus System Blame

Four Forced-choice items, each asking for the statement most agreed with (1) "The attempt to `fit in' and do what's proper hasn't paid off for Blacks. It doesn't matter how `proper' you are, you'll still face serious discrimination if you are Black;" or (2) "The problem for many Blacks is that they really are not acceptable by American standards; or (3) "Many Blacks have only themselves to blame for not doing better in life. If they tried harder, they would do better;" or (4) "When two qualified people, one Black and one White, are considered for the same job, the Black will not get the job no matter how hard she/he tries."

Modifiability of Discrimination

Two Forced-choice items, each asking for the statement most agreed with (1) "The recent upsurge in conservatism shows once again that Whites are so opposed to Blacks getting their rights that it is practically impossible to end discrimination in America;" or (2) "The recent upsurge in conservatism has been exaggerated. Certainly enough Whites support the goals of the Black cause for Americans to see considerable progress in wiping out discrimination."

Individual Mobility versus Collective Action

Two Forced-choice items, each asking for the statement most agreed with (1) "The best way to overcome discrimination is through pressure and social action;" or (2) "The best way to overcome discrimination is for each individual Black to be even better trained and more qualified than the most qualified White person."

Internal-External Control Ideology

Two Forced-choice items, each asking for the statement most agreed with (1) "People who do not do well in life often work hard, but the breaks just do not come their way;" or (2) "Some people just do not use the breaks that come their way. If they do not do well, it is their own fault."

REFERENCES

Abramowitz, E. (1976). *Equal educational opportunity for Blacks in U.S. higher education.* Washington, DC: Institute for the Study of Educational Policy, Howard University.

Allen, W. R., & Jewell, J. O. (1995). African American education since "An American dilemma": An American dilemma revisited. *Daedalus, 124*(1), 77–100.

Carmichael, S., & Hamilton, C. (1967). *Black power: The politics of liberation in America.* New York: Vintage Books.

Cross, W. E., Jr. (1991). *Shades of Black: Diversity in African-American identity.* Philadelphia: Temple University.

Deskins, D. (1983). *Minority recruitment data: An analysis of baccalaureate degree production in the United States.* Totawa, NJ: Rowman and Allanheld.

DuBois, W.E.B., et al. (1903). The talented tenth. In B. T. Washington (Ed.), *The negro problem: A series of articles by representative negroes of today* (pp. 33–75). New York: James Pott and Company. (Reprinted in J. Lester [Ed.], *The seventh son: The thought and writings of W.E.B. DuBois,* Vol. 1 [pp. 385–403]. New York: Vintage Books, 1971).

DuBois, W.E.B., et al. (1973). *The education of Black people: Ten critiques 1906–1960*. H. Aptheker (Ed.). New York: Monthly Review Press.

Farley, R., & Allen, W. R. (1989). *The color line and the quality of life in America*. New York: Oxford University Press.

Franklin, V. P. (1984). *Black self-determination: A cultural history of the faith of the fathers*. Westport, CT: Lawrence Hill.

Gurin, P., & Epps, E. (1975). *Black consciousness, identity and achievement: A study of students in historically Black colleges*. New York: Wiley.

Gwaltney, J. (1980). *Drylongso: A self-portrait of Black America*. New York: Vintage Books.

Hare, B. R., & Castenell, L. (1985). No place to run, no place to hide: Comparative status and future prospects of Black boys. In M. Spencer, G. Brookins, & W. Allen (Eds.), *Beginnings: The social and affective development of Black children* (pp. 201–214). Hillsdale, NJ: Erlbaum.

Lincoln, C. E. (1979). The new Black estate: The coming of age of Black America. In M. Namorato (Ed.), *Have we overcome?: Race relations since Brown* (pp. 3–30). Jackson: University of Mississippi Press.

Morris, A. (1984). *Origins of the civil rights movement: Black communities organizing for change*. New York: Free Press.

Ogbu, J. (1978). *Minority education and caste: The American system in cross-cultural prospective*. New York: Academic Press.

Pitts, J. P. (1975). The politicalization of Black students: Northwestern University. *Journal of Black Studies, 5*(3), 277–319.

Reid, J. (1982). Black America in the 1980's. *Population Bulletin, 37*(4), 1–38.

Schumann, H., & Hatchett, S. (1974). *Black racial attitudes: Trends and complexities*. Ann Arbor: Institute for Social Research, University of Michigan.

Sowell, T. (1980). *Knowledge and decisions*. New York: Basic Books.

Willie, C. V. (1979). *The caste and class controversy*. Bayside, NY: General Hall.

Wilson, W. J. (1978). *The declining significance of race: Blacks and changing American institutions*. Chicago: University of Chicago Press.

Wojniusz, H. (1979). Racial hostility among Blacks in Chicago. *Journal of Black Studies, 10*(1), 40–59.

Woodson, C. G. (1933). *The mis-education of the negro*. Washington, DC: Associated.

6

The College Experience: A Conceptual Framework to Consider for Enhancing Students' Educational Gains

Lemuel W. Watson

INTRODUCTION

Sociologists Pierre Bourdieu and Jean Claude Passeron are known for their work in social, class, and cultural reproduction within the educational systems. Bourdieu (1977) view education as an important social and political force in the process of class reproduction. By appearing to be an impartial and neutral "transmitter" of the benefits of a valued culture, schools are able to promote inequality in the name of fairness and objectivity. Bourdieu refers to this inequality as cultural capital, which is central to his argument. Bourdieu's (1977) concept of cultural capital refers to the different sets of linguistics and cultural competencies that individuals inherit by way of the class-location boundaries of their families.

In more specific terms, a child inherits from his or her family sets of meanings, quality of style, modes of thinking, and types of dispositions that are accorded a certain social value and status as a result of what the dominant class or classes label as the most valued cultural capital. Schools play a particularly important role in both legitimating and reproducing the dominant culture, especially at the level of higher education, and embody class interest and ideologies that capitalize on a kind of familiarity and set of skills that only specific students have received by means of their family backgrounds and class relation (Bourdieu, 1977). A four-year college degree has often been referred to as a ticket into the American middle class (Bowles & Gintis, 1976). Upward mobility in American society is defined by changes in occupational status and income and is inextricably aligned to postsecondary education in modern American society (Pascarella & Terenzini, 1991).

How does this cultural capital affect college students and their educational gains? What can be done in institutions of higher education to assist students in their learning and development? More importantly, are there differences between historically Black colleges and universities (HBCUs) and predominantly White institutions (PWIs) and Black and White students' educational outcomes from their undergraduate experiences based on the type of institution? A framework is introduced next in this chapter to address some of the posed questions.

Drawing from the work of Pace (1984) and Astin (1984), Watson's (1994, 1996) conceptual framework for student learning, involvement, and gains was developed to encourage a critical perspective for professionals when planning and addressing students' learning and educational gains. While the model employs familiar theories and concepts, it is unique in proposing a simple and practical framework to spark a holistic, creative, systematic, and critical thinking process that may be applied by educators to enhance student learning. The conceptual framework is to be used as a planning tool and is composed of three basic and dynamic components (Figure 6.1).

1. Input includes characteristics and experiences that students bring with them to college. We seem to do a great job of examining grade point averages (GPAs) and standardized test scores: however, we know little about the students as we move away from these factors. For example, students' experiences in secondary institutions, home, and community environments, as well as, their age, sex, marital status, college class, housing, major, parents' schooling, and race influence their college experience.

2. Process includes behavioral involvement of students on campus; quality of effort (scholarly and intellectual activities, informal personal activities, use of group facilities, organizational activities); and college environment (agents, peers, resources, and places on campus where students expend time and energies). Other environments represent agents, peers, resources, and places off campus where students might spend their time and energies. These places may include off-campus housing, churches, community centers, bars, and sports centers. The process section, the "what" student do, of the framework is an extremely important component of students' lives. It is equally important to understand that both the campus community and general community offer a vast array of activities. More time and energy could be invested in building partnerships in order to share resources and facilities to enhance learning and the educational gains of students and citizens. This component of the framework encourages us as professionals to expand our notions of designing environments to include other influential factors that may affect learning and educational gains.

3. Output represents educational gains in personal, social, intellectual, vocational, and cultural preparation while attending an institution of higher education (Pace, 1988), as well as societal benefits and intergenerational effects. The literature on educational outcomes is plentiful. We know that as students proceed through college from their first year to their senior year, they develop along many dimensions (Pascarella & Terenzini, 1991). In fact, central to most development theories is the notion of identity. Hence, part of the definite benefits of college is to develop those values and principles by which students live their lives. Raising the consciousness to a higher level of understanding regarding the value and respect of human existence, collective and individual, is a major contribution to society.

This framework is employed here to demonstrate the importance of consider-ing multiple factors for research, programming, curriculum, and services for students. However, for this chapter a research study is the focus while employing

Figure 6.1
Conceptual Framework for Student Learning, Involvement, and Gains

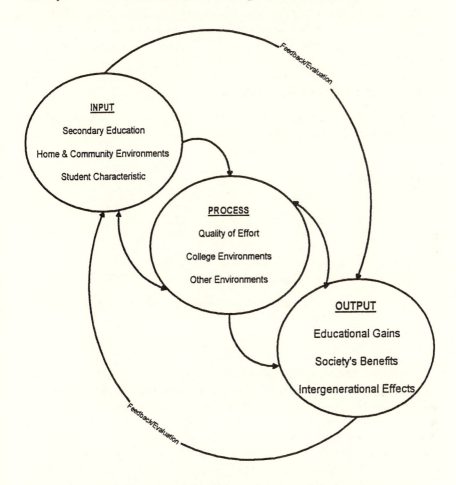

Source: L. W. Watson (1996). Learning in institutions of higher education. *Planning and Changing: An Educational Leadership and Policy Journal, 27(*3/4).

the guidance of the framework. The study that is used in this chapter includes a target sample of 1,600 Black and White undergraduate students enrolled in two HBCUs and two PWIs for the 1993–1994 academic school year. For the PWIs, a random sampling of students was drawn, while the instrument was administered at the HBCUs in compliance with the policies of the United Negro College Fund (UNCF) which prohibits the institutions from revealing students' names and addresses. A total of 862 completed and returned questionnaires were usable. The College Student Experience Questionnaire (CSEQ) was used, which measures the quality of student effort by levels of involvement in the institution, student perceptions of their campus environment, and their belief of how much they have gained across various cognitive and affective skills. The framework helps in identifying the difference between dominant race environments and why various factors in the environment affect the quality of the educational experiences and gains for Black students at PWIs and HBCUs.

INPUT—STUDENT CHARACTERISTICS

Therefore, does background affect who goes to college, where one goes to college, and how well one performs in college? (See Figure 6.2.)

Figure 6.2
The Effect of Input

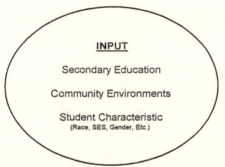

To discuss student characteristics, one must consider the student's family background, socioeconomic status or social class, parental education and income, and the student's preparation to enter college. The most commonly observed background characteristics that are related to the gains and experiences of the student in college are social class, parental education, parental income, and academic preparedness (Nettles & Johnson, 1987; Pascarella, Ethington, & Smart, 1988; Tinto, 1975). However, Terenzini and Pascarella (1980) and Bean (1980) have concluded that student background characteristics are insignificant to student performance in college.

The literature on student background characteristics is mixed in regard to student effort, persistence, and gains in college. However, educators cannot ignore the economic conditions of Black students compared to White students and how such conditions impact the college experience. According to a report in 1985 by the College Entrance Examination Board, in 1982, 48% of Black children below the age of 18 lived in households below the poverty line, compared to 17% of White children. In addition, the report found that Black students were more likely to come from a one-parent household compared to White students (Nettles & Johnson, 1987). One out of every five Blacks in the labor market was unemployed in 1982. In addition, statistics show that "70 percent of all Black students who enroll in four

year colleges dropout at some point, as compared to 45 percent of white students"
(Steele, 1992, p. 70).

The Scholastic Aptitude Test (SAT) is a major determining factor for students'
acceptance into college and can be classified as a cultural capital instrument (Hurn,
1985). For example, in 1992, 12 out of nearly 100,000 Black students who took the
SAT scored above 750 on the verbal portion of the test, and 520 scored over 700
on the math portion. Yet, only 1% of all Blacks who took the SAT scored over 600
on verbal, and only 2% scored above 600 on the math. White students were 12
times as likely as Blacks to score over 750 on the verbal and 16 times more likely
as Blacks to score over 750 on the math portion of the SAT. "Scholastic Aptitude
Test scores are profoundly affected by parental incomes and education, books in
the home, quality of schooling, ability to purchase SAT coaching aid, cultural
differences in the knowledge of words and other nonracial factors" (Goldsby, 1993,
pp. 20–21). For these reasons, SAT scores are poor measures of academic ability.
Data given in the previous sentence are mention only "because SAT scores are a
deciding factor, to a very great degree, on who will be admitted to higher
education" (Goldsby, 1993, pp. 20–21; Hurn, 1985).

In this study, the background factors had little effect on students' involvement
or educational gains. In a similar study, MacKay and Kuh (1994) found that the
level of education for parents was not a significant factor in the educational
outcomes of students. The literature on parents' education as a contributing factor
to educational gains and success is mixed and indicates different findings for race
and sex (Gruca, 1988; Pascarella & Terenzini, 1991).

In summary, one can clearly see how background factors may influence the
likelihood of students getting into institutions of higher education. Based on the
educational sociologists and reports about the SAT, the argument of cultural capital
certainly has merit in a capitalist society like the United States. However, a
capitalist society also allows one to rise out of poverty and oppression to achieve
a dream. Regardless of background or SAT scores, many students have been
accepted into institutions of higher education and perform quite well (Pascarella &
Terenzini, 1991). Yet, there are mixed reports on various institutions of higher
education and their students' success and gains in regard to student characteristics.

PROCESS—QUALITY OF EFFORT, COLLEGE ENVIRONMENTS, AND OTHER ENVIRONMENTS

Does it really matter where a student attends college? Does it affect his or her
educational outcomes? For Black students, is there really a difference between
Black and White institutions regarding their educational experience? (See Figure
6.3.)

Much of the literature of student involvement and persistence mentions the
importance of a supportive environment (Astin, 1984, 1993; Bean, 1980; Fleming,
1984; Kuh et al., 1991; Pascarella & Terenzini, 1991; Thompson & Fretz, 1991;
Tinto, 1975). Also, various students experience the campus in different ways,

Figure 6.3
The Effect of Process

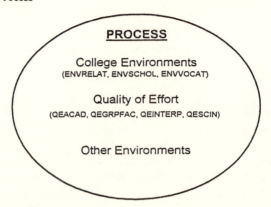

which may affect how they invest their time and effort in utilizing institutional resources and agents and, therefore, their educational gains. It is important to find out how the university environment can be made into a place of comfort and warmth for those students who do not feel welcome. Students are often expected to adjust and accommodate themselves to the physical and social environments, and they are rarely given the chance to redesign the environment to meet their desires. Therefore, students, especially Black students, pay a high adaptation cost in terms of dissatisfaction, marginal performance, instability, and avoidance of the environment (Fleming, 1984).

White Institutions (PWIs)

Research on the concerns that Black students face on the campuses at PWIs indicates that some problems are unique to them and other minorities. Because White students are part of the majority and dominant culture, the issue of assimilation does not emerge for them. However, many Black students at PWIs have reported that they have not really felt welcome on campus and have been treated like uninvited guests in a strange land (Livingston & Stewart, 1987). Therefore, before most Black students in PWIs can begin to concentrate on academics, they must first feel comfortable in the residence halls, the classrooms, and social settings. One assumption for the adjustment problem is that the expectations of most Black students are not met at PWIs. Black students go to the institution thinking there will be less racism; yet when they arrive on campus, there is a discrepancy between their ideal environment and reality (Fleming, 1984).

It is important to understand that regardless of ethnicity, most students will encounter problems adjusting to college (Plinar & Brown, 1985; Webster, Sedlacek, & Miyares, 1979). However, since they are the dominant culture at a PWI, most White students do not face racial harassment or individual, cultural, or institutional racism, as do minority groups at PWIs. The struggles that Black students face at PWIs are qualitatively and quantitatively different from those faced by White students (Baum & Lamb, 1983; Fleming, 1984; Ponce, 1988; Sedlacek, 1987).

Black Institutions (HBCUs)

In contrast to the experiences of Black students at PWIs, Allen (1986), Fleming (1984), Watson (1994), and Watson and Kuh (1996) found that at HBCUs Black students experienced more positive psychosocial development and academic achievement. In addition, Black students were supported and encouraged to a greater degree by faculty, and they reported higher satisfaction with the social aspects of the college environment.

Davis (1991) stressed how HBCUs afford the Black students more opportunities to become integrated in the campus life. Fleming (1984) emphasized that the ingredients of social connectedness are present within the HBCU settings because "an individual can achieve feelings of progress, gain a sense of recognition, and know that there are people who will provide an attentive ear" (p. 152).

The positive attributes of HBCUs have a positive impact on the overall development of Black students. Black students show stronger intellectual confidence and a greater feeling of success and satisfaction with academic life than Blacks attending PWIs. The issue of race is less of a concern, and students are able to develop and learn as individuals without having to worry about representing their race (Whiting, 1991). The developmental progress and patterns of Black students at HBCUS are parallel to those of White students in PWIs (Allen, 1992; Fleming, 1984; Watson, 1994; Watson & Kuh, 1996).

In returning to a previous question, does it make a difference where a student, especially a Black student, attends college with regard to that student's involvement and educational gains? According to the findings of the study in this chapter, there is a definite difference for Black students.

Analysis of variance was conducted on the environmental factors for Black majority (Black students at HBCUs), White majority (White students at PWIs), and Black minority (Black students at PWIs) students. (See Figure 6.4.)

Figure 6.4
College Environmental Factors

ENVRELAT	Represents the scholarly and intellectual emphasis of the campus environment
ENVSCHOL	Represents the vocational and practical emphasis of the campus environment
ENVVOC	Represents the supportive personal relationships of the campus environment

Black majority students showed one significant difference on the three environmental factors compared to White majority and Black minority students. Table 6.1 shows that the mean for Black majority students (M=4.72) was the lowest of the three groups, which indicates that students at the HBCUs in this study perceived their institutional environment to place less emphasis on ENVSCHOL, the development of academic, scholarly, and intellectual qualities; the development of esthetics, expressive, and creative qualities; and being critical, valuative, and analytical. Figure 6.5 defines the quality of effort factors.

Table 6.1
Group Comparison of Means and Standard Deviations by Racial Status for the Quality of Effort Factors, Environmental Factors, and Gains Factors

Factors	Black Majority $n = 502$		White Majority $n = 214$		Black Minority $n = 83$		F
	M	SD	M	SD	M	SD	
QEACAD	2.51	.47	2.28	.44^	2.44	.46	.000 ***
QEGRPFAC	2.28	.57	2.13	.47^	2.36	.62	.000 ***
QEINTERP	2.20	.46	2.05	.42^	2.22	.51	.000 ***
QESCIN	2.02	.70	1.88	.75	1.97	.80	.059
ENVRELAT	4.88	1.33	5.11	1.05	5.04	1.37	.064
ENVSCHOL	4.72	1.31^	5.35	.90	5.47	1.04	.000 ***
ENVVOCAT	4.67	1.41	4.85	1.25	4.95	1.25	.118

$*p < .05. **p < .01. ***p < .001.$
Note: "^" indicates the group that significantly differs from the others.
   Black Majority = Black students at predominantly Black institutions.
   White Majority = White students at predominantly White institutions.
   Black Minority = Black students at predominantly White institutions.

Figure 6.5
Quality of Effort Factors

QEACAD	Represents the scholarly/intellectual activities
QEINTERP	Represents the informal interpersonal activities
QEGRPFAC	Represents the activities in the use of group facilities
QESCIN	Represents the activities related to science

The literature on the subject supports this finding and suggests that it may be due to the historical mission of some private Black colleges. In fact, Allen (1987) and Fleming (1984) have stated in their work on Black colleges that Black students exchange psychological wellbeing, cultural likeness, and supportive academic relations for poor physical facilities and restricted academic programs. In Table 6.1, no other factors were shown to be significant between the groups, which is a surprise. Given the literature of Black students at PWIs, one would expect that at least one environmental factor would have been significant for Black minority students. The research on the experiences of Black students at PWIs reports that these students often experience feelings of social alienation, intense academic competition, racial stress, lack of campus integration, and isolation (Allen, 1987; Fleming, 1984; Rooney, 1985; Thomas & Hill, 1987).

The results of the analysis of variance show that White majority students differed from Black majority and minority students on three of the four quality of effort factors. (See Table 6.1.)

White majority students had a lower mean for all three groups, which indicates that they were less involved in QEACAD (academic activities), QEGRPFAC (group and campus facilities), and QEINTERP (informal interpersonal relations) at PWIs. Black majority students had a higher mean for QEACAD than Black minority students, and Black minority students had a higher mean for QEGRPFAC and QEINTERP. What this could signify is that the Black students at HBCUs were more involved in academic activities than Black and White students at PWIs. However, one could also conclude from the study that Black students at HBCUs would be more involved and more active in an environment where their race is dominant versus their counterparts in PWIs. In addition, one would also expect White students to be more involved with their campus resources and agents than other minority groups at PWIs.

OUTPUT—EDUCATIONAL GAINS

What makes a difference in students' educational gains at HBCUs and PWIs? (See Figure 6.6.) The educational outcomes from this study are concerned with the output section of the conceptual framework. (See Figure 6.7.)

Figure 6.6
The Effect of Output

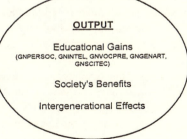

OUTPUT

Educational Gains
(GNPERSOC, GNINTEL, GNVOCPRE, GNGENART, GNSCITEC)

Society's Benefits

Intergenerational Effects

Figure 6.7
Educational Gain Factor

GAIN PERS/SOC	Represents the personal and social development gains that students believe they have made while attending an institution.
GAIN SCI/TECH	Represents the science and technology gains that students believe they have made while attending an institution.
GAIN GE,LIT,ARTS	Represents the gains one believes he or she has made in their knowledge of general education, literature, and art while attending an institution.
GAIN INTEL SKILL	Represents intellectual and analytical skills gained.
GAIN VOC PREP	Represents vocational preparation gained while attending an institution.

ENVRELAT represents an environment that emphasizes positive relationships with other students, faculty members, and administrative personnel. As was expected from numerous studies on the effects of the environment on student outcomes, Black majority students rank their environmental relationship as contributing to four out of the five gains for educational outcomes. (See Table 6.1.) As expected, in an environment where Black students are the predominant race, their educational gains are impacted positively (Allen, 1992; Fleming, 1984; Gurin & Epps, 1975). ENVRELAT was more significant in gains for Black majority students than for White majority students.

ENVRELAT influenced gains only in personal and social development for Black minority students. Compared to Black and White majority students, one may conclude that being a minority on a campus inhibits other educational gains for students. For example, the two majority groups perceive their environment to value supportive and personal relationships within the campus community, and this factor contributes more to gains for the majority students than for the minority students. (See Table 6.1.) Allen (1992) reports in his study of Black students on HBCU and PWI campuses that Black students who attend PWIs reported lower academic achievement. Fleming (1984) points out that a supportive community for Black students on HBCUs (1) provides opportunities for friendships of various kinds with various personnel, (2) affords students opportunities to participate in campus life, and (3) allows them to feel a sense of progress and success in their academic pursuits.

ENVSCHOL is an environment that emphasizes the development of academic, scholarly, and intellectual quantities; esthetics, expressive, and creative quantitative; and critical, valuative, and analytical skills. For the majority student groups, ENVSCHOL was the only factor influencing gains in general education, literature, and the arts. However, ENVSCHOL was the greatest contributing factor for gains compared to all other factors for minority students. ENVSCHOL contributed to gains in personal and social development, gains in intellectual skills, and gains in vocation and career options for Black minority students.

Therefore, it seems that Black students at PWIs obtain greater negative educational outcomes than both Black students at HBCUs and White students at PWIs when they perceive the environment to value academic excellence. This finding could also indicate that Black students at PWIs suffer in both personal and social aspects in order to have better programs and facilities, which may or may not increase their educational outcomes in the end. To the contrary, Astin (1977) states that Black students at HBCUs tend to have higher grades and are less satisfied and less likely to persist to the completion of a baccalaureate than Black students at PWIs.

Quality of effort in academic activities is shown to be significant for Black students at HBCUs for all of the gains factors, GNPERSOC, GNINTEL, GNVOCPRE, GNGENART, and GNSCITEC (see Table 6.2). Quality of effort in academic activities includes tasks related to library experiences, experiences with faculty, course learning, and writing. It was expected that QEACAD would be significant for all of the gains for Black majority students because of the relationships and support that students have from the faculty at HBCUs (Allen, 1992; Anderson, 1992).

One factor that has an overall influence on the cognitive and affective gains of students in institutions of higher education is student—faculty contact and the quality of that interaction. Talking with faculty outside the classroom, and being a guest in a faculty member's home are associated with the overall satisfaction of the college experiences. Having a class paper criticized by an instructor has a positive partial correlation with gains in general knowledge, knowledge of field or major, analytical and problem-solving skills, writing skills, and preparation for graduate or professional programs (Astin, 1993; Pascarella & Terenzini, 1991).

Also, faculty expectations and attitudes are major issues for the retention and involvement of all students, especially Black students. A study about the college experience of Black undergraduates who attend HBCUs and PWIs found that academic achievement is highest for students who report positive relationships with faculty (Allen, 1992). Likewise, Black students on PWI campuses must rely on White students and professors in making their adjustments to campus life; therefore, the support systems and other coping skills are developed within a White environment with White participants. Black students on HBCUs do not have to deal with the unfamiliar and stressful situation of being a minority (Davis, 1991).

Although the study shows that Black majority students in HBCUs perceived their institutional environment to be less scholarly and intellectual (ENVSCHOL) than that of their White and Black colleagues at PWIs, they were heavily involved with academic activities. This high involvement in academic activities at HBCUs may help explain why HBCUs tend to graduate more Black students than PWIs (Braddock, 1981; Fleming, 1984). This high involvement with academic activities

Table 6.2

Regression Analyses for Racial Majority and Minority Students' Quality of Effort Factors, Environmental Factors, and Gains Factors

	Black Majority n = 502			White Majority n = 214			Black Minority n = 83		
Gains	**B**	**Beta**	**F**	**B**	**Beta**	**F**	**B**	**Beta**	**F**
GNPERSOC									
(Personal & Social)									
QEACAD	.03	.19	.000***	.02	.13	.120	.02	.16	.240
QEGRPFAC	.01	.10	.094	.02	.12	.122	.01	.01	.933
QEINTERP	.01	.10	.118	.02	.01	.138	.02	.16	.410
QESCIN	.01	.05	.261	-.00	-.01	.936	.02	.20	.074
ENVRELAT	.08	.16	.000***	.13	.24	.001***	.17	.35	.002**
ENVSCHOL	.03	.05	.333	-.02	-.03	.694	.22	.31	.003**
ENVVOCAT	.03	.06	.288	.07	.15	.060	-.03	-.05	.629
(Constant)	.23		.289	.50		.146	-.17	.74	
R²		.31			.33			.52	
Adjusted R²		.29			.29			.43	
GNINTEL									
(Intellectual Skills)									
QEACAD	.04	.26	.000***	.02	.15	.043*	.01	.07	.647
QEGRPFAC	-.00	-.00	.943	.02	.13	.068	.03	.23	.200
QEINTERP	.02	.12	.049*	.00	.03	.709	.00	.01	.970
QESCIN	.01	.09	.039*	.03	.35	.000***	.02	.20	.022*
ENVRELAT	.10	.17	.000***	.06	.09	.120	.05	.09	.421
ENVSCHOL	.04	.06	.231	.07	.09	.182	.26	.33	.003*
ENVVOCAT	.01	.02	.716	.16	.28	.000***	.05	.08	.438
(Constant)	.07		.766	.76		.034	-.60		.318
R²		.34			.50		.47		
Adjusted R²		.33			.47			.38	
GNVOCPRE									
(Vocational Preparation)									
QEACAD	.03	.20	.000***	.03	.15	.033*	-.01	-.04	.798
QEGRPFAC	-.00	-.00	.977	.00	.01	.923	.00	.04	.842
QEINTERP	.01	.07	.274	.01	.05	.495	.04	.29	.202
QESCIN	.02	.14	.002***	.01	.06	.251	.02	.19	.130
ENVRELAT	.05	.09	.061	-.06	-.08	.185	.05	.11	.363
ENVSCHOL	-.00	-.01	.915	-.01	-.01	.905	.17	.25	.034*
ENVVOCAT	.14	.27	.000***	.26	.42	.000***	-.04	-.08	.499
(Constant)	-.00		.995	-.39		.301	.07		.908
R²		.31			.54			.38	
Adjusted R²		.29			.51			.27	
GNGENART									
(General Education, Literature, & Arts)									
QEACAD	.03	.22	.000***	.04	.24	.001***	.01	.10	.426
QEGRPFAC	-.01	-.10	.101	-.01	-.08	.238	.01	.10	.514

QEINTERP	.05	.35	.000***	.05	.36	.000***	.06	.50	.009**
QESCIN	.00	.04	.319	-.03	-.31	.000***	-.00	-.05	.633
ENVRELAT	.05	.11	.006***	.14	.23	.000***	.08	.18	.073
ENVSCHOL	.06	.15	.003***	.15	.22	.001***	.05	.09	.370
ENVVOCAT	.03	.06	.259	.01	.03	.623	.04	.09	.334
(Constant)	.04		.805	-.46	.		.138	-.52	.240
R^2		.42			.52			.58	
Adjusted R^2		.40			.49			.50	

GNSCITEC
(Science & Technology)

QEACAD	.02	.12	.027*	.00	.00	.948	.04	.25	.095
QEGRPFAC	-.01	-.08	.172	-.02	-.09	.147	-.05	-.38	.044*
QEINTERP	.02	.14	.024*	.02	.09	.188	.05	.36	.095
QESCIN	.04	.38	.000***	.09	.75	.000***	.04	.43	.001***
ENVRELAT	.09	.15	.001**	.02	.03	.613	.09	.16	.166
ENVSCHOL	-.01	-.01	.863	-.04	-.04	.487	.15	.18	.111
ENVVOCAT	.06	.10	.062	.12	.16	.014*	-.05	-.08	.428
(Constant)	-.04		.863	.10		.820	.38		.566
R^2		.33			.58			.44	
Adjusted R^2		.31			.55			.33	

$^*p < .05. ^{**}p < .01. ^{***}p < .001.$

Note: Black Majority = Black students at predominantly Black institutions.

   White Majority = White students at predominantly White institutions.

   Black Minority = Black students at predominantly White institutions.

also is associated with every aspect of educational gains for Black students at HBCUs (Fleming, 1984).

Quality of effort in academic activities was one of the two strongest factors for White majority students in regard to gains in GNINTEL, GNVOCPRE, and GNGENART. Most of the research on the in-class experiences between students and faculty points to the relationship that faculty and students have with one another and how the quality of that relationship is related to success in college (Pascarella & Terenzini, 1991). In contrast to majority groups, QEACAD was not a contributing factor to any gains for minority students, and this indicates that Black minority students do not receive the educational gains or payoffs that White students at PWIs receive for their involvement. For example, although Table 1.1 indicates that Black minority students are more involved than White majority students, Table 6.1 shows that the quality of effort for White majority students is significant and influences gains. However, for Black minority students, it is not clear why their greater involvement in QEACAD does not influence gains. This is the most disturbing finding and perhaps gives merit to the rationale for using the framework proposed to explore an in-depth examination for an explanation.

Although Fleming (1977) reports that the evaluation of faculty and administration by White students became more positive from the freshman year to senior year, the evaluation made by Black students became more negative at PWIs.

Yet, MacKay and Kuh's (1994) study shows that the QEACAD of Black students contributed to three of the five gains factors, GNGENART, GNINTEL, and GNVOCPRE, which were the same factors that are presented as contributing factors for White majority students. However, for White majority students, QEACAD was significant only in influencing GNVOCPRE. In summary, when interaction between faculty and students is enhanced and increased in the classroom and out of the classroom, the gains of students are greatly increased.

Activities related to QEINTERP include involvement in art, music, theater, personal experiences, student acquaintances, topics of conversations, and information in conversations. The study shows that QEINTERP was very significant for the Black majority student's GNINTEL (intellectual skills), GNGENART (general education, literature, and the arts), and GNSCITEC (understanding science and new technology). This is not surprising for Black majority students at HBCUs. Fleming (1984) reports that Black students at HBCUs have more positive psychosocial experiences than Black students at PWIs. The literature shows that Black students at HBCUs have higher involvement and gains when studying in their dominant race environment (Allen, 1987, 1992; Fleming, 1984; Watson, 1994; Watson & Kuh, 1996).

However, it was unexpected for QEINTERP not to contribute to gains in GNPERSOC of Black students because of the positive experiences of dating, social, and other interpersonal incidents that are reported at HBCUs. Fleming (1984) also reported that Black students at HBCUs experienced positive psychosocial development due to a critical mass of Black students, staff, administrators, and faculty within a culture more compatible for Black students. The factor QEINTERP also influenced GNGENART (gains in general education, literature, and arts) for both Black and White students at PWIs. MacKay and Kuh (1994) revealed that for Black and White students QEINTERP was the greatest contributing factor across the five gains for both Black and White students.

QESCIN was a contributing factor for gains in all groups in intellectual skills (GNINTEL) and understanding science and new technology (GNSCITEC). For Black majority students, QESCIN was also significant for gains in vocational and career preparation probably because Black students at HBCUs were found to be more focused in the career for science and technology than White majority and Black minority students at PWIs. QESCIN also was a contributing factor for gains in general education for White students in PWIs.

Intergenerational Gains

The evidence to support a connection between the college experiences and long-term gains and "quality of life indexes" is not very strong. While holding economic resources constant, many "quality of life indexes" still exist (Pascarella & Terenzini, 1991). College experiences have a moderate effect on one's health status, family size, consumer behavior, savings and investment, marital satisfaction, and life satisfaction index; they have a weak effect on marital stability, nurturance of children, cultured leisure, and job satisfaction (Pascarella & Terenzini, 1991).

There is some evidence to support that having college-educated parents positively affects the socioeconomic achievement of sons and daughters and the educational attainment of children. It is likely that

> having college-educated parents may enhance the cognitive development of young children through the indirect route of the home environment. Compared to those with less education, college-educated parents, particularly mothers, spend more time with their children in developmental activities such as reading and teaching. The long-term trend of these intergenerational legacies appears to be not only toward greater socioeconomic security and well- being but also toward greater cognitive growth and openness, tolerance, and concern for human rights and liberties. (Pascarella & Terenzini, 1991, p. 586)

RECOMMENDATIONS AND SUGGESTIONS

Policy decisions at the national, state, and local levels that address the functions and purposes of private HBCUs should focus on matters that are related to students' educational gains. Black students at HBCUs report richer educational experiences than Black students at HBCUs, given their quality of effort, their perceptions of the college environment, and their educational gains. Policymakers and practitioners who work with, and in, HBCUs must understand and recognize that these colleges and universities provide Black students with an avenue that might have been closed for them if it were not for their existence. The findings show that activities related to academic involvement, interpersonal involvement, and relationships with faculty, administrators, and students have a greater influence on educational gains of Black students at HBCUs than at PWIs. Therefore, HBCUs seem to effectively provide Black students with the skills they need to function within the general society.

Exchange programs between private HBCUs and private PWIs should be developed so that minority and majority students and faculty may become aware of practices and relationships that encourage students to succeed. Given that exposure to different people and ways of life influences a number of gains, an exchange program might provide students from HBCUs and PWIs opportunities to experience different cultures and institutions. An exchange program for students at PWIs and HBCUs should allow them to reflect on prejudices and stereotypes and appreciate their educational experiences at both types of institutions.

Because of the quality of effort that Black majority students expend on academic activities at PWIs, faculty and students from PWIs should learn new ways of interacting with Black students who choose to go to HBCUs and use that knowledge to build programs at PWIs for their own students. Faculty from PWIs should also be given the opportunity to participate in an exchange program to observe teaching styles and other interactions of the faculty at HBCUs that allow them to become more involved academically with students. For example, Butler University and Shaw University might consider an exchange program so that students and faculty from a PWI can experience being in a different environment, even as a minority, and increase their awareness and understanding of the differences that exist in an HBCU. This program would help them appreciate and recognize how students of a different race and culture feel in a similar situation and why.

PWIs should find ways of encouraging faculty to become more involved with Black students. In this study, Black and White majority students benefited more from their academic activities than did Black minority students. A key influence in the success of Black students in institutions of higher education is the faculty. Therefore, the mentoring, teaching, and servicing role of faculty in PWIs may need to be encouraged and rewarded for such related activities.

PWIs may need to increase their minority faculty, staff, and student population in order to provide Black students with the support they need to consider themselves a part of the campus community. Fleming (1984) believes that at times of frustration and alienation Black students on PWI campuses need to delve into academic activities instead of allowing those times to divert them from academic pursuits.

A two-way interaction needs to be developed where institutions and students become partners in maximizing educational gains. Perhaps programs need to be developed to teach all students how to take responsibility for their lives. In return, the institution should make sure that support, programming, and appropriate personnel are provided to assist students in utilizing the institution's resources to enhance their educational gains.

REFERENCES

Allen, W. (1986). *Gender and campus race differences in Black student academic performance, racial attitudes and college satisfaction.* Atlanta, GA: Southern Education Foundation

Allen, W. (1987). Black colleges vs. White colleges. *Change, 19*(3), 28–34.

Allen, W. (1992). The color of success: African-American college student outcomes at predominantly White and historically Black public colleges and universities. *Harvard Educational Review, 62*(1), 26–44.

Anderson, J. (1988). *The education of Blacks in the south, 1860–1935.* London: University of North Carolina.

Anderson, J., & Adams, M. (1992). Acknowledging the learning styles of diverse student populations: Implications for instructional design. *New directions for teaching and learning.* San Francisco: Jossey-Bass.

Astin, A. (1977). *Four critical years: Effects of coolege on beliefs, attitudes, and knowledge.* San Francisco: Jossey-Bass.

Astin, A. W. (1982). *Minorities in American higher education.* San Francisco: Jossey-Bass.

Astin, A. W. (1984). Student involvement: A developmental theory for higher education. *Journal of College Student Development, 26,* 297–308.

Astin, A. W. (1993). *What matters in college?* San Francisco: Jossey-Bass.

Baum, M., & Lamb, D. (1983). A comparison of concerns presented by Black and White students to a university counseling center. *Journal of College Student Personnel, 24,* 127–131.

Bean, J. P. (1980). Dropout and turnover: The synthesis and test of a causal model of student attrition. *Research in Higher Education, 12*(2), 155–187.

Bourdieu, P. (1977). The cultural transmission of social inequality. *Harvard Educational Review, 47,* 545–555.

Bowles, S., & Gintis, H. (1976). *Schooling in capitalist America.* New York: Basic Books.

Braddock, J. (1981). Desegregation and Black student attrition. *Urban Education, 15,* 178–186.

Cross, W., Jr. (1971). Discovering the Black referent: The psychology of Black liberation. In J. Dixon & B. Foster (Eds.), *Beyond Black or White* (n.p.). Boston: Little, Brown.

Davis, R. (1991). Social support networks and undergraduate student academic success-related outcomes: A comparison of Black students on Black and White campuses. In W. R. Allen, E. G. Epps, & N. Z. Haniff (Eds.), *College in Black and White* (pp. 143–157). New York: State University of New York Press.

Fleming, J. (1977). The impact of predominately white and predominately Black environments on the functioning of Black students. In *Second annual report to the Carnegie Corporation.* New York: Carnegie Corporation.

Fleming, J. (1984). *Blacks in college.* San Francisco: Jossey-Bass.

Gruca, J. (1988). Intergenerational effects of college graduation on career sex atypicality in women. *Research in Higher Education, 29,* 99–124.

Gurin, P., & Epps, E. (1975). *Black consciousness, identity, and achievement: A study of students in historically Black colleges.* New York: John Wiley & Sons.

Hurn, C. J. (1985). *The limits and possibilities of schooling: An introduction to the sociology of education* (3rd ed.). Boston: Allyn & Bacon.

Kuh, G., Schuh, J., Whitt, E., Andreas, R., Lyons, J., Strange, C., Krehbiel, L., & Mackay, K. (1991). *Involving colleges: Successful approaches to fostering student learning and development outside the classroom.* San Francisco: Jossey-Bass.

Livingston, M. D., & Stewart, M. A. (1987). Minority students on a white campus: Perception is truth. *NASPA Journal, 24,* 39–48.

MacKay, K., & Kuh, G. (1994). A comparison of student effort and educational gains of Caucasian and African-American students in predominantly White colleges and universities. *Journal of College Student Development, 35,* 217–223.

Nettles, M., & Johnson, J. (1987). Race, sex, and other factors as determinant of college students' socialization. *Journal of College Student Personnel, 28,* 512–524.

Nettles, M. T. (1988). *Toward Black undergraduate student equality in American higher education.* New York: Greenwood Press.

Pace, C. R. (1984). *Measuring the quality of college student experiences.* Los Angeles: University of California Higher Education Research Institute.

Pace, C. R. (1988). *CSEQ: Test manual and norms.* Los Angeles: University of California Center for the Study of Evaluation.

Pascarella, E., Ethington, C., & Smart, J. (1988). The influence of college on humanitarian/civic involvement values. *Journal of Higher Education, 59,* 412–437.

Pascarella, E. T., & Terenzini, P. (1991). *How college affects students.* San Francisco: Jossey-Bass.

Plinar, J. E., & Brown, D. (1985). Projections of reactions to stress and preferences for helpers among students from four ethnic groups. *Journal of College Student Personnel, 26,* 147–151.

Ponce, F. Q. (1988). Minority student retention: A moral and legal imperative. In M. C. Terrell & D. J. Wright (Eds.), *From survival to success: Promoting minority student retention* (pp. 25–54). Washington, DC: National Association of Student Personnel Administrators.

Rooney, G. (1985). Minority students' involvement in minority student organizations: An exploratory study. *Journal of College Student Personnel, 26,* 450–455.

Sedlacek, W. (1987). Black students on White campuses: 20 years of research. *Journal of College Student Personnel, 28,* 484–494.

Steele, C. M. (1992). Race and the schooling of Black Americans. *The Atlantic Monthly,* pp. 68–78.

Thomas, G,. & Hill, S. (1987). Black institutions in U.S. higher education: Present roles, contributions, future projections. *Journal of College Student Personnel, 28,* 532–545.

Thompson, C. E., & Fretz, B. R. (1991). Predicting the adjustment of Black students at predominantly White institutions. *Journal of Higher Education, 62*(4), 437–450.

Tinto, V. (1975). Dropouts from higher education: A theoretical synthesis of recent research. *Review of Educational Research, 45,* 89–125.

Watson, L. W. (1994). An analysis of Black and White students' perceptions, involvement, and educational gains in private historically Black and White liberal arts institutions. Unpublished doctoral dissertation, Indiana University. Bloomington.

Watson, L. W. (1996). Learning in institutions of higher education. *Planning and Changing: An Educational Leadership and Policy Journal, 27(* 3/4).

Watson, L. W., & Kuh, G. D. (1996). The influence of dominant race environments on student involvement, perceptions, and educational gains: A look at historically Black and predominantly White liberal arts institutions. *Journal of College Student Development, 37,* 4.

Watson, L. W., & Stage, F. (under review). A conceptual framework for student learning, involvement, and educational gains. In F. Stage, L. Watson, & M. Terrell (Eds.), Enhancing student learning: Setting the campus context (n.p.). San Francisco: Jossey-Bass.

Webster, D., Sedlacek, W. E., & Miyares, J. (1979). A comparison of problems perceived by minority and White university students. *Journal of College Student Personnel, 20,* 120–165.

Whiting, A. (1991). *Guardians of the flame: Historically Black colleges yesterday, today, and tomorrow.* Washington, DC: American Association of State Colleges and Universities.

7

"Am I Black Enuf fo Ya?" Black Student Diversity: Issues of Identity and Community

Lori S. White

INTRODUCTION

Black students in the 1990s who attend institutions of higher education in America come from a variety of socioeconomic backgrounds and precollege experiences. Some have lived in predominantly Black communities, some in predominantly White communities, and some in communities with people from a variety of ethnic and cultural groups. Some students are Black American, others are from Africa or the Caribbean, and others are biracial.

As a group, Black college students and their experiences have been the subject of a great deal of research. However, as the introductory chapter to this book indicates, most research on Black college students focuses on comparisons of their experiences to those of White students or other minority students. Very little of this research focuses on within-group differences among Black students.[1] Given that, as a group, Black students are not a homogenous population (Allen, 1985; McEwen, Roper, Bryant, & Langa, 1990; Pounds, 1987), the characterization or definition of a "Black student" is certainly much more complex than most of the college student literature would lead us to believe.

What challenges does this Black student diversity present to higher education researchers and practitioners? For example, how does one take within-group differences into account when developing theoretical models to understand issues related to Black students in institutions of higher education (e.g., social and academic integration, retention, identity development)? How does the director of a campus Black cultural center provide support services to Black students if Black students from different countries, states, and socioeconomic backgrounds have different needs, perspectives, and campus friendship networks and affinity groups? Are there particular aspects of Black student experiences on campus (e.g., Black peer group relationships) where within-group differences are more salient than others?

In this chapter, I focus on the diversity of experiences around Black student involvement and noninvolvement in Black campus organizations (student associations, cultural centers, residence hall theme houses, student affairs offices, etc.)[2] at one predominantly White institution (PWI). Through the use of personal narratives and other interview data, I illustrate how Black students differently construct their Black identity and their relationships to other Black students on campus. I rely on personal narratives as the method for exploring within-group differences in Black student experiences because the use of such narratives "give[s] primacy to individuals' accounts in order to convey a range of human experiences" (Gumport, 1993). Although survey methods (generally questionnaires with a fixed number of closed-ended questions) allow researchers to study large populations, survey data generally do not provide an in-depth understanding or any sense of the complexities of the people and the behavior being studied (Bangura, 1992; Bryman, 1988; Denzin, 1989). At least one researcher believes that survey methods, because "the data gathered through survey research simply can not talk" (Bangura 1992, p. xii), are particularly limiting in studies of Black students in institutions of higher education.

The students whose personal narratives are presented in this chapter participated in a 1995 survey of Black student experiences at Western University (a pseudonym), a private PWI. Black students make up approximately 8% of Western's undergraduate enrollment.[3] Of the 219 students who completed surveys and who were involved in at least one campus organization (student or administrative campus involvement opportunity), 34% were involved exclusively in Black organizations; 24% were involved exclusively in non-Black organizations, and 42% were involved in both Black and non-Black campus organizations.[4]

According to Rooney (1985), Black organizations exist at almost every PWI with a sizable enrollment of Black students. However, the preceding data on student involvement in Black organizations show that while some Black students participate in these organizations, other Black students do not. Since these data showed different patterns of Black organization involvement for Black students at Western, I was interested in understanding whether or not student involvement or noninvolvement in these organizations was based on more than simply random or happenstance student involvement choices.

During my semistructured interviews with 22 Western students,[5] I discovered that asking students about their involvement in Black organizations became a vehicle for students to have larger conversations with me about issues related to their own Black identity, their relationships with other Black students, and their perceptions of whether they were a part of, or apart from, their definition of the Black community on campus. I believe these conversations demonstrate, at least for these students, that within-group differences have a powerful effect on their self-perceptions and their overall campus experience. Both researchers and practitioners should find valuable messages related to their respective endeavors as a result of reading these students' personal narratives.

As a Black female from a middle-class background, I cannot claim knowledge or speak for all aspects of the Black cultural diaspora. However, my own "once upon a time" experiences as a Black student at a PWI enabled me to develop a particular connection to my interviewees and gave me a cultural framework for analyzing my interviewees' "stories." My connection and framework are obviously different from those of others not similarly situated. As an outsider, it is often difficult for a researcher to "penetrate and understand the meanings and symbols of a group" (Denzin, 1989).

Thus, it is important for a researcher to have more than a tacit understanding of the population being studied and to be trusted by the individuals being interviewed. Interviews and other ethnographic research methods, particularly when conducted by Black researchers with knowledge of Black culture, offer a strategy for combating the aforementioned limitations of survey data in representing the complexity of Black student experiences in higher education.

The five students whose personal narratives were selected for inclusion in this chapter represent a balance of men and women, first-year students and seniors, Black organization participants and nonparticipants, students from predominantly White and mixed-race communities and students from predominantly Black communities, and the particular richness with which the student described his or her experiences. Simone is a first-year student from a predominantly White community who is involved only in Black organizations on campus. Deborah is a senior who is also from a predominantly White community but who has not been involved in any Black organizations on campus. Greg is a first-year student from a predominantly Black community who attended a White private high school. All of Greg's extracurricular involvement, with the exception of one non-Black community service organization, is in Black organizations. Wanda, is a senior who has been primarily involved in mixed-race community service organizations during her four years at Western. Wanda says that until the sixth grade she lived and attended school in a predominantly White community; from the sixth grade on, she lived and attended school in a predominantly Black community. Broderick, who is biracial (one his parents is Black), wrote a note on the back of his survey that said, "I am only half-Black." Broderick attended what he describes as a "multicultural, inner-city" high school and is not involved in any Black organizations. Broderick is a senior.

The two themes that are most prominent in the subsequent personal narratives of Simone, Deborah, Greg, Wanda, and Broderick, and in the other interview data presented in this chapter, are "identity" and "community." These narratives suggest that (1) for Black students, Black identity is complex, ever-present, and situationally determined; (2) Black students who have not been around a Black peer group before college may have different social adjustment issues than Black students from predominantly Black environments; and (3) Black students have dual social relationships to the campus—their relationship to the campus as "a student" and their relationship to the campus as "a Black student." "Am I Black Enuf fo Ya," the title for this chapter, is my characterization of how Black students at Western perceive their racial identity and their interactions with other Black students on campus.

Simone

Simone is from a predominantly White community in the Southwest. She describes herself as "one of those Black students at Western who is only involved in the Black community." Most of the organizations that Simone is involved in are Black social or performance-oriented groups. According to Simone, the reason that she has only been involved in only Black organizations at Western is that, as she says, "in high school, I had always not been involved in the Black community."

Simone spent her first year living in King House, the Black theme residence hall on campus. Simone says that her family did not know if she would survive in King House because, as she says, "except for the Black church, I had never been in the Black community." She says that she chose to live in King House because she thought that it would be a good introduction to the Black community.

Simone believes that it is difficult for Black students at Western to be involved in both the Black and the non-Black community on campus. "Maybe," she says, "it is because the worlds [Black and non-Black] are so different. You either have to be in one or the other; it is definitely difficult to do both." She describes Black students who are not involved in the Black community on campus as "random" and says that once a student has been labeled "random" by the Black community, it is difficult for that student to be accepted by other Blacks. Simone thinks that "random" students do not become involved in the Black community because they do not feel comfortable. She thinks that because other Black students question "how Black" random students are, the random students are "alienated" and "driven further from the Black community." In describing her perceptions of how random students experience the Black community on campus, Simone says, "It is more a discomfort level, a feeling of rejection from a community that is supposed to be supportive."

Simone does believe, though, that there are some students, athletes primarily, whose involvement in both the Black and non-Black community on campus is accepted. Says Simone, "If you play a sport or something that kind of mandates that you be in another community, you get more support [for being in both the Black and non-Black community]." Simone thinks this is because "athletes are put on such a high pedestal in the Black community. . . . [A] lot of stuff [that athletes do] is going to be unconditionally accepted." From Simone's perspective, it also seems to be important for Black students who do join non-Black organizations to have been involved in the Black community first and to make sure that their Black friends are not forgotten when they participate in non-Black organizations. In describing some athletes who joined a non-Black fraternity, Simone says that "they were involved in the Black community [before]. When they joined this fraternity they had a party and they made sure the Black community knew about it, so it was not like they were trying to get away from the Black community." Simone does say, though, that to ensure that "the Black student voice" is heard on campus, Black students are encouraged by the Black community at large to participate in non-Black organizations such as the student government.

Simone describes the Black community at Western as being centered primarily around King House, the Black theme residence hall. But Simone feels that "being in the Black community means that you are comfortable." Simone says, "I know a lot of students that feel that they are outside the Black community, who don't feel comfortable coming to King House, who don't feel like King House and the Black Cultural Center are their organizations. I don't think it is a question of how Black you are, I think it is whether you are comfortable with the programs that are for Black students." But Simone also feels that because so many Black activities on campus are centered around King House, for those students who do not live in King, "it takes extra effort" for them to become involved in the Black community on campus.

Prior to her matriculation at Western, Simone describes herself as "being on the outside of the Black community looking in," painting a picture of the Black community as an entity with a tangible set of boundaries between Black and non-Black. Says Simone,

> I think I have always been on the other side, always looking into the Black community. Even at my high school where there were only 12 Black students, I was a random because I didn't agree with the things that they [the other Black students on campus] did, and they all hung out together. I didn't really make that effort [to hang out with other Blacks] because I knew that they didn't approve of me in the first place.

Simone feels that at Western it is much easier to get involved in the Black community because "there are so many aspects of the community. You can be in the community and you don't have to dress a certain way, or to talk a certain way." She says that in her high school this was not the case. Simone said, "In my high school you had to just be, quote, unquote, a stereotypical Black person' to be in that community." Simone says that at Western she does not know of any Black persons who would not be accepted or could not be involved in the Black community if they really wanted to.

Simone says that she has not been involved in non-Black organizations at Western because she has been in the White community for most of her life, and she wants to spend the time she is at Western involved in Black activities; nothing in the White community at Western interests her; she doesn't have enough time. Simone feels that the Black community organizations fulfill her affiliation needs. Further, Simone says, "If there was an organization that I wanted to be in, I certainly would get involved, but just the fact that it is in the White community stops me—the fact that I like community service and there are community service organizations in the Black community—there is basically something for everyone in the Black community."

Simone feels that, even though she is involved only in Black organizations, she is very much a part of the general campus life at Western. Says Simone, "I don't think that there is just one 'Western' experience. . . . There are just so many lives here. It [Western] is a very diverse experience; there are a lot of [majority culture] campus traditions that I have never done here. But I don't feel that I am missing out. I think that every student is unique to Western, so if you are a part of a community, then you are a part of Western."

Greg

Greg is from a predominantly Black community on the East Coast. His family is originally from the Caribbean. He attended a predominantly White private day school. Except for one non-Black community service organization, all of the organizations in which Greg is involved in at Western arc Black.

Greg says that it was a big change "socially" coming from the East Coast to the West Coast. "The West Coast is more laid back," says Greg. "Little things were uncomfortable at first, but as I adjusted, and it became more comfortable; it became more fun."

Greg lived in King House his first year. He says he decided to live in King House because, "I felt like my first year I needed to be around the Black community cause there were so few of us on a major White campus."

Greg says that he primarily has Black friends. Says Greg, "That's who I've surrounded myself with. It's not like I can't rap to White people; I just prefer to be around Black people. My culture is more fun. I am not a separatist or anything. It's just more comfortable with Black people."

In talking about attitudes of non-Black students toward Black students, Greg says, "The White students that I have messed with have been on the level with me. They talk to me and say that everyone deserves to be here." Greg goes on to say:

> Since this is Western, more of these students who have come from little towns in the Midwest are willing to learn about minorities once they start to get off the surface. There is always going to be bigotry and prejudice. I can deal with that, but the overall campus feeling, since this [sic] is highly intellectual people, not just academically, but socially, they will also be after the ability to learn about other cultures.

Greg says that one of the difficulties of being a Black student at Western is the pressure to be active in the Black community and to do well academically, which is something that Greg believes White students on campus do not have to contend with. Describing this pressure, Greg says:

You [a Black student] are required to do more for the community as well as try to achieve academically. Some students can deal with this; some can't. We may not come from the best neighborhoods sometimes; that's why we have to somehow give back by doing community service, trying to do something in the Black community. But then there is the added pressure of trying to do well academically. That's one of the hardest things at Western. And then to deal with the added pressure of trying to achieve something within the Black community and then trying to deal with working on campus, living in general, just the added pressure. That's a lot that White students don't have to deal with.

According to Greg, some Black students are more comfortable being involved with Black activities than other Black students. Greg thinks this is because some Black students have never been around other Black people. In talking about a particular (Black) student that he knows at Western, Greg says, "He didn't understand what it means to be Black. He had an identity crisis. That's understandable; he didn't grow up like I did, surrounded by Black people every day." But Greg feels that the Black community "shouldn't isolate someone who doesn't become involved right away in the Black scheme of things." Greg discusses the reasons Black students who are not involved in the Black community are ostracized by other Black students:

We are depending on each other to achieve something—for someone who has not been there before—for someone to just subtly come in, Black people see that as an insult. [They say,] "What are you doing here now, where were you before." It's the struggle, the so-called struggle on campus. We need to be more understanding and willing to accept. . . . Some of us are going to take a little more time than others to get involved. Some may not even become involved.

Greg says that the role of Black organizations should be "to promote Black unity and to keep everybody together and focused." Greg says that other Black students on campus are a source of support for him and that a lot of White students do not understand why many Black students on campus hang out with one another. Says Greg, "As long as [we] have someone to relate to, as long as we stick together, we can make it."

Greg says that he does not see himself becoming involved in non-Black organizations on campus because he is not the type to "do the multicultural thing." He feels that he can be successful even if he is involved only in Black organizations. Says Greg, "I definitely think I can make it. I don't think anyone is going to look down on me because I kept it Black—White people keep it White; why can't I keep it Black and still achieve?"

Greg says that his goal for his remaining years at Western is "to just do the best that I can academically." Greg adds:

I want to leave here knowing that I came to the most prestigious university in the world and I achieved here; I didn't flunk out. That Greg had his fun, but he got his grades and he did well, and he went to medical school and he became a doctor, and Western got him there. I would like to leave that as a legacy—another African American male who could achieve, when it was doubted by society that he would achieve.

Deborah

Deborah is originally from a predominantly White neighborhood on the West Coast. She has not been involved in any Black organizations during her four years at Western, although she has been involved in a number of non-Black organizations on campus. She is an athlete who describes herself as "doing a lot of water sports—things that are not traditionally Black."

During her first year at Western, Deborah was a member of the volleyball team. After she stopped playing volleyball, she looked for other activities to fill her time. Deborah says that the organizations she joined "post-volleyball" were those that her friends were a part of. "Once I quit [volleyball] . . . I realized I would need something to take the place of it. I started looking more toward people that I knew were involved in things. My roommate was involved in [a non-Black community service organization] so she pulled me into it; initially it is the people that I knew who were involved [that get her interested in the organization or activity]."

Although Deborah has not been involved in any Black organizations during the four years she has been at Western, she says that she and a Black friend (who lived in her first-year residence hall) tried to get involved in the Black community at many different times during her first year. Deborah said that neither she nor her friend felt completely comfortable or accepted by other Black students. Deborah believes that part of the reason for these feelings of discomfort and nonacceptance was that both she and her friend grew up in White neighborhoods. Says Deborah:

> All year long we [Deborah and her friend] would go to the sorority and fraternity dances. . . . We would spend most of the time talking to each other. We would see people from our classes; we would say hi, but that was it—it was like a five-minute conversation. We never felt welcome; we both felt kind of strange. The other thing about both of us is we grew up in neighborhoods that were primarily White so we weren't used to hanging out with Black people anyway. But we both wanted to meet Black people and whoever else was out there—but we didn't feel particularly welcome.

In describing her perceptions of the differences between students who grew up in White or mixed-race neighborhoods and students who grew up in Black neighborhoods, Deborah says:

You can tell. I get the feeling that Blacks who come from mostly Black environments dress differently, talk differently, tend to hang out with other Blacks—those are the ones that will nod and say hi to you—versus the ones from other [White/mixed-race] neighborhoods, [who] say, "Why is another Black person sitting next to me?" The ones that come up from mostly White environments tend to hang out with mostly White friends and don't speak to other Blacks on campus. They dress differently and act differently (it is something that I do, too), and try to do activities to separate themselves [from other Black students]. Part of it is that you [Blacks who grew up in White environments] are used to being the sort of model Black, [and other people tell you that] you are different from other Blacks. I think that I and a lot of other Blacks are used to being considered that way.

Deborah feels that there should be some way to bridge what she terms a "gap" between these two groups of students (those who have grown up in Black neighborhoods and those who have grown up in White or "mixed" neighborhoods) but says that there are a lot of barriers to bringing the two groups together. Says Deborah, "Because they don't see eye to eye, neither one understands the way the other one thinks, and why they can't see it our [each other's] way. I don't think they'll ever get together. They should look at it less as a sort of competition—all or nothing. [I think] you can do things this way, or you can do things that way. The message you get now is that either you are down with us, or you're not."

With respect to student participation in Black organizations and general Black activities on campus, Deborah believes that there is a short "window of time" for Black students to become involved in the Black community and that if students do not participate in Black activities early on in their frosh year, it is very difficult for those students both to be accepted by the Black community and to become involved in subsequent years. Describing this difficulty, Deborah says:

After freshman year, at the beginning of sophomore year, I kind of stopped trying. It wasn't working. . . . We tried. It seems like there is a really short window of time in the first two or three weeks that you arrive at Western, when you either decide that you are going to be with Black people, and I think you get sort of accepted by them, or pretty much you spend the rest of your years meeting them, but not really feeling like you're wanted there, like you're part of it.

For students who live in King House, Deborah says that it is easier to know about, and become involved in, Black activities on campus:

I think it's true that if you live in King your freshman year, you're very aware and it's all around you, and I think it makes it a lot easier to step right in. I think if you don't live in King, you definitely have to make a decision or you have to actively try. If you live in King, it's more passive—you live there; they are going to come knock down on your door [to get you involved]. But if you don't live in King, then I think it's more up to you to go out and actually find other Black people and get to know them.

Deborah describes the purposes of Black organizations as varied, depending on the organization. She perceives the Black Student Union (BSU), in particular, as providing a "niche" and a "comfort level for people who grew up in environments where there were mostly Black people" but also feels that the BSU is a "little too political in terms of pushing a certain agenda. She does not specify what this agenda is but compares King House, which she feels is a social/cultural organization, to the BSU, which she partially perceives to be a political organization. She also says that she feels Black organizations are "pursuing things that some Black students need" but that "you can't lump them [all Black students] together and say this is what all Black students need." Deborah believes that Black students who are primarily involved in Black activities should be aware of the "spectrum of activities that are available to them, and not just what is going on in King House."

In talking about the concept of racial identity, Deborah describes her family as the "Rainbow Coalition" and says that she never thought about race until she got to Western. She says that a Black psychology class she took made her "think more about my own life, and myself as a Black person." Says Deborah:

I never made a lot of distinctions about myself and what was distinctly Black. I'm trying to fit that into my whole world picture. I think I am still searching, and I am pretty screwed up about the whole thing. . . . Most people wake up and realize at some point, I am Black, what does that mean to me, what does it mean to my world? I would feel comfortable talking to someone about it, but I don't want to feel pressured. . . . Also, it is ignorant to assume that one person's Black experience is everyone's Black experience.

In looking back on her experiences at Western, Deborah says:

I love Western. The emphasis is on personal individual achievement. I still believe it's true—you are whatever race you are, but that can't possibly be the first thing that comes to your mind. How hard you work, the things that you do to prove what type of person you are and what you are capable of, will always come first in my mind. I spend more time thinking about that! Some people spend more time thinking that Blacks shouldn't have to work twice as hard just to prove that they are equal; I believe that, but I'm not going to spend time thinking about it. I want to go make my millions; I'm going to go do it! I'm not going to let being Black stand in my way, but I think I need to spend a little more time realizing exactly what that's going to mean as time goes on.

Wanda

Wanda is a senior who has been primarily involved in community service activities during her four years at Western. Wanda came to Western from southern California and says that until the 6th grade she lived and attended school in a predominantly White community; from the 6th grade on she lived and attended school in a predominantly Black community.

Wanda says that she was attracted to community service activities because she felt that those were the only campus organizations that met her particular affiliation needs. Says Wanda, "I looked around—nothing on campus sort of fit with my background and who I am and things like that. It [community service] was sort of my outlet to reality and getting back to where I am from, to ground myself more than anything."

Wanda believes that the Black students at Western do not come from the same type of community (predominantly Black) that she is from and that when she came to Western for the Black orientation weekend, her initial impressions were that "the Black folks at Western really don't seem Black." Wanda chose not to live in King House her frosh year because, says Wanda, "I didn't want to live with a whole lot of Black folks trying hard to find themselves." Wanda says that when she told other Black students her reasons for not wanting to live in King House her frosh year, they labeled her "militant."

From Wanda's viewpoint, "the majority of Black students at Western come from non-Black environments," and they (the students from non-Black environments) are the most likely to isolate or label the Black students who don't participate in the Black community. Says Wanda:

The majority of Black folks are coming from non-Black environ-ments—they come here and want to say that they are so Black, and those [Black] people that they see as what they are, or what they used to be, they isolate. These Black folks [the Black students from non-Black environments] are just trying to talk about other Black folks—who are what they see themselves as, and what they are scared that they are. The Black folks who are coming from predominantly Black environments, they are not isolating folks. If they [the students from Black environments] are [isolating other Black students], it is by joining certain Black organizations, more so than by saying you [other Black students] are not Black enough. Those who are talking about people not being Black enough are those coming from White environments.

Wanda believes that part of the college culture for Black students, particularly those from White environments, is to become involved in Black organizations.

Wanda says that "people struggling with identity are those who jump most into [Black] organizations." Wanda also feels that many Black students are involved in Black organizations primarily to be accepted by other Black students on campus, not because they are committed to supporting the Black community. Says Wanda:

> People [Black students] have different ideas and expectations when they come to college. There are some things you think you are supposed to do—you are supposed to give back to the community, you are supposed to identify with being Black—there are things you are supposed to do so as not to be socially stigmatized. It's all about "stylin' and profilin'"—it's not like they are really committed to helping anybody or doing anything. You know what you are supposed to say, to get into what you want to get into. I think it's a college culture thing.

Wanda says that people choose to be outside the community for different reasons. Some are uncomfortable with their color; some people honestly deserve that label (being outside the community) because, if they could choose to remove it, they would remove their color.

As examples of these students, Wanda points to students who, "if you say hello . . . and they don't speak to you," and "people who request NOT to have a Black roommate." Wanda says she chooses to be "outside of the Black community" because she does not "click with the folks [other Black students] here [at Western]." But Wanda also says that because she is "confrontational," people perceive her as being "deep in the core" of the Black community. Says Wanda, "There are clumps of Black people who choose not to be deep in the core of the Black community. I choose not to be deep in the core—but just because of how confrontational I am, people kind of put me there."

Wanda thinks that Black organizations should be a link to the surrounding Black communities. She also says that they should serve to "ground people in Black identity" and that she has "seen a lot of people grow through their involvement in the Black organizations at Western." In talking about her lack of involvement in Black organizations at Western, Wanda says that the Black organizations on campus "haven't done much for me. I could have done without most of the speakers and the soul food dinners and established a deeper relationship with other individuals—faculty and staff of color." Wanda adds, "I think it's good to have those things for folks who don't know who they are—for me, I needed more support." Wanda says that she has been able to use some of the speakers that came for different events sponsored by Black organizations as "an avenue to get to Black folks outside of the Western community." Adds Wanda, "I identified more with Black folks in [a local Black community off-campus] than I did with Black folks here [at Western]."

In describing her relationships (or nonrelationships) with Black students on campus, Wanda says, "It's stressful; it's bothersome; it's a tragic shame that I feel as though I couldn't click with the folks here." During this, her senior year, Wanda says, "I started chillin' with people who don't go here. I couldn't really get into the folks here."

As Wanda reflects on her experiences at Western and thinks about the future, she says she sees herself developing links with other ethnic groups—"It may not just be Black folks I am working with"—and that she has grown to see herself not just as a Black person but "more as a Black woman."

Broderick

Broderick is a senior from a multicultural, inner-city community in southern California. During his years at Western, Broderick has been primarily involved in organizations related to his academic interests. None of the organizations that Broderick has been involved in have been Black. On the back of his survey, Broderick wrote a note that said, "I am only half-Black."

Broderick says that he is open to the idea of joining groups but that he doesn't *have* to be in one. He says he joins groups because of "people with similar interests and backgrounds—people that I can relate to." He says that involvement in extracurricular activities "helps buffer the stress level and makes my academics more endurable." Broderick also says, "I would join something that had a race component, if it was something related to my fundamental interests like academics or career." But, says Broderick, "I wouldn't go to a group just for the race component. If there was something else that attracted me—common interests, and it was Black, then that would be great."

Broderick says he did not live in King House because "I didn't think I'd fit in." He also says that he went to some of the Black Student Union meetings and also to a group for "people who are mixed," but, says Broderick, "I tried them out, but none of them seemed to fit me." At the "all-Black meetings," Broderick says, "It seems like I stuck out like a sore thumb. They subtly made me feel out of place—I didn't think I could relate, as much as they could among themselves. I stood out; it felt kind of uncomfortable."

Describing his ethnic identity, Broderick says: "Genetically I am half White and mostly Black, and also Native American. If they ask what I am in terms of what I feel I am—I say that I am `a-racial.' I think I am pretty color blind. I grew up in a diverse environment. It was never an issue with my family. It was never brought up. They looked at everyone the same." He goes on to say: "I don't feel like I have a foot in either door. But partly the impetus for me trying was my Black [ex] girlfriend. She said I should acknowledge my Blackness. I thought I would give it a try. She thought I should identify as a Black—at the expense of ignoring the other. I tried to open up my mind, but it seemed like a little too much pressure from her." Broderick describes his ex-girlfriend as "very in touch" with Black culture. Says Broderick, "[S]he has a Black brother and sister; her family tried to make her consciously aware of the history of the Black race and aspects of Black culture."

Broderick says that there are "distinct social skills" for the "Black group" and the "White group" and that many of these skills are acquired on the "playground."

Broderick says that he does not have the "Black group" skills, which he describes as the following: "[J]ust the manner of speaking—the subtle ways that you relate to each other—even the dancing—I don't have those skills, specifically for that group. That's not necessarily fundamental like I have to have those skills in order to interact, but it just makes it a little less comfortable, whereas I've learned the White ways a lot better." But he also says, "I don't know if I stand out more with the White group, or with the Black group" and adds, "If I had to choose—I feel like I fit in better with the Black group, because even though I'm not considered Black or White—I feel like I'm considered a minority, more than a non-minority."

Speaking about Black organizations specifically, Broderick feels that they are "narrow in their focus and in who they try to serve." But he also says that this narrow focus is "not necessarily intentional or negative." He feels that "the groups [Black organizations] should be open to everyone. If people have similar interests, they should be encouraged to come also." Broderick also believes that there is "merit in groups that separate themselves because group members can learn from each other, feel that special bond" but adds that, "since I am not 100% of any group, I don't feel that special bond; all I feel is separatism."

Broderick believes that it is particularly important for non-White students on campus to "find people who are like themselves, for social support, who can understand the things that aren't really the academics." He says "For a lot of Black students, I'm sure that the Black student groups help them that way." He also says that he doesn't see becoming involved in Black organizations and getting involved in other activities on campus as "mutually exclusive." Says Broderick, "Obviously you only have so much time away from classes." However, "I don't think the Black student groups are giving Black students skills that are going to transfer later on—those groups just help them deal with the present situation. The only place I have found I can get those skills is by doing the thesis, paying attention in classes, seeking out study partners—social groups don't give you any skills that will transfer later." In talking about interactions between Black students and non-Black students, Broderick says that "students at Western mix in classes, but not outside" and that because "Black students are more of a minority than other groups, there is this pressure to stick together to try to get through."

Broderick says that a research program for minority students in which he was involved in the summer before his senior year made him more interested in "cultural issues" and is an example of "a perfect way to combine minority cultural themes with academics." He says "I wasn't really interested in academically studying minority issues, but the project that I studied this past summer compared minorities' and non-minorities' views and perceptions in situations of discrimination. That project really encouraged me to think more about cultural issues. It opened my eyes!"

DISCUSSION

The original purpose in conducting the semistructured interviews with the students whose narratives are profiled in this chapter was to gain more in-depth understanding of their perceptions of Black organizations on campus. Certainly, the student profiles do provide insight into student views of these organizations. However, as indicated in this chapter's introductory paragraphs, these student profiles highlight some overarching themes relative to student participation or nonparticipation in Black organizations at Western and illuminate differences in Black student experiences on campus. The two themes that are most prominent in these student profiles are issues of *Black student identity* and perceptions of the Black community on campus. Table 7.1 summarizes the particular perspective vis-à-vis these themes and the type of pre-Western neighborhood or community represented by the profiled students. To provide additional illumination of these themes, I include selected quotes from the 17 students who were also interviewed as part of this study but not profiled in this chapter (Brief descriptions of these additional students are contained in the Appendix).

Racial Identity

The student profiles suggest that Black students are engaged in an ongoing search for the meaning of "being Black" as it relates both to how they see themselves and to how they see the world. Students use such phrases as "acknowledging it" (Broderick), "contemplating the meaning of it" (Deborah), "having or not having it" (Greg), "trying to find or struggling with it" (Simone) in discussing their attitudes toward "it," their own Black/racial identity and that of other Black students on campus. *The* or *a* definition of Black racial identity is made more complex by the diversity of backgrounds that the Black students at Western come from and for students who are interracial (Broderick) or who are not African American: "I used to think of myself as being Black AND White; I used to separate those two things. I would visualize it in my mind as more the *Ying* and *Yang*, separate but equal—me kind of split in half . . . . Now I have gone with [describing myself] as a "swirl" (Jacob).

"When I am with Whites, I consider myself African American; when I am with Blacks, I consider myself Eritrean. Because I am from Africa—so there is not necessarily a bond [with American Blacks]" (Johannes).

Some students from predominantly White environments (Deborah) seem to be engaged in a continual struggle to come to terms with the meaning of Black identity to their sense of self-identity. For these students, Western is the first time that they have had to confront within-group issues with regard to race and/or to evaluate themselves on a racial dimension against a Black peer group.

The majority of people here are "bougie" [boo-jhee], middle-class Black people, and there is this whole competition thing, like who's Black and sort of what the definition of Black is (Wilmetta).

A large percentage of Black students here come from predominantly White backgrounds. . . . It's really weird because people ascribe to some Black identity that they don't really know about—it's like [she describes the Black students from predominantly White neighborhoods] you are not from the "hood"; you wouldn't even know what to do there (Brianna).

Everybody is trying to fit into what this idea of being Black is. You would never know it unless they told you [which students are from Black communities and which students are from non-Black communities] cause everybody tries to act like they been around Black people all their life (Malik).

The student profiles also suggest that students spend a great deal of time evaluating the "Blackness" of other Black students, labeling students who do not participate in the Black community as "random" or "miscellaneous."[6] Wanda in particular believes that the harshest critics are those students from predominantly White backgrounds who are insecure with their own lack of "a Black experience." From Wanda's perspective, these students are the most likely to participate heavily in Black organizations. Another interviewee, from a predominantly White environment, says: "But a lot of people here are questioning their Blackness, or their involvement in the Black community, and how that determines how Black they are—they project that on to other people, creating standards. I did the same thing—he's a Tom [a Black person who acts White]—and then you think, they could be saying the same thing about me" (Wilmetta).

As a student from an all Black environment, an interviewee says: "Some students, especially light-skinned students, think that joining certain Black organizations (Black Greek organizations specifically) gives them their cultural license" (Malik).

As a psychological construct, adolescent and college student identity development has yielded a number of theoretical models and a large body of research (see Pascarella & Terenzini, 1991, for an overview). However, the unique developmental needs of Black students, particularly as this development relates to the issue of *Black racial identity,* are an area where there is an absence of study and attention (McEwen et al., 1990; Pascarella & Terenzini 1991). McEwen et al. contend that developing ethnic and racial identity is an important part of the unique developmental tasks of Black/African American students and has not been adequately addressed by current psychosocial student development theories (she cites as examples Chickering, 1969; Coons, 1970; King, 1973; Sanford, 1962). Although not a "traditional" student development theory, the Cross (1978) model of psychological Nigrescence, from which Parham and Helms (1981) developed the racial identity attitude scale (RIAS), is one model that does offer a conceptualization of racial identity development for Blacks.[7]

Students profiled appear to be at various levels of awareness, comfort, acceptance, and integration of the meaning of "Blackness" to their sense of

Table 7.1

Type of Pre-Western Community and Perspectives of Self and Community Identity for Students Profiled

	Type of Pre-Western Community	Racial Identity (Self)	Perception of which Black Students Make up Western's Black Community	Community Insider/ Outsider
Simone	Predom. White	Exploring Blackness by immersing herself in Black community on campus	Black students involved in Black campus activities say any Black students can be a part of them if they want to	Insider (but an outsider in school)
Greg	Predom. Black	Says he "understands what it means to be Black because he grew up surrounded by Black people"	Black students who serve the Black community	Insider
Deborah	Predom. White	Trying to understand what being Black means	Black students from all-Black communities	Outsider
Wanda	Predom. Black (did spend some time in predom. White neighborhood)	Strong Black identity but also interested in developing links with other ethnic groups	Black Students who are learning how to be Black	Outsider (but says other students see her as "deep in the core") of the community
Broderick	Multi-cultural	Half-Black; other students tell him he needs to acknowledge his Blackness	Black students with "distinctly Black social skills"	Outsider

self-identity, in ways that correspond closely to the RIAS *preencounter* (anti-Black or Black unaware), *encounter* (exploring Blackness), *immersion* (strong pro-Black), and *internalization* (incorporation of Black and non-Black values) stages. For example, Deborah says that many Blacks from predominantly White environments, herself included, are more comfortable around Whites than around other Blacks *(preencounter)*. Simone, also from a predominantly White environment, talks about Western's presenting an opportunity to explore her Black culture or be a part of a Black community for the first time *(encounter)*. Simone also says that she is involved only in Black organizations at Western because, prior to Western, she had been involved only in non-Black organizations. Wanda believes that other students see her as militant and "deep in the core" of the Black community *(immersion)*. Wanda also sees herself working and developing links with other ethnic groups, and Greg says that, though he chooses to socialize almost exclusively with Black students, he is comfortable with both Black and non-Black students on campus *(internalization)*. However, what the profiles and other interviews show are that racial identity development issues are even more complex for students whose heritage is biracial and that particular attention to these students, as well as to other students who have multiple self-identities or "self-referents" (e.g., Black women, Black students from other countries), is also important. For many of these students identity is situational (e.g., the Black student interviewee from Eritrea who identifies himself as African American around Whites but as Eritrean around African Americans or a Black female student for whom the salience of gender and race is different in different contexts). These are issues that the RIAS scale does not account for or is not able to capture as currently constructed.

Additionally, issues related to "being Black" seem to be of particular concern to students who come to Western from a predominantly White or non-Black environment (Simone, Broderick). For many of these students, the meaning of being Black beyond simply skin color became salient only when these students, through their enrollment at Western, became part of a Black peer group for the first time. Although Black students from predominantly Black environments who attend a PWI such as Western may have adjustment issues related to moving from a Black environment to a predominantly White environment, these students (Greg) appear to be more comfortable with their Black identity (at least to the extent that this identity means that they feel comfortable or accepted by other Black students). The issue of how Black students from predominantly White backgrounds experience a Black peer group at a PWI has not been the subject of in-depth analysis by higher education researchers. The notion of a Black peer group at a PWI has an important relationship to both the psychological (self-identity) and social experiences (student-to-student relationships) of Black students on campus.

Black Community

Students use the notion of the "Black community" as a reference point for evaluating their own Black identity and that of other Black students on campus. In fact, student perceptions and expectations of this "Black community," in combination with other factors (e.g., affiliation needs and interests, perceptions of the roles of various organizations on campus), play a major role in influencing student involvement choices.

The Black community at Western is collectively defined as a particular place, made up of particular types of people, a particular set of attitudes and behaviors, an abstract, yet tangible, entity with boundaries that separate "insiders" from "outsiders." Although King House (the Black theme dorm on campus) is the acknowledged center of the Black community, students vary in their definitions as to who is actually a member of the Black community on campus.

Some students (Broderick, Simone) perceive the Black community as made up of students largely from all-Black environments; others (Wanda) see the community as made up of students from predominantly White environments who are experiencing a significant Black peer group for the first time. Students from either environment will be "counted" (identified) by other students as "in the community" based on some combination of the factors that students use to define Black community. For example, one of the non-profiled students said, "Just by my name being African and being from the South, I never felt like I had to prove my Blackness" (Malik). However, it does seem that students from all-Black environments (e.g., Greg and Wanda) are perceived by other students to be "in the Black community," regardless of whether or not these students identify themselves as "in the Black community."

> There are people who grew up in Black communities and there are people who grew up in White communities. They [the people who grew up in White communities] don't talk much about where they grew up—there is this perception that people who grew up in Black communities know more about being Black (Wendy).

> If you grew up in the "hood," and you walk a certain way and talk a certain way, then you are [perceived as] really Black (Wilmetta).

Students describe a number of norms, primarily *attitudes and behaviors* that signal "in the community" status. Although, again, individual student perceptions determine what and how important particular attitudes and behaviors might be, some of the behaviors and attitudes mentioned by students include feeling comfortable in the Black community, speaking to other Black students on campus, going to Black activities, joining Black organizations, speaking and dressing certain ways, having "distinctly Black" social skills.

As an *entity,* students describe their relationship with the community in an active way, using such phrases as "surviving it," "getting to know it," "being a part of it," "fitting in to it." There is also a perception that the Black community has a tangible set of boundaries where some combination of where one lives, where one is from, and how one thinks and behaves separates "outsiders" from "insiders." One of the students profiled, Simone, particularly captures the sentiment that the Black community is defined as an entity with particular boundaries, describing herself prior to Western as having "always been on the other side, always looking into the Black community."

The self-perception of a student's own insider or outsider status many times does not match the perception of other students. Wanda is a student who does not formally participate in Black organizations on campus but says that other students perceive her to be "deep in the core" of the Black community because of her personality, which Wanda describes as "confrontational." Jamilla, one of the students interviewed but not profiled in this chapter, says that she gets "flak" from other Black students because they do not see her at King House, but she feels that the definition of Black community should not be limited to only those students who actively participate in Black activities:

> I was going to a lot of things with my [White] friends in the hall last year and I got some flak for not going over to King House all the time and for not going to the parties and the steps shows . . . but, if the Black community only includes those who are part of certain organizations and activities, then the community would not include me. I am not a part of a [Black] sorority, I am not yet as involved in one of the organizations, and I don't live in King.

Any notion of a community identity confers on its "members" certain behavioral norms and expectations for being part of that community, expectations that many Black students interpret as *pressure*. Students perceive that there are pressure to acknowledge and/or declare one's Black identity (Broderick, Deborah); pressure to serve the Black community *and* do well academically (Greg); pressure from Blacks to participate in Black activities; pressure from Whites not to participate in Black activities; pressure to "be Black" and be a student. Says Jamilla:

> I would like to be a part of the Black community because I haven't been a part of that community yet. But my White friends pressure me not to go to Black activities. . . . I feel there is a gap between the Black community and White community. It is hard because I have been a part of both and I feel like I want to be a part of the Black community especially since I haven't been, but there is also a tug, because it is seen [by Whites] like you are going to the other side.

Jamilla says that another Black student gave her "flak" for not being in the Black community. She says that she was not trying to be a "sellout" by not participating in the Black community but that "I was just trying to be a student first and foremost." She goes on to say, "I was really hurt when I got that kind of pressure and negativity from people. It is definitely hard for minority students to deal with that kind of tug."

Other, nonprofiled interviewees also used the word "pressure" in describing particular aspects of their experiences on campus:

My parents were concerned about—like I guess maybe the whole stereotypical Black college student is always worried about going to the BSU meeting—they were worried because they knew my upbringing—they were worried about me feeling pressured or feeling somehow insecure or inferior to other Blacks because I hadn't had the same Black experiences as them (Michelle).

It's [the pressure] not spoken—it's more like so and so never talks to Black people, or so and so is always with their White friends, or you hear about what they say about other people who do do that [are always with their White friends] so in a way they feel the pressure anyway, they are going to talk about me if I do this or they are going to think I sold out or I'm "random" (Wendy).

For some students, pressure translates into joining or contemplating joining Black organizations as a means of signaling some measure of Black identity to other Black students: "People walk around feeling like they need to go to these [Black] things, because there is an identity complex on this campus" (Samantha). Pressure may be perceived by students (Wanda) as the reason other students, specifically those from predominantly White environments, join Black organizations. For other students, particularly for those students whose heritage is biracial (Broderick), pressure results in an uneasiness about participating formally • in Black activities.

The student interviews suggest that Black students, at a minimum, have dual social relationships to the campus: their relationship to the campus as *a student* and their relationship to the campus as *a Black student.* The notion that Black students have both a "personal" and a "collective" identity is something that Gurin and Epps (1975) discuss in their often cited book titled *Black Consciousness, Identity and Achievement.*

Black students, like other students on campus, must find ways to negotiate and survive in the campus mainstream, if not socially, certainly academically. However, these interviews also indicate that, in addition to interacting at some level in mainstream academic and social environments, many Black students feel that they must negotiate the Black social network on campus. Again, students from predominantly Black environments appear to be more easily or readily accepted as part of the Black community or Black collectivity on campus—either because their prior "Black" experiences give them a greater degree of comfort in interacting with other Black students or because Black students on campus perceive these students to know more about being Black. For students from predominantly White environments, one senses from reading the student interviews that many of these students worry about being labeled "miscellaneous" or "random" by the Black community because they do not participate in Black activities and/or do not have the combination of behaviors and attitudes that grant them "in the community" status.

CONCLUSION

"Am I Black enuf fo ya?" The personal narratives and interview data presented in this chapter illustrate the diversity that encompasses the definition of a Black student and of Black student experiences on one campus. The keys to the experiences of the students profiled at Western are the issues of Black student identity development, Black student perceptions, and their definitions of the Black community on campus.

For researchers, the data presented in this chapter suggest that gaining a greater insight into the increased diversity that encompasses the definition of a "Black student" will result in the creation of more accurate models to understand Black student development experiences and outcomes. For example, the data suggest that current Black racial identity development models (e.g., the Parham and Helms RIAS) should be reformulated to account for biracial and non-African American heritage, the situational nature of Black identity for students, and the relationship between students' perception of the Black community on campus and their self-evaluation of their Black identity.[8] The data also support McEwen et al.'s (1990) contention that resolving racial identity issues is an important aspect of the developmental process for Black students and should be accounted for in evaluating the fit of traditional psychosocial student development models (e.g., Chickering, 1969) for understanding Black student development. Additionally, though a sense of the collective identity of Black students on any campus will be influenced by the individual students who are part of the community, it seems important to develop a greater understanding as to where definitions regarding "being Black" originate on a campus and how these definitions, in turn, differentially affect student experiences. Some thoughts in this regard include exploring the ways in which societal-level cultural and political definitions of Black people influence the perceptions of what being Black is on a campus. For example, in describing what it means to be Black at Western, one of the students interviewed says that "there is this whole competition to be either rappers, or what Hollywood envisions as being Black."

The experiences of Black students encountering a Black peer group for the first time were another important issue raised in this study. Additional research and exploration should consider the question of how Black students from predominantly White environments experience Black peer groups. Multi-institutional studies on this subject should include students from HBCUs as well as PWIs. Finally, if researchers believe that Black students are not a completely homogeneous population, then it must be determined what is unique to being a Black student (as opposed to being a White student or a Latino student) but is not experienced equally or in the same way by all Black students or by all Black students who are similarly situated. For example, though all of the students profiled included their own socially constructed descriptions and definitions of Black community on campus in reference to their perceptions of their own identity (something that, in all likelihood, White students would not point to in White students' respective definitions of their identity), student perceptions of their "in the community status" were not the same for all the Black students from predominantly Black environments or for all of the Black students from predominantly White environments.

For administrators, within-group diversity among Black students presents a number of challenges to a PWI such as Western. These challenges include issues related to what administrators think about designing services and programs for "Black" students on campus; how the nature of the Black community is affected by a mix of students on campus from different environments; and who are at various degrees of comfort and acceptance with issues related to racial identity. In addition to playing their historical support role for students from predominantly Black environments, Black organizations at Western provide what appears to be an important racial identity exploration and development role for Black students from predominantly White communities. This suggests that the presence of Black organizations at PWIs should be supported and encouraged. However, for those students who have not been able to access the Black community on campus or who choose not to participate in Black organizations because of the perceived lack of fit between the organizations and their self-identities or experiences, there are few other places (cocurricular or within the academy) where students can explore what appears to be an important part of their identity development. It would seem that, in addition to student organizations, academic courses and the presence of Black faculty and staff would be important resources for students in processing the complex issues related to racial identity development. Additionally, the added layer of "the Black community" to their Western experiences means that the lives of many Black students are, in some ways, more complicated than the lives of White students on campus. Recognition that Black students may have differential experiences at campuses such as Western and the availability of appropriate health and counseling services for Black students may be critical components for ensuring that the expectations or pressure Black students experience or exert on one another as part of the Black community identity do not adversely affect their student-life experiences or their academic progress. It would also seem worthwhile to understand the ways in which campuses reinforce the homogeneity of the Black student population. Although Black students may have many common needs based on their racial heritage, it is also important to recognize and respond to the increased diversity of backgrounds and experiences that Black students bring with them to a college environment and to recognize that when a Black student talks about wanting to "fit in" on campus, he or she could be referring to the White community on campus, the Black community on campus, or both.

APPENDIX: INTERVIEWEES NOT FORMALLY PROFILED IN CHAPTER

Brianna: A senior who grew up in New York and California. Brianna attended a predominantly White and a multicultural school. Brianna is not formally involved in Black organizations but does, on occasion, attend Black activities on campus.

Clifford: A senior from the North. Clifford attended a high school that was over 90% Black. Except for one non-Black community service activity, Clifford is exclusively involved in Black organizations.

Danisha: A first-year student who is minimally involved in one organization—a Black organization. Danisha is from a largely Black, interracial community within close proximity to Western and goes home a lot on the weekends. She attended both private and public schools; the school she attended immediately before Western was public. She did not live in King House her first year.

Francesca: A first-year student originally from the South. She attended high school with both Black and White students but describes her high school and her community as segregated racially. She is extensively involved in a non-Black sorority and a club sports team. Francesca lists minimal participation in a Black academic organization.

Georg: A biracial student who does not feel comfortable identifying himself as either Black or White. He is originally from Germany and attended a college-prep boarding school on the East Coast. Georg says that, even though he does not identify himself culturally as either Black or White, he thinks about his identity a lot.

Jacob: A first-year student whose father is African American and whose mother is White. He is uncomfortable describing himself in terms of race and describes himself as a "swirl." Jacob is from a predominantly Jewish neighborhood in Chicago. He attended a public high school but did not have many classes with non-White students. Jacob is not involved in any Black organizations.

Jamilla: A first-year student originally from a predominantly White community on the West Coast who attended a college-prep boarding school. Jamilla says that she has spent her entire life in schools where there have been few minorities and that she looked at Western as an opportunity to have a culture and become a part of the BSU (Black Student Union).

Johannes: A first-year student whose family is from Eritrea. Until junior high school, he lived in Libya, at which time his family moved to central California, where he attended a predominantly White high school. Johannes says that when he is with Whites, he considers himself African American, but when he is with Blacks, he considers himself Eritrean. He is not involved in any Black organizations.

Malik: A fifth-year senior from a predominantly Black community in the South. He attended a high school that he describes as 98% Black. Malik lived in King House his freshman year. Throughout his years at Western, Malik has been involved in a number of Black and non-Black organizations, particularly other (non-Black) ethnic organizations on campus.

Michelle: A first-year student originally from a predominantly White community in the South. She lived in King House her first year. Michelle is involved only in Black organizations but has very low levels of involvement in these organizations. Michelle describes her high school as mostly White. Both of Michelle's parents are Western alumni.

Patricia: A first-year student who did not live in King House. Her family is from the West Coast, but she attended a predominantly White boarding school on the East Coast. Patricia says she lived in the "ghetto" until she was 9, at which time her family moved to the suburbs. Patricia is involved in both Black and non-Black organizations.

Richard: A first-year student from the North. Richard attended what he describes as an "all-White high school." He was involved in two organizations during his first year at Western, one a Black academic organization and the other a non-Black campus service organization. Richard did not live in the King House his first year.

Rochelle: A first-year student originally from a predominantly White community in the South. She attended a boarding school that was a math/science magnet. Rochelle lived in King House her first year and is extensively involved in a number of Black and non-Black organizations.

Samantha: A senior from a middle-class, predominantly Black community in northern California. She attended both a public and a private high school. She is involved in Black and non-Black organizations on campus.

Sondra: A first-year student from a predominantly Black, middle-class environment in southern California. She attended a racially diverse high school. Sondra did not live in King House but did have a Black roommate. She is involved in both Black and non-Black organizations.

Wendy: A senior who is from a predominantly White community. She is involved in one Black and one non-Black organization. Wendy lived in King House her first year.

Wilmetta: A senior who is from a predominantly White community in southern California. She is biracial; her mother is Pilipino, and her father is African American. She is involved in a Black sorority as well as the Pilipino student organization on campus.

NOTES

1. Allen (1988, 1991) and Fleming (1984) are two researchers whose work does focus on within-group differences in Black student experiences in higher education.

2. I define a "Black campus organization" as any campus organization (student or administratively run) that includes African American as part of its name or whose mission is focused on providing support or service to Black students or the Black community.

3. The breakdown for other ethnic groups is as follows: White, 52%; Asian, 23%; Hispanic, 11%; American Indian/Alaskan Native, 1%; International, 4%). The undergraduate degrees conferred in 1993–94 were 1,470 (Western University Public Information Office).

4. Of the 510 self-identified Black students attending Western University in 1993–94, 507 were mailed questionnaires. Three students listed out-of-state addresses, so questionnaires were not mailed to them.

5. Of the 219 students who completed the 1995 survey of Black student experiences at Western, 22 were invited to be interviewed.

6. Adjectives such as "random" and "miscellaneous" are similar in meaning to the phrase "Uncle Tom" and are used by some Black students at Western to describe those Black students who associate primarily with Whites.

7. There are four stages to the Racial Identity Attitude Scale (RIAS)—preencounter, encounter, immersion/emersion, and internalization. The RIAS was developed by Parham and Helms to measure racial identity attitudes reflective of four of the five stages of racial identity proposed by Cross (1971, 1978) in his model of psychological Nigrescense. The first stage, Preencounter, is characterized by the belief that Blacks are inferior to Whites and a preference for the values and behaviors associated with Whites. Stage two, encounter, is an exploring stage where the individual begins the transition from an anti-Black to a pro-Black stance. Stage three, immersion/emersion, is the complete endorsement of Black values to the exclusion of those perceived to be White and an all-consuming urge to understand, incorporate, and relate to the experience of being Black. The fourth stage, internalization, is a selective acceptance of values from both Black and White cultures. Although these stages can be thought of as a progression from stage one to stage four, individuals can also remain at a particular stage indefinitely.

8. One might be tempted to explain within-group diversity among Black students, particularly with respect to racial identity attitudes, as reflective of socioeconomic class differences. However, Carter and Helms (1988) found that socioeconomic status did not predict differences in racial identity attitudes among Black students.

REFERENCES

Allen, W. (1985). Black student, White campus: Structural, interpersonal, and psychological correlates of success. *Journal of Negro Education, 54*(2), 134–147.

Allen, W. (1988). The education of Black students on White college campuses: What Quality the experience? In M. Nettles (Ed.), *Toward Black undergraduate student equality in American higher education* (pp. 57–86). Westport, CT: Greenwood Press.

Allen, W., Epps, E. G., & Haniff, N. (Eds.). (1991). *College in Black and White: African American students in predominantly White and in historically Black public universities.* Albany: State University of New York Press.

Bangura, A. (1992). *The limitations of survey research methods in assessing the problem of minority student retention in higher education.* San Francisco: Mellen Research University Press.

Bryman, A. (1988). Quantity and quality in social research. Boston: Unwin Hyman.

Carter, R., & Helms, J. (1988). The relationship between racial identity attitudes and social class. *Journal of Negro Education, 57*(1), 22–30.

Chickering, A. W. (1969). *Education and identity.* San Francisco: Jossey-Bass.

Coons, F. (1970). The resolution of adolescence in college. *The Personnel and Guidance Journal, 48,* 533–541.

Cross, W. F. (1978). The negro to Black conversion experience: Towards a psychology of Black liberation. *Black World, 20*(9), 13–27.

Denzin, N. K. (1989). *The research act.* Englewood Cliffs, NJ: Prentice-Hall.

Fleming, J. (1984). *Blacks in college: A comparative study of students' success in Black and White institutions.* San Francisco: Jossey-Bass.

Gumport, P. (1993). Fired faculty: Reflections on marginalization and academic identity. In D. McLaughlin & W. Tierney (Eds.), *Naming silence lives: Personal narratives and processes of education change* (pp. 135–154). New York: Routledge.

Gurin, P., & Epps, E. (1975). *Black consciousness, identity and achievement.* New York: John Wiley & Sons.

Helms, J., & Parham, T. (1985). *The racial identity attitude scale-RIAS.* Unpublished summary of RIAS survey instrument. (Available from J. Helms, University of Maryland; T. Parham, University of California, Irvine).

King, S. H. (1973). *Five lives at Harvard: Personality change during college.* Cambridge: Harvard University Press.

McEwen, M., Roper, L., Bryant D., & Langa, M. (1990). Incorporating the development of African-American students into psychosocial theories of student development. *Journal of College Student Development, 31,* 429–436.

Parham, T., & Helms, J. (1981). The influence of Black students' racial identity attitudes on preferences for counselor's race. *Journal of Counseling Psychology, 28*(3), 250–257.

Pascarella, E., & Terenzini, P. (1991). *How college affects students.* San Francisco: Jossey-Bass.

Pounds, A. (1987). Black student needs on predominantly White campuses. In D. J. Wright (Ed.), *Responding to the needs of today's minority students: New directions for student services, no. 38* (pp. 23–38). San Francisco: Jossey-Bass.

Rooney, G. (1985). Minority students' involvement in minority student organizations: An exploratory study. *Journal of College Student Development, 26*(5), 450–456.

Yin, R. (1989). *Case study research: Design and methods.* Newbury Park, CA: Sage.

8

Self-Segregation: An Oxymoron in Black and White

Sybril M. Bennett

A HISTORIC SEPARATION

On December 1, 1955, a young seamstress, with her refusal to give up her seat, permanently altered the course of history. Rosa Parks, who was sitting in the section designated for "Coloreds," was ordered by the bus driver to move to a seat farther back to allow a White man to have her seat because the White section of the bus was full. Parks and Reed (1994) say, "Bus drivers then had police powers, under both municipal and state laws, to enforce racial segregation. However, we were sitting in the section designated for colored" (p. 22). In other words, Mrs. Parks was being told to get up out of the area that the White authorities had already assigned to her to sit and relocate to another location where Whites wanted her to sit for their immediate convenience. This may sound perplexing, but it is historically accurate. Since that time, the reason Mrs. Parks challenged segregation and did not give up her seat has been the subject of individual and societal interpretations. Many have stated that she was physically weary and that her feet were tired from a long day's work. Mrs. Parks refutes this: "My feet were not tired, but I was tired—tired of unfair treatment" (Parks & Reed, 1994, p. 25).

Affectionately known as the "Mother of the civil rights movement," Mrs. Parks' noncompliance with the bus driver's order for her to yield her seat to a White man was the catalyst for the Montgomery, Alabama, bus boycott. As a result, on December 21, 1956, the city buses in Montgomery were legally desegregated. This meant that Blacks could choose to sit anywhere that they wanted to sit on a bus. They were no longer relegated to sitting in the area specified for Blacks or forced to relinquish their seats to White patrons. According to the legal system, it was then up to individual Blacks to decide whether to sit next to Whites or Blacks. As such, it became evident that the intent of the boycott was not to have the socially constructed "privilege" of sitting next to Whites but rather to be able to exercise freedom of choice.

Five years prior to the Montgomery bus boycott, G. W. McLaurin had taken action against the Oklahoma State Regents for Higher Education for similar reasons. He had already been admitted to pursue his doctorate in education at the University of Oklahoma. Though he was allowed to attend classes with White students, he was assigned to sit in an area designated "Reserved for Coloreds." In addition, he was forbidden to sit near or with other White students in the library, cafeteria, or classroom. This differential treatment provided the grounds for his lawsuit. The Oklahoma Supreme Court ruled in the plaintiff's favor. Chief Justice Vinson delivered the Court's opinion: "There is a vast difference—a Constitutional difference—between restrictions imposed by the state which prohibit the intellectual commingling of students, and the refusal of students to mingle where the state presents no such bar" (*McLaurin v. Oklahoma State Regents for Higher Ed.* [339 U.S. 637, 641, 70 S.Ct. 851, 855, 94 L.Ed. 1149, 1154 (1950)] [citations omitted]). Justice Vinson could not ensure that McLaurin would be accepted by his White classmates because the White students could elect not to associate with him. In essence, the formal blockade was removed, but the individually imposed separation remained. That was nearly 50 years ago.

Today, students of color, Black students in particular, legally have the personal right to sit where they please. Likewise, White students are afforded the same option. However, on predominantly White campuses (PWIs), members of both races most frequently choose to sit near their respective same-race peers. Ironically, although both races can exercise their freedom of choice, Black students are often accused of self-segregating. Therefore, the purpose of this chapter is to (1) revisit the concepts of integration, segregation, and their variations; (2) explore the notions of self-segregation and resegregation and how they apply to Black and White students; and (3) offer suggestions that promote positive interracial interactions.

SEGREGATION REDEFINED

African American students were not legally permitted to attend predominately White institutions (PWIs) until the late 1960s when Title VI of the Civil Rights Act of 1964 prohibited colleges and universities from discriminating against these students in admissions solely because of the color of their skin. Until that time, institutions of higher education were legally segregated by race. It is imperative that scholars understand exactly what segregation and its variations mean and meant. According to *Black's Law Dictionary* (Campbell, 1990), *segregation* is the act or process of separation. It is the unconstitutional policy and practice of separating people on the basis of color, nationality, religion, and so on, in housing and schooling. *Desegregation* means to abolish the segregation of the races. *De jure segregation* usually refers to segregation that is mandated by law. *De facto segregation* is segregation based on social, economic, and other reasons not based on laws imposed by the state. Although segregation and de jure segregation are, indeed, illegal according to the letter of the law, de facto segregation continues to flourish as an inescapable reality in America. Moreover, scholars across the country are justifiably concerned about the seemingly inevitable return to segregation in light of the crusade to dismantle affirmative action programs.

According to Marcus (1997), a writer for the Associated Press (AP), at a conference held at Harvard University to assess the state of higher education, scholars articulated their concerns that, indeed, colleges and universities will "resegregate" as affirmative action programs are ruled unconstitutional. Further-more, they expressed extreme dismay that civil rights progress, which took 30 years to achieve, would be eroded in less than 2 years. Scholars in attendance assert that since the passing of Proposition 209 in California and the *Hopwood v. State of Texas*, 1994 W.L 242362 (W.D. Tex., Jan 20, 1994) (NO. CIV. A-92-CA-563-SS), decision in Texas, Black and Hispanic enrollment has already declined. In an AP news release, the reporter cites Gary Orfield, a professor of education and social policy at Harvard, as having stated that Black and Hispanic students may reason, "I'm not going to be welcomed, I'm not going to get in, I'm not going to get finan-cial aid, so I might as well not apply" (Marcus, 1997). This speculated lack of hope is startling. The diminishing enrollment of racial minorities is cause for alarm. It warrants a closer look. However, this is not the express purpose of this discus-sion—the emergence of this conceptualization of "resegregation" is. Have PWIs desegregated? What is integration? Has full integration occurred? If not, how can practitioners promote positive interracial interaction on campus? Colleges and universities have superficially and cosmetically desegregated, but not ideologically.

INTEGRATION: A QUESTION OF EQUALITY OR AMBIGUITY

According to *Black's Law Dictionary* (Campbell, 1990), *integration* is the act or process of making whole or entire. It is the bringing together of groups (as races) as equals. Hurtado (1992) conducted a thorough literature review and found that in the early 1970s colleges employed several programs to service African American students when they were legally permitted to enroll. However, they did not address the strained relations between majority and minority members or the psychological climate. In addition, Hurtado states that, according to race relations theorists, racial tension increases when the privileged group's position of power is threatened. For this hegemonic reason, some Whites find viewing Blacks as equals problematic. Equality is a central component of integration.

According to *Webster's New World Dictionary* (1966), *equal* means having the same rights, privileges, abilities, rank, and so on. *Equality* is a state or instance of being equal, especially the state of being equal in political, economic, and social rights. The realization of this ideological conceptualization has been compromised, according to Forbes (1990), beginning in the late eighteenth century when White writers began to degrade non-Whites: "I am apt to suspect the negroes, and in general all the other species [for there are four or five different kinds] [at that time humankind had been divided into Caucasian, Mongolian, Ethiopian, American and Malay] to be naturally inferior to the whites. There scarcely ever was a civilized nation of any other complexion than white." (David Hume, 1770, cited in Forbes, 1990, p. 8). Although these assertions were never empirically proven, this self-proclaimed superiority became the law of the land. It continues to be promulgated on many college campuses through the curriculum, administrative policies, campus publications, and other dominant-ruled entities.

Colleges and universities have not achieved more than perfunctory levels of integration. Black students integrate as soon as they matriculate at PWIs. This is what is known as cosmetic integration. They are physically on the campus and can be seen intermixing with White students in classroom situations in particular. Unfortunately, those interrace interactions are often superficial. For example, when Blacks and Whites are compelled to collaborate in a study group for class, the goal is to achieve a high score on a test, not for them to become better acquainted. Sports events provide another arena for superficial contact. Students attend a game to cheer their team to victory, but they seldom socialize interracially after the final buzzer. Yet another potential place where integration could occur is the student dining hall. All students have to satisfy what Maslow calls a basic need, the need for food. In spite of having to meet this physiological necessity within the same food service areas, both races have the right to choose where they will sit when they dine. More often than not, both races choose to sit with members of their own race. Barnett (1995) clarifies this occurrence: "The cafeteria interaction is merely a snapshot of what is actually a very intricate and carefully orchestrated social interaction; for often this is the only time throughout the entire day when the student will interact with other Black students" (p. 115). However, Black students continue to be condemned for self-segregating. Barnett explains: "It is often discussed that Black students have a tendency to separate themselves from the rest of the campus community. Often this is pointed out simply because it is the Black students who are readily visible and identifiable. Although White students sit together in dining commons, live together, and enjoy membership in all White student organizations, it is often perceived that the Black students, who behave in a similar manner, are the primary hindrance in achieving a unified campus" (p. 114). By blaming Black students only, a potentially volatile dichotomy is created. Therefore, instead of placing the onus upon Black students for allegedly being separatists and expecting them to correct the perceived problem alone, both Black and White students (with the help of faculty, staff, and administrators) should equally strive to rectify the situation.

Hurtado, Dey, and Trevino (1994) explored this ideological concept that students of color self-segregate on PWI campuses. Though they do not explicitly define self-segregation, it is implied throughout the paper. For the purpose of this chapter, self-segregation is being defined as the majority-ascribed belief that non-White individuals or groups who choose to socialize and/or associate with same-race/ethnic members (in clubs, fraternities, sororities, seating choice, ethnic houses, cultural centers, theme dorms, etc.) are separating and are doing so because of their personal wish to be separate from the dominant culture. Using data from the Cooperative Institutional Research Program (CIRP), Hurtado and colleagues analyzed the interracial interactions between Whites and several racial minorities. Their findings show that students of color interact cross-racially more often than Whites when it comes to dining, studying, dating, and general on-campus contact. To be more specific, they found that 55% of African Americans frequently dined with members from a different racial/ethnic group. Only 21% of Whites did the same. They found similar patterns of intergroup interactions among Whites and Asian Americans and Chicanos. Hurtado and colleagues (1994) assert, "These basic patterns of interaction suggest that the current concern may simply be an expression of a majority perspective, where intragroup activity labeled as 'self-segregation' may be more visible among students of color, even though it is *actually higher* among White students in these informal social situations" (p. 11).

CONTRIBUTING FACTORS FOR INTRAGROUP RELATIONS

Person (1990) examined the Black student culture on a predominantly White campus. She found that, indeed, a distinct African American culture did exist. Moreover, this culture was partially formulated by internal pressure. For example, Person talks about how the incoming Black freshmen felt pressure from current students to participate in, and support, Black-oriented activities. When coming in contact with prospective students, students who already attend, Person says, "lay the groundwork for establishing the limits and expectations of frequency of interactions and behavioral norms acceptable to this culture, which was determined by its members" (p. 119). More recently, White (1995) and Barnett (1995) also reported that one of the factors that influenced Black students to participate in Black organizations and in the Black community was pressure from other Black students to do so. Page (1996) states that Black students are obligated by the color of their skin to be loyal to their heritage. "Black students on a campus with very many other black students might find themselves suddenly pinched under the thumb of social fascism that forbids their making White friends, sitting at any but the 'black tables' in dining halls, or presenting anything to the rest of the world but a 'united front' in the cause of blackness" (p. 268). The numbers of Black students who attend PWIs are usually very low. As such, it is very noticeable when a Black student does not espouse Black views. Therefore, one reason for Black students to associate with other Black students may be peer pressure.

Another explanation for Black students' seeking other Black students is for survival. Allen and Haniff (1991) state, "Black students on White campuses have been shown to experience considerable difficulty in making the adjustment to an environment which is culturally different, academically demanding, and socially alienating" (p. 96). This need to seek solace in other Black students is what Page (1996) calls the affinity impulse. "Tis human to follow the natural affinity impulse that lures us into cliques and associations with others who are as much like ourselves as possible" (p. 269).

"Hanging out with other Blacks is just natural" (Barnett, 1995, p. 115). This may be the result of what Feagin, Vera, and Imani (1996) call "collective memory." African American students share a common history, experience, and understanding. This familiarity leads students to create fictive kinships. According to Barnett, it is common for Black students to include other Black students, faculty, staff, and administrators as part of their newfound family. Thus, this is an additional rationale for Black students to establish bonds with other Black students.

Cultural preservation is yet another rationale for Black students to yearn for the companionship of their same-race peers. "Black students often find it necessary to create their own social and cultural networks in order to remedy their exclusion from the wider, White-oriented university community" (Allen, 1992, p. 29). Black students are choosing voluntary separation for cultural purposes to the dismay of many educators. The disappointment is inevitable when some view embracing the African American culture as automatically denouncing the European culture. This sentiment could not be further from the truth. Some African American students need a sense of identity and pride to persist and graduate. To deny their cultural heritage because of unsubstantiated paranoia is a travesty and an injustice. Kochman (1981) states that the fact that "no consideration should be granted Blacks when they behave in accordance with their cultural norms, when this violates White norms and reinforces a pattern of Black cultural subordination" (p. 159) proves to be detrimental to both Blacks and Whites.

Willie and McCord (1972) assert that "black separatism is a function of White racism. It represents failure in the relationship between the Black individual and the White society. The Black experience at a White college is a story of hope, frustration, and disillusionment. It is a story of acceptance and rejection. It is a story of individual and institutional racism. It is a story that is important to every member of the community" (p. 3). In addition, Allen (1992) adds that "on predominantly White campuses, Black students emphasize feelings of alienation, sensed hostility, racial discrimination, and lack of integration" (p. 39). Therefore, Black student relationships may be sought to combat real or perceived acts of racism or discrimination.

Environmental cues, like paintings of Whites that may adorn the campus walls while excluding people of color, African Americans overrepresented in menial jobs, all-White fraternity and sorority row houses, and White senior administrators, ostracize the phenotypically visible minority. These overt environmental cues, which Feagin et al. (1996) write about, dishearten and alienate African American students. It is necessary for African Americans, as Maslow asserts, to feel that they belong. Ultimately, for some Black students, that sense of belonging comes from their ability to fraternize with other African American students.

Moreover, by sitting in the same area day after day and year after year in the cafeteria, Black students establish boundaries. Feagin and colleagues (1996) use the concept of the "territorial imperative" to explain this phenomenon: "Humans seek to conquer territory and maintain dominion over territory that can be used to demarcate in-groups and out-groups" (p. 50). They also discuss what they call "racialized space." These are areas that embody the essence of Whiteness and are culturally biased against non-Whites. Black students are made to feel like intruders upon sacred White space. They are often excluded from the yearbook, newspaper, and other such publications on PWI campuses. As a result, they look to one another for support, validation, and reassurance. Much of this support, as previously mentioned, takes place when they sit together in the cafeteria.

Yes, the American society was founded on the White middle-class belief system. For years, Blacks have tried to emulate this class. "Implicit is the idea that the closer you get to Whiteness, the better you are" (Carmichael & Hamilton, 1967, p. 159). Integration was established based on this premise. However, now some Black college students are refusing to sacrifice and deny their culture toward that end. Some may hypothesize that Blacks are associating with other Blacks to buck the system. This view is inherently laced with racial connotations because it once again relegates Blacks to a position dictated by White societal norms. According to Hurtado et al. (1994), "[P]eer groups on campus may exclude members because they do not consider individuals who seek acceptance as having equal or comparable social status" (p. 3). For the most part, White peer groups have the power to exclude non-Whites.

"Opponents of what is perceived as self-segregation believe that students who dine with members of the same ethnic group, participate in ethnic student organizations, and participate in university programs established for minorities contribute to a decline of race/ethnic relations on campus" (Hurtado et al., 1994, p. 1). It is more common to see Whites separate themselves from Blacks. For example, when the Supreme Court ruled that segregation was illegal, Whites began to flee to the suburbs. Their "White flight" produced ghettos and slums for racial minorities because the government officials (who were mainly White) allocated monetary resources to the suburbs where the Whites had relocated. By so doing, the officials neglected to give funds to the inner city. Ironically, "White flight" is a classic form of segregation, but it is accepted as status quo.

Some White students may be quite perturbed just because some Blacks are choosing not to socialize with them. "Colonial subjects have their political decisions made for them by the colonial masters, and those decisions are handed down directly or through a process of 'indirect rule.' Politically, decisions which affect Black lives have been made by White people—the White power structure" (Carmichael & Hamilton, 1967, p. 7). For Whites, Kochman (1981) says that self-assertion (in this case, the right to choose) occurs as a function of higher status entitlement. He illustrates this notion when he discusses how Blacks and Whites view taking turns. Whites approach taking turns as a cultural imperative. Teachers have control of the discussion and they can decide whom to call on when students raise their hands. They become flustered when Black students ascribe to their cultural norm by speaking out without being recognized by the instructor. This leaves the White teacher frustrated. In a similar vein, White students may be displeased because Black students have opted to sit with other students instead of with them. They are not able to exert their power or control over the individual choice of some Black students. "Segregation is back, except this time it's voluntary" (Page, 1996, p. 28). It never disappeared. It has just resurfaced in a different form—Black students are consciously separating from White students.

Finally, the precarious relationship between Black and White students on PWI campuses may be a semblance of egoism. Some members of each group may self-select for self-interest. Others may fall prey to *groupthink*. Since everyone else is sitting with members of his or her race, the student may feel that he or she will violate an unspoken social norm to dine cross-racially. Still others may sit with people with whom they are most familiar (i.e., hometown or high school friends, roommate[s], etc.).

SEGREGATION IN PERSPECTIVE

A little more than 30 years ago, Black students were legally segregated in public education. They did not have the right to attend White institutions. When they were admitted, they were often banished to areas that were designated for "Coloreds." As the late Rev. Dr. Martin Luther King, Jr., wrote, while serving time in the Birmingham City Jail, "All segregation statutes are unjust because segregation distorts the soul and damages the personality. It gives the segregator a false sense of superiority, and the segregated a false sense of inferiority" (King, 1963, p. 12). In 1954, when *Brown v. Board of Education* (347 U.S. 483, 74 S.Ct. 686, 98 L.Ed 873 [1954]) ended legalized segregation, Blacks were bused to White schools. The dominant culture presumed that by giving Blacks access to White education (and consequently to their quality of life), the condition of Blacks would automatically improve. Now, once again, Blacks are being told by external factions that they are self-segregating. In other words, they are separating themselves from the culture that they are expected to emulate. Some scholars suggest that this alleged self-segregation is a response to the hostility that is often present on PWI campuses. In each of these situations, Blacks have been viewed as reactionary and powerless. This categorization reeks of White superiority and privilege.

The reason that self-segregation is an issue is that Black students and other students of color are finally exercising their right to choose. Some Blacks are not giving Whites the chance to alienate and ostracize them. They are actively seeking intragroup validation. Scholars are alarmed because they realize the burden of integration will now fall on the White students. Given that the White majority has the power, it is only logical for them to contribute to, and initiate, the integration process. When Black students are accused of self-segregation, and their White counterparts are not, they are being accused of breaking a law they did not create and one that no longer exists. "Black students sitting with one another is called 'self-segregating' or 'balkanizing.' White students sitting together is called 'normal.' If self-segregation is not a virtue, it also must be remembered that, alas, students of color didn't invent it" (Page, 1996, p. 263).

According to Page (1996), true integration is a two-way street. It entails cultural sharing and mutual respect. No one involved is expected to assimilate or deny his or her heritage. This proves to be challenging for African American students who attend PWIs because they feel estranged and may take refuge in the company of other same-race students. Page also asserts that it would be unnatural to eradicate more than 300 years of slavery and segregation in little more than a quarter of a century. "Students have always balkanized themselves. It just appears more visible today because greater numbers of students of color are enrolled" (p. 266). It is curious that educators expect students to solve a problem that many courts in America have been grappling with since the 1960s—self-segregation.

TOWARD A TRULY INTEGRATED CAMPUS

In searching for solutions to remedy the separation of the races on PWI campuses, scholars should begin by acknowledging that this is an issue. Next, they may need to assess how prominent the separations are on their particular campus. This may be accomplished by conducting a survey and following up with personal interviews with a representative sample. Also, practitioners should assess whether or not this is an institutional priority, what resources are available to commit to finding a solution, and how much of a priority finding a solution really is. Following the assessment, preparations should be made for implementations and interventions. These planning sessions should include representatives from numerous entities on campus, including students. Implementation is the next step, followed by an in-depth evaluation that should employ quantitative as well as qualitative measures to assess progress. Possible strategies to employ include:

1. Talk with all students about the issue, not just Black and White students.
2. Adjust the curriculum to encompass all student histories and experiences with accurate representations. This will help to foster a climate for mutual respect.
3. Model the desired behavior. Faculty, staff, and administrators will need to practice what they preach. They also should work on not stratifying across racial lines.
4. Advocate "switch race days." Encourage students to sit with members of other racial/ethnic groups in the cafeteria on specified days. Extra class credit should be offered for students who write a report on their experiences. They could also give oral presentations on their findings. Their work should be in line with their chosen discipline (philosophy, biology, etc.).
5. Promote collaboration on projects between student organizations, in particular, between sororities and fraternities. Have race workshops before and after the initiatives. Faculty, staff, and administrators should also attend.
6. Do something: Do not allow the issue to just go on without being challenged. Also do not place the burden upon students to initially delve into this problem.
7. Make a conscious effort to represent students of non-White ethnic groups fairly in the campus physical and existential environments (i.e., on the newspaper staff and in the newspaper articles, in the display of artwork).

FINAL COMMENTS

On most PWI campuses, African American students constitute less than 4% of the undergraduate population. It is commonplace for people who have similar characteristics to seek others with the same attributes. African American students are often ridiculed for what has been empirically proven to be normal. They are persecuted for seeking the companionship of those who are most like them on campus. Some White students express fear when they see groups of African American students congregating on campus. They accuse African American students of self-segregating—a charge that African American students vehemently denounce. This accusatory position is contradictory. African American students who attend predominantly White campuses integrate by enrolling at the institution.

African American students are not segregating themselves by choosing to associate with other African American students. They choose to associate with people who make them feel the most comfortable. As Duster (1991) writes in *The Chronicle of Higher Education*, Black students are not different from any other ethnic group: "Just as the Jewish students have found Hillel and a common ethnic/cultural identity [to be] the basis for self-affirmation, so too do today's ethnic and racial 'minorities' often need to draw upon the social, cultural, and moral resources of their respective communities" (p. B2). Furthermore, he states that White, Jewish, and Catholic students segregated themselves earlier in this century. When White students choose to have relations with one another every day, they are not accused of segregating. As members of the dominant race, White privilege protects White students from such accusations.

Blacks and Whites obviously view the issue of self-segregation from culturally influenced perspectives. But it is imperative that both groups learn how to compromise. As Kochman (1981) asserts, "A culturally pluralistic society must find ways to incorporate these differences into the system, so that they can also influence the formation of social policy, social intervention, and the social interpretation of behavior and events" (p. 62).

REFERENCES

Allen, W. R. (1992). The color of success: African American college student outcomes at predominantly White and historically Black public colleges and universities. *Harvard Educational Review, 62*(1), 26–44.

Allen, W. R., & Haniff, N. Z. (1991). Race, gender, and academic performance in U.S. higher education. In W. R. Allen, E. G. Epps, & N. Z. Haniff (Eds.), *College in Black and White: African American students in predominantly White and in historically Black public universities* (pp. 95–109). Albany: State University of New York Press.

Barnett, M. C. (1995). *We are family: Social supports and family interaction among Black college students*. Unpublished doctoral dissertation, University of Pennsylvania.

Brown v. Board of Education, 347 U.S. 483, 74 S.Ct. 686, 98 l.Ed. 873 (1954).

Campbell, H. C. (1990). *Black's law dictionary: Definitions of the terms and phrases of American and English jurisprudence, ancient and modern*. St. Paul, MN: West.

Carmichael, S., & Hamilton, C. V. (1967). *Black power: The politics of liberation in America*. New York: Vintage Books.

Duster, T. (1991, September 25). Understanding self-segregation on the campus. *The Chronicle of Higher Education, 38*(5), B1–B2.

Feagin, J. R., Vera, H., & Imani, N. (1996). *The agony of education: Black students at White colleges and universities.* New York: Routledge.

Forbes, J. D. (1990). The manipulation of race, caste, and identity: Classifying Afroamericans, Native Americans, and Re-Black people. *The Journal of Ethnic Studies, 17*(4), 1–51.

Hurtado, S. (1992). The campus racial climate. *Journal of Higher Education, 63*(5), 539–568.

Hurtado, S., Dey, E. L., & Trevino, J. G. (1994). *Exclusion or self-segregation? Interaction across racial/ethnic groups on college campuses.* Paper presented at the annual meeting of the American Educational Research Association, New Orleans.

King, M. L., Jr. *Letter from Birmingham City Jail.* (1963, April 16). (n.p.)

Kochman, T. (1981). *Black and White: Styles in conflict.* Chicago: University of Chicago Press.

Marcus, J. (1997, April 11) *Conference warns of return to segregation at universities and colleges.* Associated Press Wires.

McLaurin v. Oklahoma State Regents for Higher Ed., 339 U.S. 637, 641, 70 S.Ct. 851, 855, 94 L.Ed. 1149, 1154 (1950).

Page, C. (1996). *Showing my color: Impolite essays on race and identity.* New York: HarperCollins.

Parks, R., & Reed, G. J. (1994). *Quiet strength.* Grand Rapids, MI: Zondervan.

Person, D. R. (1990). *The Black student culture of Lafayette College.* Unpublished doctoral dissertation, Teachers College, Columbia University.

White, L. S. (1995). *Hanging Black: Social and psychological factors influencing Black student participation in Black campus organizations at a historically White university.* Unpublished doctoral dissertation, Stanford, CA: Stanford University.

Willie, C. V., & McCord, A. S. (1972). *Black students at White colleges.* New York: Praeger.

9

Doing What Comes Unnaturally: Increasing African American Faculty Presence in Predominantly White Colleges and Universities

William B. Harvey

Life for me ain't been no crystal staircase.—Langston Hughes

Some 30 years ago, the noted African American scholar Harold Cruse offered the following observation in his groundbreaking book *The Crisis of the Negro Intellectual*. Cruse (1967) wrote that "in the detached social world of the intellectuals, a considerable degree of racial integration and ethnic intermingling does take place on a social level. While the Negro intellectual is not fully integrated into the intellectual class stratum, he is, in the main, socially detached from his own Negro ethnic world" (p. 9). The positive transitions in identification that have occurred for people of African descent are obvious as we have evolved from being Negroes to Blacks to African Americans. But it is not clear over this 30-year period how much progress, or lack of same, the men and women who are considered intellectuals have made in reattaching themselves to, as Cruse put it, their own ethnic world.

Are African American intellectuals, who presumably are mostly academicians, connected to the world in which their brothers and sisters work, live, and play? Or are they detached, physically and psychologically, from the African American multitude, wandering about their ivory towers and engaging only those people who are in their intellectual class stratum? If they are detached, how can they become reconnected to the African American community? These are provocative questions, for they touch on considerations of leadership and solidarity among African Americans, and attempts to answer them necessitate understanding the changes that have occurred in the larger culture as well as on the higher education landscape since Cruse presented his assessment of the situation.

When Cruse made his comment back in 1967, almost all African American faculty members were employed in historically Black colleges and universities (HBCUs). By ignoring the availability of African Americans who were qualified to join their faculties, colleges and universities that were predominantly White institutions (PWIs) had managed to maintain racial homogeneity among their instructional personnel, and thus the HBCUs presented the only significant academic employment possibilities of the day. At the time, affirmative action was a brand-new concept and was in its earliest stage of application in the world of higher education (Washington & Harvey, 1989). Given that reality, one is particularly struck by the part of Cruse's statement regarding detachment, for it suggests that many members of the professorate were only nominally involved with the "regular" people—a point that would certainly be contested by some social observers. But surely, the statement is a relative one, for most higher education professionals would acknowledge that the academic world is, in many respects, a place of escape and privilege. A faculty or administrative position in an institution of higher education takes one into a quasi-protected environment where some of the significant issues and concerns of the real world can be evaded, at least on a temporary basis.

The implicit dichotomy of the situation generates two questions. At this time, can contemporary African American academicians afford to experience the proverbial "life of the mind"? Can they lose themselves in the luxury of contemplation and repose that is one of the great seductive elements of an academic career, without regard or concern for what happens in the "real world"? From this author's perspective, both questions have a single answer—Absolutely not. Because, while academic intellectuals carry out the duties of their profession in libraries and laboratories, transmit the benefit of their wisdom and knowledge through lectures and seminars, and monitor the effectiveness of the process through exams and papers, life outside the sanctity of the college campus goes on, and the ugly reality of racism continues to manifest itself. For African American academicians, there is the ultimate recognition that, like their nonacademic brothers and sisters, whatever the level of their standing, reputation, or selected area of expertise within the boundaries of their institutions, they will continue to face discrimination and prejudice when they exit the refuge of the sanctuaries where they work. Those African Americans who work at PWIs are likely to face the indignities of racism even without having to leave their places of employment.

Each African American faculty member and administrator ultimately will decide for himself or herself what efforts he or she can make to bring about changes in the larger society—to help achieve a greater measure of equality for all people. While the American legacy of systematic, unequal treatment of African Americans would hopefully compel every citizen to help transform the society into a more equitable one, some individuals are more prone than others to contribute their efforts toward raising the quality of life in their communities. For members of the professorate, their willingness to be involved in such efforts may be influenced, in varying degrees, by their areas of academic specialization. Psychologists, for example, may see more opportunity to apply their skills in everyday situations than geologists would, and physical therapists may be more directly involved in specific actions on behalf of African Americans than are physicists. However, no matter what the area of expertise, every African American who works in a PWI can assist in making these institutions more representative and diverse. In that sense, the activities that African American intellectuals engage in to bring about changes in the academy may be the most meaningful way for them to reestablish their ties to their communities. Instigating change in the existing state of affairs in postsecondary institutions to increase African American faculty presence could become an important contribution that leads to higher comfort and success levels for African American students who are in those settings. Based on education and income comparisons, African Americans continue to lag substantially behind Whites in high school completion levels, college completion rates, and family income figures (Carter & Wilson, 1996). Since nearly 85% of African American students experience their postsecondary education at PWIs (Carter & Wilson, 1996, p. 15), ease of access to, and more hospitable treatment within, these environments would be an important step in the preparation of the next generation of African American leaders. The educational enhancement of these students would lead to the betterment of African American populations, as they successfully negotiate their chosen academic institutions, pursue careers, become productive citizens, and then give something back to their communities.

INDUCING CHANGE

Colleges and universities are tradition-bound settings that are resistant to change. During a period of widespread social upheaval in the 1960s and 1970s, mass media portrayals of these institutions resulted in their being regarded as hotbeds of activism where students and faculty were constantly engaged in challenging the status quo. Certainly, there were protests and direct action on a substantial number of college campuses during this period, but much of the activity was directed toward bringing about a greater measure of autonomy and personal freedom for the students themselves, rather than the achievement of a broader social agenda. However, while the general public may still hold the view of academic institutions as liberal, left-wing bastions, over the past 25 years, the prevailing attitudes on college and university campuses have become increasingly conservative. Recently, the same backlash that has been directed at affirmative action efforts in the larger society has begun to curtail the limited inroads that African Americans were making toward greater representation in the academy. "Angry White men," upset at having their historical positions of privilege challenged by affirmative action, have curtailed these diversity initiatives. Kent (1996) contends that the national debate has shifted from the historic foundations of minority poverty and disadvantage toward the twin myths of total individual responsibility and "color-blindness" (p. 48).

To make PWIs more amenable and accepting of an African American presence, these institutions must change their values and practices. But, given the current conservative political posture both on and off the campus based on the leadership of White faculty, it is unlikely that a significant transformation will take place in academe. In fact, the greatest increases in representation that have occurred as a result of affirmative action have been experienced not by African Americans but by White women. In addition, higher education's pathetic record of employing African American faculty and senior-level administrators hardly suggests that White faculty members have a serious and sustained commitment to making their institutions more racially diverse. It is sobering to note that from 1983 to 1993 the national representation of African American faculty in higher education increased from 4.0% to 4.8%, less than 1% (Carter & Wilson, 1996, p. 96). Similarly, the African American representation among full-time administrators rose less than 2% during that same period (Carter & Wilson, 1996, p. 84). Further, it must be noted that these figures are not disaggregated by types of institutions, and therefore they also include gains in these categories that might have occurred at the HBCUs. Since enrollment at the HBCUs has risen by 26% since 1976, with most of the growth occurring after 1986 (JBHE, 1996–97, p. 78), it would be reasonable to presume that there has been a corresponding increase in faculty and administrative hiring at these institutions and that the majority of those persons hired would be African American. This effort to increase African American faculty representation at PWIs is an extension of the civil rights movement. It is the latest phase of an ongoing struggle to secure equal treatment and justice for all African Americans. For better or worse, it has become apparent that initiating and sustaining efforts to change the higher education community to make it more representative fall most heavily on those African Americans who have been able to scale the wall of discrimination that has customarily surrounded these institutions.

IDENTIFYING THE PLAYERS

African American faculty, particularly those who are not tenured, are at risk in the academy, and their rates of receiving tenure are lower than those of any other race or ethnic group (Carter & Wilson, 1996, p. 84). Still, the special status that faculty members have within colleges and universities (Harvey, 1991) means that these are the men and women who will have to be the front-line troops in the campaign to complete the desegregation of higher education. The academic "pecking order" is apparent and enduring, since faculty members who do not measure up to institutional expectations do not receive tenure. Beyond earning tenure, the next watershed accomplishment for a faculty member is to be endorsed by one's professional peers and colleagues as having compiled a record of distinction that is worthy of holding the rank of full professor. Those African Americans who have earned tenure, especially those who have reached the rank of full professor, have to assume the primary responsibility and the leadership role in lowering the color bar at their institutions. Full professors, particularly, are considered less susceptible to punitive or retaliatory action, either real or imagined, than other members of the academic community. Though the small numbers of African Americans who have reached this plateau have done so through long years of intense work and sacrifice, they would not have been able to ascend to these lofty positions had not numerous other African American trailblazers pushed open the gates to the institutions where they practice their profession.

So that others might also advance, African American faculty must use their knowledge of academic culture and process to aggressively induce their institutions into actually realizing the kinds of diversity that institutional officials so often claim they would like to have within their environment. In undertaking this quest, it is important to remember that institutions of higher education are much more than simply places where individuals absorb information for a certain period of time and then proceed on to employment. They are also the settings where the values and attitudes of the next generation's leaders are shaped and honed (Harvey, 1991). If American society is to transcend the racism that is woven throughout the fabric of its culture, the banner of change will have to be carried by enlightened Whites who can lead their fellow citizens forward to a less discriminatory future. The college experience represents the ideal setting where influence can be exerted on the manner in which the future policymakers and opinionsetters establish their patterns of analysis and decisionmaking, and thus it is critical that African Americans be represented among the faculty in these institutions so that they can provide their insights, perspectives, and experiences.

African Americans who hold administrative positions on the campuses of PWIs are another key group in the change process, particularly if they have reached positions of dean or higher levels in the hierarchy. If these individuals are involved in academic administration, as opposed to student affairs or administrative affairs, it is likely that they also have faculty experience and a certain measure of credibility with their White faculty colleagues. These senior-level administrative positions carry status within and outside the academic arena, and they are usually salaried at levels that place their recipients comfortably within the upper levels of the middle class. For these reasons, some African Americans who have gained such positions have shown reluctance to challenge their institutions to be more aggressive in achieving greater levels of diversity among the faculty, though they will often complain in safe circles about the lack of institutional commitment and follow-through in this regard.   Since the African American administrative personnel who hold lower-level positions are more vulnerable to punitive reprisals if they are considered too aggressive or outspoken with regard to institutional practices, they often take their cues concerning appropriate institutional behavior from their higher-ranking brothers and sisters. Frequently, African American administrators have access to information and sometimes even to resources that can be used to influence and affect institutional behavior. Though there are risks involved, and in spite of the fact that they are not likely to gain favor for doing so, these African American administrators must join hands with their faculty colleagues to develop cohesive internal strategies that will bring more African Americans into the faculty ranks and ultimately into administrative positions as well.

CULTIVATING EXTERNAL ALLIES

Perhaps to a greater degree than other organizations, colleges and universities resist changes that are initiated from outside the institutions. The academic mindset tends to ignore or diminish perspectives when their origin is external to the academy, and this is why it is so important that African American faculty lead the efforts to transform these institutions from within. While the significance of having members of the professorate articulate the importance of diversity within the institutional governance bodies and processes cannot be overstated, it would be naive and foolish to think that these individuals can bring about substantive and lasting change within the institutions without active support from other groups and individuals, including students, community organizations, and advocacy groups. In addition, a media strategy is an important component of the overall plan because the probability, or even the likelihood, of negative public relations will often cause officials in higher education to be more responsive to concerns that are placed before them than they might otherwise be.

African American faculty should offer more than nominal support for African American student organizations—they should work closely with them in pursuit of the common goal of a more diverse campus community. The members of these organizations represent an important constituency at any college or university, one that the campus administration often tends to deal with in a cautious, deliberate manner. Thus, informed and active students can be an important force in helping to present and press the case for a larger African American faculty presence on the campus because they can capitalize on their identity as consumers who expect to receive a quality product for the tuition and fees that they are paying to their institutions. Like other organizations, colleges and universities tend to be sensitive to issues and concerns that are presented to them by their customers and to respond to them out of institutional self-interest. When students and faculty join forces, they represent two important interest groups working from within to underscore the importance of having a critical mass of African American faculty members.

In academic environments, the sense of distance from the real world is not only an individual but an institutional phenomenon; and, as such, colleges and universities are frequently dismissive of criticism from nonacademic groups, unless those groups have the potential to disrupt the serenity of the campus. Institutions of higher education feel a certain vulnerability to negative observations that are made by critics from the worlds of politics and/or journalism, and so the success of any campaign to increase African American faculty representation is likely to be enhanced if there is active support from within these arenas. Colleges and universities are sensitive about their public perception, and they work hard to maintain an image that reflects positively on the institution and that elicits favorable reactions from prospective students, parents of already enrolled students, alumni, and possible donors. African American faculty can help their institutions to develop and implement plans and procedures to increase their presence, using their own networks and contacts to facilitate a flow of appropriate candidates.

When such cooperative activity occurs and results in additional hiring, then the colleges and universities involved deserve to be praised in the media and in political circles for their enlightened behavior, and the African American faculty members should be actively engaged in disseminating this information. On the other hand, when little or no progress is made by their institutions in increasing the numbers of African Americans who hold faculty positions, there should be no hesitation among the African American faculty who are at the college or university in making the unsatisfactory nature of the situation known to appropriate legislative or journalistic figures.

National organizations that have the realization of racial equality as part of their goals should also be sought as partners in the development of strategies to increase the presence of African American faculty members in those colleges and universities where they are underrepresented. Groups such as the National Association for the Advancement of Colored People (NAACP) and the Urban League can sometimes exert influence or leverage that helps institutions of higher education to become more active and more innovative in their efforts to hire and retain African American faculty. In communities where chapters of these national organizations do not exist, there may be local or regional groups that can satisfy the same purpose of serving as a resolute, stimulating external force to help recalcitrant institutional officials within the college or university understand the importance of increasing the numbers of African Americans who hold faculty positions. Social, economic, political, and demographic considerations are all part of the mix of factors that influence faculty hiring decisions; and African Americans should not be hesitant about making their voices heard and their needs known as faculty vacancies are filled.

The idea, then, in terms of instigating a larger African American faculty presence is that various points of influence and pressure need to be brought to bear and consolidated into a broad-based plan of action if the prevailing tradition in PWIs of appointing faculty members who come from the same racial background as those persons who already hold such positions is to be changed. Various interpretations, ranging from justification to condemnation, have been presented to explain these hiring patterns. Some observers see the situation as an effort to maintain a certain comfort level among individuals who already hold positions within these institutions; others see the assignment of less value and significance to candidates who represent "nontraditional" perspectives or frames of reference; while still others see a manifestation of racist behavior, either covertly or overtly practiced. Whatever the underlying ideological, personal, or psychological considerations, the result is that all throughout this country and across the various categorical levels of institutions of higher education African Americans still experience difficulty in securing and holding faculty positions in PWIs. As the nation moves rapidly toward the twenty-first century, this situation is a travesty that must be addressed and resolved.

BECOMING SCHOLAR-ACTIVISTS

Undoubtedly, some African American academicians will be uncomfortable with the notion of reaching outside the academy to bring about a change of behavior within institutions of higher education. Certainly, some of our White faculty colleagues will consider such a tactic to be inappropriate and ill considered. Perspectives such as these ignore the reality that external forces, organizations, and individuals have been routinely solicited to help guide colleges and universities in a certain direction or in pursuit of specific agendas. Whether the reference is to foundations, legislators, benefactors, or prominent alumni, administrators and faculty members have assiduously courted those persons or groups who have influence and resources to bring to bear in regard to a particular interest or cause. It is disingenuous to suggest that this same strategy should not be employed as a means of increasing African American faculty representation in institutions that have somehow managed not to realize this worthy goal through means that are more acceptable to them. For African American faculty at PWIs to assume the responsibility of being scholar-activists and to be willing to challenge their institutions in this effort, reflects a sense of intellectual maturity as well as a realization of social commitment. At Yale University, one sees a chilling example of what can happen if African American faculty do not step forward to hold their pronouncements of concern up against the actual records of performance.

One of the most prestigious and highly recognized institutions of higher education in the world, Yale University, employed 34 African American tenured or tenure-track professors in 1973, representing 2.7% of all such faculty at the institution (JBHE, 1997). In 1995, the university employed exactly the same number of African Americans in tenured or tenure-track positions, but because the overall number of faculty at the university increased during this period of time, the representation of African Americans actually dropped to 1.9%. One might presume that an institution with the tradition and resources of Yale, located in a city that has a sizable African American population and being a short distance away from the nation's largest metropolitan area, would be able to employ African American faculty at a level that would be in keeping with its elevated standing in the academic world, but obviously this is not the case. Among the reasons that have been offered by members of the Yale administration to defend the absence of progress in hiring African American faculty are a woeful scarcity of appropriate candidates and concern about their salary expectations.

But perhaps the most creative explanation of why Yale has not been able to increase the number of African American faculty was presented by Professor Sharon Oster, who serves the University as affirmative action deputy. Oster (JBHE, 1997) contends that Yale's diversity efforts have not been successful because of a lack of comparable higher education institutions nearby that could serve as alternative employers for the spouses of prospective faculty members. This statement discounts the fact that there are several public and private institutions within a reasonable driving distance of Yale and that New York City with its multiplicity of academic institutions is only 70 miles away. Apparently, this problem does not hold true for the recruitment of White faculty, since the university has been able to increase their numbers over the past two decades. Yale President Richard Levin has publicly declared his interest in hiring African American faculty, but, as is the case with many other PWIs, there is a monumental gap between what is claimed to be desirable for the institution and the behavior that is manifested. Over a period of more than 20 years, it would seem that the collective brilliance of the White Yale faculty members would have been able to devise a workable strategy to increase the number of African American faculty, provided, of course, that this goal was truly important to these highly accomplished academicians. Presidential proclamations aside, the outcomes of the Yale faculty hiring processes suggest that increased diversity was not a particularly significant consideration for the individuals who were involved in the screening and selection activities.

The academic culture at Yale and certainly at numerous other PWIs does not truly value the presence of African American faculty. For this reason, African American scholar-activists who already hold faculty positions on the campuses are best suited to initiate actions that will help their institutions become more diverse, with a little help, as needed, from outside the academy. White faculty members are so immersed in their culture of privilege that some of them may not even be conscious of the ways in which they practice their exclusionary tactics until such behavior is brought to their attention. When their idyllic serenity of sameness is shattered, and they realize they cannot escape it, they eventually accept the reality of change within these havens of tradition. One highly accomplished African American sociologist who had a long and distinguished career retired a few years ago from a professorship that he had held for several years at an urban campus of a public university system in the Northeast. Upon recounting his years at the institution, this person recalled that when the first woman was hired in the Sociology Department, several of the faculty members complained bitterly and openly, sometimes using demeaning language to describe their colleague-to-be. Observing the situation with some concern, this individual said that he later shared his concern with his friends that if his fellow department members were making such comments about someone who was of the same race but of different gender, he could only imagine what they were saying when he was hired. This situation was part of his personal awakening, and it helped to transform him into a scholar-activist, who for many years afterward worked with, through, and around the faculty and administration at this institution, alone and with others, to increase the African American faculty presence at the university where he was employed.

To some degree, the detachment among African American intellectuals that Cruse (1967) identified over 30 years ago continues into the present. Given increased access to housing outside African American neighborhoods, academicians are more likely to be physically separated from their communities than they were in the past. But those African American intellectuals who hold faculty positions at PWIs can reduce their sense of detachment from their own ethnic world by functioning as scholar-activists to increase African American faculty representation in their institutions. By addressing this important issue of systematic exclusion from the faculty ranks and demonstrating that they understand the importance of ensuring access to and representation within, institutions of higher education, African American academic intellectuals can reconnect with their communities. If successful, their fight to increase the African American faculty presence within their respective colleges and universities will also make these institutions more welcoming places for African American students. The efforts show, in dramatic fashion, that they are willing to jeopardize their relatively comfortable positions to try to improve the circumstances and the futures of their brothers and sisters.

REFERENCES

Carter, D., & Wilson, R. (1996). *Minorities in higher education*. Washington, DC: American Council on Education.

Cruse, H. (1967). *The crisis of the negro intellectual*. New York: William Morrow Books.

The current state of America's Black colleges and universities. (1996–97). *Journal of Blacks in Higher Education*, 78–79.

Harvey, W. (1991). Faculty responsibility and racism. *Thought and Action*, Fall, 115–136.

Kent, N. (1996). The new campus racism: What's going on? *Thought and Action*, Fall, 45–57.

Washington, V., & Harvey, W. (1989). *Affirmative rhetoric, negative action: African American and Hispanic faculty at predominantly White colleges and universities*. Washington, DC: George Washington University Press.

Yale's substandard record in hiring Black faculty. (1997). *Journal of Blacks in Higher Education*, 16–17.

Cultural Capital and the Role of Historically Black Colleges and Universities in Educational Reproduction

James Earl Davis

The role of schools in the generation of cultural knowledge and cultural connectedness to family, community, and the African diaspora generally is currently a major point of discussion within scholarly, policy, and practice arenas. The sources and responsibility of this cultural knowledge, however, are not fully understood or appropriately attributed. In particular, the place of historically Black colleges and universities (HBCUs) in providing cultural understanding and connection has come under closer scrutiny, particularly after school desegregation policies were enacted. Desegregation in education gave African American students legal access to formerly all-White educational experiences and consequent effects have been most visibly seen in the shifts in enrollment patterns of Black students in higher education. During the 1960s, Black students entered colleges and universities that are predominantly White institutions (PWIs) with high expectations, but many were greeted with hostile and culturally foreign environments. Although there were quantitative changes in the number of Black students enrolled at these PWIs, qualitative changes of the institutional culture did not mirror student demographic changes. While the cultural integration of Black students into the mainstream of university life was assumed, to the dismay of many optimistic policymakers, university administrators, and students alike, the presence of African Americans on college campuses was marked by social isolation and cultural estrangement.

HBCUs, on the other hand, have historically assumed a greater responsibility for educating Black students and granting a disproportionate number of college degrees to African Americans in the country. Further, the primary responsibility for creating a Black middle class is often laid at the feet of these schools. By 1947, Black colleges had produced 90% of all HBCU graduates. However, this percentage has declined since that time to about 80% in 1967 and little over 50% in

1974 (Gurin & Epps, 1975). Given other higher educational options, enrollment in HBCUs fluctuated in the 1970s and 1980s; yet, they still grant a disproportional share of undergraduate degrees to African Americans (Hoffman, Snyder, & Sonneberg, 1992). The continued preference of Black students for an HBCU environment still evidences itself in recent increases in undergraduate enrollment at the 105 HBCUs. About one-fifth of all African Americans enrolled in institutions of higher education make their collegiate home at one of these institutions. While 83% of all students attending these schools are African Americans, there is tremendous variation in the racial makeup of student populations at these schools—the enrollment of non-Black students ranges from zero to over 20% (Hoffman et al., 1992). These institutions, without a doubt, not only occupy significant space in diversifying the nation's higher educational landscape but also play a critical role in the cultural lives of their students and within African American communities that benefit culturally and economically from their presence.

African American cultural knowledge and reproduction are by no means peculiar to HBCUs, nor are they confined to the graduates of these schools. To the contrary, various social institutions steeped in African American community life, such as families, churches, and civic organizations, play an important role in the creation and dissemination of culture and its myriad manifestations. Research on cultural learning includes a range of studies that center on the transmission of cultural beliefs, behaviors, and attitudes among African Americans (Dyson, 1993; Semmes, 1992). Yet, even these discussions are based too often on narrow conceptual frameworks that are silent concerning issues of race and racialized histories of Black higher education. This analysis attempts to understand more fully the role of these institutions in the generation and representation of African American culture.

This chapter explores the utility of conceptualizing the historic and contemporary roles of HBCUs through the framework of cultural capital. The first section provides an historical context of the development of Black colleges and relevant research. Next, the debate surrounding the contemporary roles and benefit of attending an HBCU is presented, followed by a theoretical discussion of cultural capital and its relevance for understanding the unique role of HBCUs in educational reproduction. The final section presents a critical reading on the cultural politics of representation and Black colleges.

HISTORICAL DEVELOPMENT OF HBCUs

Historical study of HBCUs is very important because the present situation of these schools and their students cannot be completely understood and appreciated without some knowledge of historical events that influenced the development and current state of these institutions. HBCUs are products of a historic racist and rigidly segregated society. The transitions and adjustments that HBCUs have made, due, in part, to the elimination of legal segregation and improved race relations, reflect continuing changes in the relationship between higher education in America and larger social structures.

By the turn of the nineteenth century, there were very few African Americans in higher education. With the exception of a few Black college graduates from northeastern colleges and universities, there were almost no college-educated African Americans in this country. Organized efforts to provide higher education for African Americans, however, date to the 1850s, before the Civil War. During this period, almost all the Black population was located in the southern and border states. In these regions, strict social customs prohibiting African Americans from obtaining formal higher education were enforced. In the North, however, at least three colleges (Lincoln and Cheney of Pennsylvania in 1854; Wilberforce of Ohio in 1856) had been established, and in many northern states a small number of African Americans were admitted to White colleges (Browning & Williams, 1978). Yet, by the end of the Civil War in 1865, there were only 28 Black college graduates out of the nation's nearly 4 million newly freed slaves and approximately 400,000 previously free African Americans (Branson, 1978).

The post-Civil War period was the time when the greatest attempts were made to organize educational facilities that would allow newly freed slaves to participate in society as educated men and women. During the Reconstruction period, northern missionaries and southern Blacks themselves expounded the belief that emancipated slaves were fully capable of benefiting from higher education. Unlike northern missionaries, however, who advocated a liberal arts education for freed slaves, most southern Whites felt, and promoted the idea, that African Americans were less competent than Whites and thus should be granted a separate and lower-caliber education (Bullock, 1967). A group of influential citizens from northern and southern states convened in Virginia after the *Plessey v. Ferguson* (163 U.S. 537, 165 S.Ct. 1138, 41 L.Ed.2d 256 [1896]) decision of 1896 to plan the development of a separate system of education in the South (Browning & Williams, 1978). Not all participants believed that a separate system of higher education for African Americans was the best solution, but it was the general agreement of the conference that vocational education should be the focus of this eventual separate system of higher education.

It was clear that the industrial educational movement produced mixed emotions among the African American community and among some northern philanthropists. For the most part, African Americans envisioned these new Black industrial colleges as an opportunity to control their own education, although it was not intended to be equal to that received by Whites (McPherson, 1970). In 1890, a new and separate system of higher education in the South was officially established under the Morrill Land Grant Act of 1890. The federally supported system presented a vocational model of education that had the political and economic support of southern Whites at the time. Some private Black colleges that were established before the Morrill Act of 1890 found themselves competing against a powerful and generally accepted "new" model of Black higher education. Even some Black colleges that were founded as private institutions became public, state-supported schools after the passage of legislation creating Black land-grant colleges.

Colleges that developed during this period were generally of poor quality with inadequately trained faculty and instructional facilities, relative to White institutions. Many of these institutions were initially founded as nondegree-granting schools focusing primarily on agricultural, mechanical, and industrial pedagogy. Of the 17 Black colleges established under the second Morrill Act, none offered a liberal arts education before 1916, and only 2 provided 4-year degree programs (Bowles & DeCosta, 1971). However, Black colleges made substantial progress despite many adverse circumstances during these early years of their development. Most of these institutions started as primary and secondary schools, but they gradually developed into normal schools offering college-level programs for training teachers and preachers. Early studies of these institutions attempted to assess the quality and contributions of these schools and their students. Two of the earliest examples of research devoted to examining Black colleges were conducted by W.E.B. DuBois; the first published was *The College-Bred Negro*, in 1900. Here, DuBois surveyed the social and economic conditions of Black college graduates in the South. The second study, *The College-Bred Negro American*, examined the quality and content of education provided by Black colleges (DuBois, 1910). DuBois' analysis, although at times accusatory and highly critical, generally presented a favorable picture of Black colleges—focusing on the educational and cultural contributions of these schools and their graduates. These studies, like others during this era, were principally funded by northern philanthropic interests concerned with the efficient use and influence of their contributions.

After the early part of the century and continuing to the end of World War II, many Black colleges suffered from acute fluctuations in enrollment and inadequate financial resources. As a result, several institutions were forced to close their doors to students. Many other Black colleges, however, against daunting odds, continued to progress and build academic programs and enrollment.

CONTEMPORARY ROLES OF HBCUs

The contemporary role of HBCUs has been a point of intense discussion in the academic literature and within public policy debates. Research in higher education has documented a link between the social and academic experiences of African American college students and whether they attend HBCUs or PWIs (Allen, Epps, & Haniff, 1991; Fleming, 1985; Gurin & Epps, 1975; Nettles, 1987). Indeed, research findings that campus environments influence the educational experience of college students are a consistent thread throughout the study of African Americans in higher education. Yet, an uneasiness surrounding public endorsement of these institutions, particularly the financial linkages to state-supported public HBCUs, continues to persist.

Increased educational opportunities for African Americans and desegregation policies have changed the demographic face of most higher education institutions.

However, only three decades after these corrective reforms began, through assaults on affirmative action and cutbacks in economic support, the nation is witnessing again a distressing ebb in the tide of increased educational opportunity for African Americans. This occurs, paradoxically, at a time when higher education desegregation policy has caused sharp increases in Black students attending PWIs (Carter & Wilson, 1993). Yet, HBCUs remain viable options for many African Americans. Actually, there has been a recent increase in enrollments at HBCUS—about a 15% increase between 1986 and 1990. Female students account for the bulk of this increase, while male enrollment experienced a slight decline during this period (Hoffman et al., 1992).

While research on the benefits and outcomes of attending an HBCU may be mixed at best, there are some consistent findings about how these schools structure and influence students' experiences. Recent studies offer some evidence of HBCUs' unique abilities to effectively structure environments that lead to greater achievement outcomes for their students. For instance, attending a HBCU at least equalizes future wages among all students (Constantine, 1994). This finding is very significant when compared to previous expectations that students attending HBCUs would actually have lower future wages. Specifically, analysis of labor market outcomes for students attending HBCUs found little to no effects: students were more likely to receive a B.A. degree, but attendance did not garner further labor market benefits such as additional wages (Erhenberg & Rothstein, 1993). In a related economic indicator, men who attended HBCUs were more likely to be married by 1986. Two-thirds of graduates of historically Black colleges were married in 1986 compared to about half of non-HBCU Black men. However, there were no differences in the marriage rates for women who attended Black institutions. Additionally, recent studies are inconsistent concerning graduate school attendance of HBCU students. In some fields, however, such as medicine, there appears to be a clear advantage in attending an HBCU when students seek admission to medical schools. Research using the National Post-Secondary Aid Study of 1990 found that African American HBCU students are more likely to pursue postgraduate education and become professionals than Black students at PWIs (Wenglinsky, 1996). To the contrary, other studies have found that HBCU graduates were less likely to continue on for graduate degrees than non-HBCU graduates (Ehrenberg & Rothstein, 1993). Even with these recent studies, there still exist conceptual problems and limitations in examining how HBCUs provide and structure these benefits to African American students.

Traditional conceptual frameworks usually present three principal domains of explaining the effectiveness of HBCUs: compensatory and remediation effectiveness, environmental support, and precollege background factors. The compensatory and remediation model focuses on the role of HBCUs' effectiveness with Black students who have relatively poor high school backgrounds and college preparation. Here, much evidence exists to show that early in students' college careers, HBCUs are able to provide effective remedial instruction that enables students to persist in college, obtain degrees, and eventually form attachment to the labor market (Davis, 1991; Constantine, 1994). Second, environmental support models argue that these schools provide support so that students will become more confident, are more involved in campus activities, and are more engaged with faculty (Allen, 1992). Another framework for explaining the role of HBCUs lies not in what actually occurs in college per se. Instead, outcomes are determined by what students bring to the college experience. These dispositions and demographics, such as whether students are inclined to concentrate in a particular field or certain study habits, academic behaviors, and characteristics related to gender and other demographics of HBCU enrollments, are primarily responsible for student outcomes in these settings (Nettles, 1987). Although these conceptual frames are useful in explaining some of the variation in the outcomes of students enrolled at Black colleges, they fail to explicitly focus on the cultural content and context of HBCUs and how the cultural milieu of these institutions affects students.

At the center of much of the research and policy discussions is whether or not African American students receive some value-added benefits from attending HBCUs. Do these institutions provide a unique, added advantage for their students that is absent from the experience of Black students attending PWIs? I would like to draw attention to the use of a culture-based, value-added framework to explain the evidence and outcomes attributed to, and circumscribed by, attendance at these HBCUs.

HBCUs AS CULTURAL CAPITAL

Cultural experiences and benefits of attending HBCUs are often cited as important justifications for the existence and survival of these schools. In essence, I argue that these institutions are sources of cultural capital. Traditionally, cultural capital has been defined as competence (e.g., behaviors, habits, attitudes) in a society's high-status culture and is considered an important mechanism in the reproduction of educational and social hierarchies. Bourdieu's (1977) cultural capital theory posits that the culture transmitted to, and rewarded by, educational systems reflects the culture of the dominant class. Here, I would like to explore historically Black colleges as contexts for the production and transmission of cultural capital of African Americans. The decoding and transmission of cultural capital are generally seen as the providence of families, not schools, although schools often implicitly demand these qualities of their students (Bourdieu & Passeron, 1977). The argument tries to establish the idea of HBCUs as potential sources of cultural capital and as vehicles for providing the techniques used in receiving and decoding African American cultural knowledge. Additionally, Bourdieu (1973) argues that social class and family background determine the sources of cultural knowledge—what is called "cultural capital." For example, high-status cultural activities, like attending the theater, opera, or ballet, are limited mostly to the economically privileged strata in society. Thus, "the ruling classes have at their disposal a much larger cultural capital than other classes" (Bourdieu, 1973, p. 85). This uneven distribution of familiarity with high-status cultural content leads to differential advantages in the school and the marketplace according to social class.

It is conceivable that the HBCUs, while not typically the domain of the "ruling class" and not necessarily the purview of traditional European class markers, such as the knowledge and exposure to the arts, including literature and music, are responsible for cultural learnings. For instance, some HBCUs were responsible for cultural "knowledge" and dispensation—positioning themselves traditionally as "finishing" schools for students of disadvantaged economic class backgrounds (Thompson, 1986). In many ways these institutions were considered "culturally starting" schools or places where students began the accumulation of cultural skills that would not only ease their transition and progression through college but also increase their social market value and employment opportunities upon graduation. For instance, Atlanta University, with its historical special connection to the Congregational Church in the city, was more deliberate in its attention to produce and reproduce an influential Black gentry (Jewell, 1996). Many other institutions, such as Fisk, Hampton, and Spelman, also come to mind as places where adherence to culturally accepted lifestyles and behaviors was viewed as a critical component in educating Black students. Various strategies, such as more explicit, direct instruction of proper etiquette and public social behavior, to the less obvious integration of African American literature and history in the curriculum, were employed to increase students' cultural capital.

Cultural resources usually refer to the extensiveness of culturally connected personal ties through which information about jobs and other opportunities can be diffused or allocated through the characteristics of the contact person who has the potential to influence access to opportunity and outcomes of these and other privileges. Although the term "cultural capital" is used often in the job search context to signify the personal or social networks that can provide information or influence, Lee and Brinton (1996) argue that it is important to delineate the social structural origin of such cultural capital. While educational institutions can generate cultural capital for their students, they purport that cultural resources or ties can be acquired only through an individual's attendance at a particular college or university. Here, institutional social capital is used to distinguish it from the social ties represented by nonuniversity friends, family members, and other resources that provide private social capital. I would like to extend this reasoning to HBCUs as a context for disseminating cultural resources to their students and graduates. This idea moves Bourdieu's notion of cultural capital away from precollege structures, such as families, communities, and previous schooling, and locates the generation of new cultural resources, such as networks, attitudes, behaviors, and expectations, within the environment and experience of attending an HBCU. Consequently, an important question arises as to whether or not the network of cultural connections and intensity has led to a greater influence of cultural capital on the outcomes of HBCU graduates.

The notion that relationships and connections, be they cultural or otherwise, among people can constitute useful resources has been widely used by researchers who have examined the role of informal personal ties in the process of job search or occupational status attainment. In this case, previous studies from secondary education demonstrate that students' social characteristics can affect their performance through teacher expectations and opportunity structures that are made available to them (Oakes, 1985; Polite, 1993). Variations in teacher expectations lead to differential treatment and outcomes for students; teachers are more likely, for instance, to encourage males to interrupt, analyze, and work more independently than females (Sacker & Sadker, 1985). Likewise, lower income students and some ethnic minorities tend to be channeled into vocational or general tracks that steer them away from the skills, knowledge, or cultural content necessary for educational and occupational success (Bowles & Gintis, 1976; Oakes, 1985). Consequently, students from higher socioeconomic backgrounds are more likely to seek out and be exposed to cultural information deemed valuable by the broader academic community for the pursuit of high-paying and more prestigious occupations and opportunities.

Within the cultural context of HBCUs, very little within race gender analysis has been done to disentangle the differential experience of African American males and females on HBCU campuses. Studies have found that African American males gain more, both socially and academically, at HBCUs relative to their female peers (Fleming, 1985). An insightful gender analysis is needed to more fully understand the differential cultural experience offered to students at HBCUs. How gender informs this discussion of cultural capital and how gendered experiences at HBCUs delimit and enhance the benefits of cultural capital need to be explored further. This discussion attempts to begin an interrogation of the constructions, meanings, and variations in cultural capital and gendered experiences in HBCU settings.

CULTURAL POLITICS AND REPRESENTING HBCUs

In research and analysis of HBCUs and their students, one major problem usually surfaces—the problem of the constructed hegemony of HBCUs and the experiences of students attending these schools. While much work has been done to investigate the relationship between cultural resources and educational achievement according to social class, race, and gender differences (Bourdieu, 1973; Bowles & Gintis, 1976; DiMaggio, 1982), little work, particularly in higher education, attempts to deconstruct historically Black colleges for their unique cultural position among postsecondary institutions. In particular, there is an urgent demand to carefully interrogate our assumptions about HBCUs, their meaning, and social representation. This urgency is reflected in current policy discussions where HBCUs have come under attack concerning their educational justification for continued existence. In some ways, I may also be guilty of perpetuating a monolithic notion of these institutions, by too often lapsing into an essentialist view of Black colleges. In considering cultural capital, I have taken some liberties in representing HBCU cultural settings as uniform entities; however, there is much variation in the character, cultural environments, and experiences of students in these schools. Indeed, a more culturally nuanced presentation of these multidimensional and diverse institutions is being demanded of higher education researchers and policy analysts. My intent, however, is to place this analysis at the center of a needed discourse on the construction, realities, and experiences of African American students attending a variety of HBCUs. For instance, particular attention should be paid to the distinction between public, private, religiously affiliated, urban, and geographically diverse HBCUs. Although most HBCUs are located in the southeastern region of the nation, not all of them are. Almost 90 of the total HBCUs are four-year institutions, while the rest are two-year or community colleges. Not surprisingly, there is much variation among enrollment sizes: four-year schools range from fewer than 800 students to campuses exceeding 8,000 students (Hoffman et al., 1992). A more critical reading of the role, function, and diversity of HBCUs will hopefully position our discourse on HBCUs more toward the center of research in higher education and make this discourse less marginalized in our theoretical understanding of the position of HBCUs in this chapter.

Within the current debate about the direction and mission of the nation's HBCUs, there appears to have surfaced a conflict between a legislative agenda and a cultural mandate for these institutions. Recent court rulings and litigation have been based on the elusive dreams of desegregating higher education institutions and creating universities that are truly "state"-controlled and -directed. Juxtaposed to these court directives, these institutions continue to adhere to community cultural mandates that focus their development and character on African American community needs and cultural experiences. While this conflict is yet to be resolved, the face of higher education in the country will never be the same, culturally or politically, with the inclusion and appreciation of HBCUs.

REFERENCES

Allen, W. R. (1992). The color of success: African American college student outcomes at predominately White and historically Black college and universities. *Harvard Educational Review, 62,* 26–44.

Allen, W. R., Epps, E. G., & Haniff, N. Z. (1991). *College in Black and White: Africans students in predominately White and in historically Black public universities.* Albany: SUNY Press.

Anderson, J. D. (1988). *The education of Blacks in the South 1860–1935.* Chapel Hill: University of North Carolina Press.

Bourdieu, P. (1973). Cultural reproduction and social reproduction. In R. Brown (Ed)., *Knowledge, education, and cultural change* (pp. 71–112). London: Tavistock.

Bourdieu, P. (1977). Cultural reproduction and social reproduction. In J. Karabel & A. H. Halsey (Eds.), *Power and ideology in education* (pp. 487–511). New York: Oxford University Press.

Bourdieu, P., & Passeron, J. C. (1977). *Reproduction in education, society, and culture.* London: Sage.

Bourdieu, P., & Passeron, J. C. (1979). *The inheritors: French students and their relation to culture.* Chicago: University of Chicago Press.

Bowles, F., & DeCosta, F. A. (1971). *Between two worlds: A profile of negro higher education.* New York: McGraw-Hill.

Bowles, S., & Gintis, H. (1976). *Schooling in capitalist America: Educational reform and the contradictions of economic life.* New York: Basic Books.

Branson, H. R. (1978). Black colleges in the North. In C. V. Willie & R. R. Edmonds (Eds.), *Black colleges in America: Challenges, development, and survival.* New York: Teachers College Press.

Browning, J. E., & Williams, J. B. (1978). History and goals of Black institutions of higher learning. In C. V. Willie & R. R. Edmonds (Eds.), *Black colleges in America: Challenges, development, and survival.* New York: Teachers College Press.

Bullock, H. A. (1967). *A history of negro education in the South: From 1619 to the present.* Cambridge: Harvard University Press.

Carter, D., & Wilson, R. (1993). *Minorities in higher education.* Washington, DC: American Council on Education.

Constantine, J. M. (1994). *Measuring the effect of attending historically Black colleges and universities on future labor market wages on Black students.* Paper presented at the Institute for Labor Market Policies Conference, Cornell University, Ithaca, New York.

Davis, R. B. (1991). Social support networks and undergraduate student academic success-related outcomes: A comparison of Black students on Black and White campuses. In W. R. Allen, E. G. Epps, & N. Z. Haniff (Eds.), *College in Black and White: African American students in predominantly White and in historically Black public universities* (pp. 143–157). Albany: SUNY Press.

DiMaggio, P. (1982). Cultural capital and school success: The impact of status culture participation on the grades of U.S. high school students. *American Sociological Review, 47,* 189–201.

DuBois, W.E.B. (1900). *The college-bred Negro.* Atlanta: Atlanta University Publications.

DuBois, W.E.B. (1910). *The college-bred Negro American.* Atlanta: Atlanta University Publications.

Dyson, M. E. (1993). *Reflecting Black: African-American cultural criticism.* Minneapolis: University of Minnesota Press.

Ehrenberg, R. G., & Rothstein, D. S. (1993). *Do historically Black institutions of higher education confer unique advantages on Black students? An initial analysis.* NBER Working Paper No. 4356.

Fleming, J. (1985). *Blacks in college: A comparative study of students' success in Black and White institutions.* San Francisco: Jossey-Bass.

Gurin, P., & Epps, E. (1975). *Black consciousness, identity, and achievement.* New York: Wiley.

Hoffman, C. M., Snyder, T. D., & Sonneberg, B. (1992). *Historically Black colleges and universities, 1976–1990.* Washington, DC: National Center for Education Statistics.

Jewell, J. (1996). *Atlanta University and the Congregational Church.* Paper presented at the annual meeting of the association for the study of Afro-American life and history Charleston.

Lee, S., & Brinton, M. C. (1996). Elite education and social capital: The case of South Korea. *Sociology of Education, 69,* 177–192.

McPherson, J. M. (1970). White liberals and Black power in negro education. *American Historical Review, 75,* 1357–1386.

Nettles, M. T. (1987). *Toward Black undergraduate student equality in American higher education.* Westport, CT: Greenwood Press.

Oakes, J. (1985). *Keeping track: How school structure inequality.* New Haven, CT: Yale University Press.

Plessy v. Ferguson, 163 U.S. 537, 165 S.Ct. 1138, 41 L.Ed.2d 256 (1896).

Polite, V. (1993). If we knew then what we know now: Foiled opportunities to learn in suburbia. *Journal of Negro Education, 62*(1), 12–23.

Semmes, C. E. (1992). *Cultural hegemony and African American development.* New York: Praeger.

Thompson, D. C. (1986). *A Black elite: A profile of graduate of UNCF colleges.* Westport, CT: Greenwood Press.

Wenglinsky, H. H. (1996). The educational justification of historically Black colleges and universities: A policy response to the U.S. Supreme Court. *Educational Evaluation and Policy Analysis, 18,* 91–103.

Part III

Addressing Higher Education Policy and Practice as They Relate to African American Culture

Policy, Practice, and Performance: Strategies to Foster the Meaningful Involvement of African Americans in Higher Education Decision-Making Processes

Wynetta Y. Lee

A case could be made that policy has been a part of the civilized world since the introduction of the Ten Commandments in biblical times. However, "policy" is a rather nebulous concept that often leaves scholars grasping at the essence of its meaning. Thoughts of policy might first draw images of powerful government officials' making laws that govern the lives of all citizens within their jurisdiction. Those oriented to the private sector might associate policy with the collage of powerful and affluent personalities who lead giant corporations. Other images might involve the purpose of policy and discern the concept as being a means of minimizing chaos by setting a standard for accepted behavior.

Students of public policy grapple with understanding what policy is, since literature on the subject presents it as both a noun (the manifestation of a decision) and a verb (repeated actions taken over time) (Anderson, 1975; Jones, 1984). For purposes of this discussion, definitions are offered by making a distinction between policy and the policy process. Policy is seen as the *articulation* of decisions made to systematically address a specific problem. Moreover, these decisions are applied consistently. The policy process, then, is the series of decisions regarding the *actions* taken to move decisions from mere articulation to a tangible reality. Figure 11.1 presents the policy process as three domains of decisions to be made to address a specific problem. The three decision domains include (1) decisions on what to do (development), (2) decisions on how to do it (implementation) and (3) decisions on how to assess outcomes (evaluation/assessment) (Anderson, 1975; Jones, 1984; Nakamura & Smallwood, 1980; Stokey & Zeckhauser, 1978). Although the decisions to be made are distinct, they tend to overlap, suggesting that the process is tightly interconnected. Thus, decisions made in each domain have an impact in each of the remaining domains of the policy process.

Figure 11.1
Policy Process

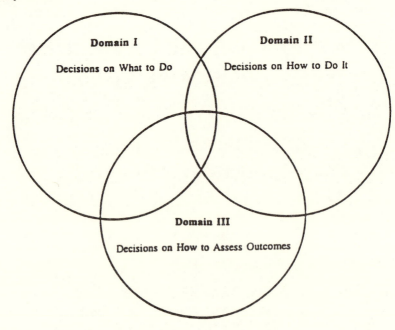

THE POLICY PROCESS

Domain I: Deciding What to Do (Policy Development)

The policy process starts with setting an agenda or making decisions regarding (1) what problems should be addressed and (2) in what order they should be addressed. This process is important because it ultimately determines where resources will be directed. These decisions involve considering the opportunity cost(s) of addressing one problem over another (Mansfield, 1982, p. 178). Once a specific problem is targeted, decisions are then made regarding what should be done about the problem. For example, if student attrition is identified as a problem for policy development, then decisions are made that are intended to lead to reducing or eliminating student attrition. One decision might be to raise admission standards so that only those with a chance of success are admitted. An alternative decision might be to provide assistance so that all students admitted will have sufficient institutional support for their success. The use of creditable data is an invaluable tool for making rational decisions with a chance of success (i.e., reducing student attrition). All policy decisions made should be informed through data pointing to (1) whether or not the decision is doable (implementation) and (2) if or when outcomes are measurable (evaluation/assessment). Otherwise, any further actions are likely to be ineffective and a tremendous waste of resources. For example, suppose that institutional data indicate that 90% of students leaving the institution are from families earning less than $15,000 annually and that, of that number, 75% of the students report that they are working two or more jobs outside the institution. To address this problem, imagine that those holding the power and authority to make institutional policy then decide to address student attrition through new financial aid programs. Then attention should be given to whether or not additional aid is available (doable). If the decision is doable (i.e., a careful review of the institutional budget indicates that millions of dollars could be directed to support all students enrolled), attention should be directed to determination as to (1) what indicators of success will be used, (2) whether or not the data are available through current record-keeping processes (e.g., student income and enrollment records) and (3) if additional data collection and analysis strategies (such as the relationship between financial aid awards and attrition) are needed to determine success. If data are not available to indicate the extent to which the policy can be implemented or to indicate whether or not the policy impact matches expectations, then decision makers should seriously consider decision alternatives. Unfortunately, not all policies are made based on data. Too often other factors, such as personal bias, political negotiations, and limited resources (i.e., time constraints, lack of data, fiscal limitations, etc.) influence decisions on what to do (Bardach, 1977).

Domain II: Deciding How to Do It (Policy Implementation)

Policies are manifested through the decisions that point to *how* to address a specific problem. These decisions reflect institutional practice and often are discernible as a program (i.e., an array of services delivered by specific institutional personnel to specific clients, in this case, students). The policy example given in domain I (development) is unusual since it indicates specific courses of action (i.e., new financial aid programs). The policy implementation domain of the policy process can be a rather difficult feat since the articulation of decisions in domain I often presents rather vague statements that leave considerable room for interpretation. For example, to address the attrition problem, the decision makers might develop a policy that says that "the institution will effectively and efficiently use institutional resources to provide assistance that fosters students' academic success." The clue for those charged with implementing the policy is "to provide assistance," since that indicates what action is to be taken; "how to provide assistance" is open for interpretation. For example, assistance could come in the form of academic counseling through peer and/or faculty mentoring programs, or staff could elect to provide assistance through the use of technology, such as establishing computer-assisted learning laboratories for tutorial services. The decisions made in this domain of the policy process, like decisions on what to do, also benefit greatly from the use of creditable data because they can illuminate the policy process. The use of good data, both quantitative and qualitative, minimizes the need "to shoot from the hip," since it provides a valid and reliable foundation for implementation decisions. For example, institutional data showing an attrition rate of 55% over the last 10 years would point to a problem and prompt institutional decision makers to develop a policy (rather vague in language as presented in an earlier example) to resolve attrition. Decision makers at the implementation level would then need to examine the data further as they ponder appropriate courses of action for program development. Imagine that upon further examination of the data, it was discovered that 90% of those who dropped out were first-term freshmen who had excessive absences from two or more classes. The descriptive statistics here clearly show a pattern of behavior but fall short of understanding why the behavior exists. The use of qualitative research techniques, such as focus group interviews and observation, can point to *why* students frequently are absent from class and can lend insights to interventions directed as the root of the problem rather than the symptom. Although it can prolong program development, the use of valid and reliable data is an efficient means for program development since it can reduce errors that result from trial-and-error strategies. The use of both quantitative data and qualitative data can lead to a comprehensive understanding of the problem, thus providing a sound foundation for the development of programs to implement policy decisions by making the best use of available resources.

Domain III: Deciding How to Assess Outcomes (Policy Evaluation/Assessment)

Public demands for institutional accountability place tremendous emphasis on the evaluation and assessment domain of the policy process. Those vesting resources (stakeholders such as taxpayers and consumers) expect evidence that the right decisions are made regarding what to do and how to do it. Thus, decisions regarding how to measure success are the most important and potentially the most challenging domain of the policy process. Policy evaluation/assessment requires a balance between adhering to the rules of research rigor and practical utility (Patton, 1982). The ease with which these decisions are made depends heavily on the clarity with which the development and implementation domain decisions are articulated. Ambiguity in the decisions to address a problem (policy statement) or in the means by which it is addressed (program implementation) poses tremendous problems for establishing expected outcomes and indicators of those outcomes. For example, if the decision is made to provide peer and faculty mentoring programs in order to reduce attrition, a clear definition of "attrition" is necessary. While such decisions appear to be obvious, establishing an operational definition of the variable is not as simple as it seems because there is no one way to measure most variables. For example, a simple calculation of the total number of students who leave the institution without receiving a degree divided by the total number of students to entered the institution is one measurement of attrition. Another approach would identify all students who enter seeking a degree and divide that number into those of that group who leave prior to degree completion. In either case, reaching consensus on the measure of attrition can be a challenge since the definition implies an institutional value. The first calculation would suggest that the institution expects all students who enter to complete a degree, while the second indicates that only those entering seeking a degree will be targeted for retention. If those responsible for making assessment decisions come to agreement about measuring the expected outcome, the next issue is to understand the program being implemented. For example, "mentoring" can be a rather abstract concept open to considerable variance in interpretation during implementation. Therefore, precision in defining the program (i.e., services provided to specific student populations through mentoring) is warranted in order to determine whether the right thing was done the right way (Chen & Rossi, 1983). The assessment domain should be tightly coupled with the development and implementation domains of the policy process. In other words, decisions on how to measure effects should be wedded to decisions on what to do and how to do it.

HIGHER EDUCATION DECISION MAKERS

Public policies are made at the federal, state, and local levels. In higher education, federal policies are formulated through the Department of Education, state policies are generated at the system level, and local policies are established at the institutional level. In this hierarchy, policies established at lower levels cannot conflict with those established at higher levels. Institutional policy cannot counter system or federal policies. At each policy level, policies are made to address specific problems by leaders who have the power, influence, and authority to make decisions; these decisions ultimately impact the lives of large numbers of people (Boone, 1996).

Martin Luther King once said, "There is nothing more dangerous than to build a society with a large segment of people in that society who feel that they have no stake in it; who feel that they have nothing to lose. People who have stake in their society, protect that society, but when they don't have it, they unconsciously want to destroy it" (Bell, 1995, p. 60). Higher education is a system in which a large population of American society is not vested. In higher education, decision makers (policymakers) are formal leaders who hold professional (presidents, faculty, administrators, etc.) positions in colleges and universities. Table 11.1 indicates that African Americans are underrepresented in higher education policy decision-making positions; conversely, the table also demonstrates that African Americans are overrepresented in positions that have little or no influence in the policy process.

Underrepresentation in the higher education policy process is likely to continue since too few African Americans are in the pipeline for having the credentials to be policy decision makers (*Digest of Education Statistics, 1995*). Table 11.2 presents African American student enrollment and graduation data for American colleges and universities. African American students are underrepresented at all levels of higher education (undergraduate, graduate, and professional), and too few of those students complete their degrees. Although the presence of African

Table 11.1
African Americans in Decision-Making Positions

	Total	African Americans	% African American
1992 U.S. Population*	255,082,000	30,316,000	11.9%
1991–92 Full-Timer Higher Education Employees**	1,786,569	219,469	12.3%
PROFESSIONALS	1,016,781	67,543	6.6%
Executives	136,908	11,886	8.7%
Faculty	520,551	24,611	4.7%
Support/Professionals	359,322	31,046	8.6%
NONPROFESSIONALS	769,788	151,926	19.7%
Technical	146,267	23,123	15.8%
Clerical	365,332	59,210	16.2%
Skilled	62,052	6,868	11.1%
Service	196,137	62,725	32.0%

Source: Statistical Abstract of the United States 1994.

**Source: The NEA 1994 Almanac of Higher Education.*

Table 11.2
African American Student Enrollments

	Total	African Americans	% African American
All Students	14,359,000	1,335,400	9.3%
4-yr. Institutions	8,707,100	757,800	8.7%
2-yr. Institutions	5,651,900	577,600	10.2%
Undergraduates	12,439,300	1,229,300	9.9%
Graduates	1,639,100	88,900	5.4%
1st Professionals	280,500	17,200	6.1%

Source: Digest of Education Statistics 1995.

Americans in the policy process currently is limited, there are strategies that could foster the representation and the meaningful involvement of African Americans in higher education decision-making processes.

Fostering the Meaningful Involvement of African Americans in the Decision-Making Process

Who is responsible for involving African Americans in higher education decision-making processes? Roueche, Baker, and Rose (1989) offer insights into this question with their notion of transformational leaders and shared vision. Transformational leaders are change agents who "exhibit leadership behaviors that reflect vision, demonstrate the ability to influence others, acknowledge the importance of attending to and motivating people, and act on the importance of modeling values conducive to institutional excellence" (p. 289). They go on to write:

> Those who dream, those who have vision have the ability to change their dreams and visions into reality. . . . Transformational leaders possess imagination and creativity that, when combined with their ability to interrelate with their organizations or institutions, provide a climate conducive to new beginnings. . . . Visions are only the seedlings of reality. We must value and cherish our dreams and visions, nurturing them into fulfillment. Most of all, we must remember that few of our visions can be accomplished alone. The key to the achievements that we strive for is the ability to share our visions and thus earn the acceptance and assistance necessary for turning them into reality. What is truly important, what is lasting, is accomplished together. (p. 289)

Transitional leaders can visualize and nurture leadership potential in those who do not see themselves as leaders. For example, professors who see students as protégés and future peers exhibit transformational leadership. Fostering the involvement of African Americans in higher education policy should *start* with those who are already policy decision makers, those with the authority to make policy decisions at all levels (federal, state, local) and in all domains of the policy process (development, implementation, and evaluation/assessment). These leaders should have a vision of increasing the meaningful involvement of African Americans in the higher education policy process. This vision should be energized with efforts to provide a climate that would support this new beginning, a climate that realizes that effective, lasting policies are created inclusively. Therefore, this vision would lead to a willingness to actively and creatively seek African American participation in the policy process.

Responsibility for the meaningful involvement of African Americans in higher education decision-making processes should be shared between those who are already policy decision makers and African Americans. Thus, the responsibility does not lie entirely on those currently in power. African Americans must be proactive by preparing for, and seeking, opportunities to participate in higher education policy processes at all levels.

Decision makers who embrace the idea of increasing the meaningful involvement of African Americans in the higher education policy process (what to do) are often left grappling for strategies to respond to the questions of how to do it and how to assess outcomes. Insights into implementation and evaluation/assessment strategies can be found in Boone's (1996) community-based programming process that promotes the empowerment of people by involving those who are often excluded from the decision-making process. Community-based programming fosters "collaboration among the people, their leaders, and other community agencies and organizations" (Boone, 1996, p. 4). Community-based programming is suited for fostering the inclusive collaboration between stakeholders (policy decision makers) and target publics (African Americans). Building on the principles of Roueche et al. (1989) and of Boone (1996), Figure 11.2 presents a model for increasing the involvement of African Americans in the higher educa-

Figure 11.2
Shared Responsibility Model

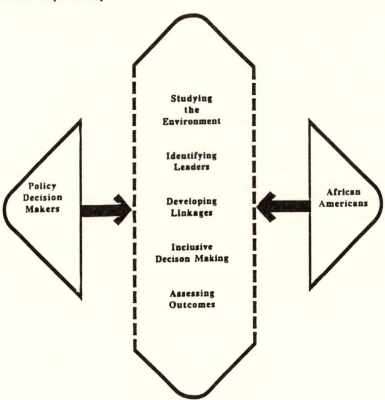

tion decision-making process. The model suggests that the responsibility for empowering African Americans in the higher education process is shared between decision makers and African Americans. By being actively involved in specific actions, such as studying the environment, identifying leaders, developing linkages, maintaining inclusive decision making, and assessing outcomes, the increased presence of African Americans in the higher education policy process can become a reality.

SHARED RESPONSIBILITY MODEL

Studying the Environment

Policy decision makers should study higher education environments to (1) determine the extent to which African Americans are either underrepresented or overrepresented in the decision-making process in all domains of the policy process, (2) identify what drives the circumstance, and (3) identify what policy issues being addressed are likely to have a disproportionate negative impact on African Americans. Admittedly, this is not an easy or quick process. To start studying the institutional environments, decision makers should be prepared to invest resources (i.e., time, money) in studying African American culture in order to gain cultural competence (Cross, Bazron, Dennis, & Issacs, 1989; Mason, Benjamin, & Lewis, 1996) for working effectively with this population and understanding policy impacts from a different perspective. Understanding African American values and norms (Bolman & Deal, 1991) is essential in organizational development, as it is a means for viewing higher education problems from the perspective of African Americans. By studying higher education environments from the perspective of African Americans, along with their own insights gained from personal values and experiences, decision makers will have a better chance of developing policies that will lead to the success of both higher education and African Americans in society.

In studying African American culture, decision makers should use quantitative and qualitative data to reflect on African American involvement in the policy process. Quantitative data provide a tangible means of identifying the scope of a condition (i.e., limited available pool with academic credentials and experience), and qualitative data lend insights to understand why the condition exists (i.e., personal and institutional barriers). Thus, a mixed-methods approach to data collection would give decision makers a complete picture of African Americans in higher education, their current involvement in decision-making processes, policy impacts on this population, and obstacles to their meaningful involvement in the policy process.

Studying environments is not the sole responsibility of decision makers. African Americans should function in a proactive mode to address policy issues, even in higher education. The first step to becoming proactive in the higher education policy process is to adopt a notion that information is power and begin using creditable information to study institutional environments and the domains of the policy process. Although anecdotal evidence is excellent for making an emotional appeal to decision makers regarding policy actions, African Americans should study higher education environments to discover policy issues (both current and coming) that impact African Americans and to understand the full impact of those policies based on valid and reliable data.

Thus, African Americans should take every opportunity to develop skills in research to build a case for policy decisions. Those who are not pursuing research careers could find the idea of developing research skills rather disconcerting, since "research" in higher education curricula tends to strike fear in the hearts of even the most academically confident students. The intent is not to turn all African Americans into scholarly researchers but rather to emphasize the importance of internalizing basic research principles in order to become informed consumers of research, fully able to distinguish between good and bad research, and able to use "not good but all there is research" appropriately. Not only does the effective use of data provide a basis for defensible arguments for increasing the involvement of African Americans in the decision-making process, but it also provides a solid foundation for understanding the policy process, issues, and appropriate positions to take.

Identifying Leaders

Decisions are made by people, usually on behalf of a group of people. For example, parents make decisions on behalf of children. Teachers make decisions on behalf of students. In the public policy process, decision makers hold formal positions as either elected or appointed leaders. This pattern carries over to higher education since policy decisions are made by those who hold formal leadership positions. For example, general institutional policies in public colleges and universities are made by those who hold formal leadership roles.

Administrative policies (e.g., those that determine how the institution will implement board policies) are made by those holding formal administrative and professional positions, such as presidents, provosts, institutional attorneys, deans, and other senior administrators. Academic policies are generally sanctioned by this group and generated from faculty. Although nonprofessionals make decisions that could bear upon the implementation of institutional policies (i.e., passive resistance), generally their participation in the policy process domains (development, implementation, and evaluation/assessment) is, at best, obscure. Since there are so few African Americans in formal leadership positions, those with the authority to make higher education decisions should broaden their concept of "leaders" to include those who carry considerable influence among a group, whether or not they hold an official position. Therefore, higher education decision makers should identify African Americans who do hold official administrative or faculty leadership positions (a process that, in most institutions, will not take long, given the sparse representation of African American officials). A more tedious task is to identify informal African American leaders (e.g., those who are a tremendous influence among the institution's African American population but who do not hold an official position). Informal African American leaders are important because they can influence reactions to policy decisions and institutional behavior. For example, Reverend Jesse Jackson does not hold an elected or appointed public policy position, yet the African American community's reaction to policy, in both the public and private sectors, is driven by his leadership. Those responsible for institutional policy would be well served to spend time identifying institutional "Jesse Jacksons" who should be involved in the policy development, implementation, and evaluation processes.

African Americans who already have reached the ranks of policy officials have a burdensome responsibility. This group is responsible for first representing the interests of those who cannot represent themselves. But, as important, this group is the best equipped to perpetuate the presence of African American leaders in the future by identifying those with leadership potential and being a professional mentor. For example, those who are in administrative positions should find a way to help other African Americans, early in their careers, to gain the kinds of credentials and experiences to prepare them for policy leadership roles. This task is not an easy one, since most administrators are busy addressing the daily crises that seem rather endless. However, keeping African Americans in the pipeline is essential so that when those in office leave, there are other African American leaders available to replace them. Therefore, there will be African American leaders qualified to increase African American representation in higher education administration and other policy positions. Maintaining a pool of qualified African Americans (with credentials and experience) is important so that when those in office leave, there are other African Americans to replace them and to increase African American representation in the policy process.

Developing Linkages

The identification of African American leaders by itself is not enough to gain their participation in the policy process. Those who are already policy decision makers should connect with those African American leaders identified in the previous process in such a way that a working relationship evolves. Since the involvement of African Americans in higher education policy domains is a fairly new experience for this group, being involved in a meaningful way is likely to be suspect. Those who are committed to a vision of a shared responsibility for higher education policy should be long on patience and short on frustration. Relationships tend to evolve over time, since they involve developing mutual trust and effective communication techniques. The qualitative paradigm offers useful strategies, since this process is like qualitative research efforts to gain entry into a new environment and establish rapport with those in the environment.

African Americans can facilitate the linkages process by being receptive to those who are seeking to foster their participation in the policy process. Reciprocity of effort is essential if decision makers and African Americans are to develop sound working relationships. Waiting for an engraved invitation to become involved in higher education policy could either not happen or not happen soon enough. African Americans who hold an interest in policy, especially those who hold credentials and experience, should be assertive in contacting those who already have policy-making authority in order to initiate a working relationship. Again, qualitative research techniques are helpful in this process since, as previously discussed, the objective is to gain entry into a new environment and to establish a rapport with strangers.

Inclusive Decision Making

Once higher education policies and their effects on African Americans have been identified, and African American leaders have been identified and recruited to participate in the policy process, the new policy-making group (previous policy leaders and new African American leaders) should work toward inclusive decision making. This is done by the group's efforts to reach consensus on higher education policy decisions. Group facilitation skills are essential in this process. Since all persons involved in the policy process at this point are vested in the outcomes, an external party could be a good investment for keeping discussions moving forward and defusing excessively passionate positions that cause the group to polarize. Policy discussions are often potentially heated, even under the best of circumstances. Discussions regarding race tend to be emotionally charged. Thus, it follows that discussions regarding the impact of policy on race will be rather volatile. Nonetheless, if policy decisions are to be made that will have a rather equal effect across groups, struggling through passionate and sometimes emotional debate is a necessary price to pay. The point is to make all involved comfortable enough to voice opinions, yet manage the group so that policy decisions are actually made, and the decisions made reflect the consensus of the group.

Decision makers can support this process by developing effective listening skills to actually hear the perspective presented by African American leaders. More often than not, the points of view could be similar since many issues apply to all humans regardless of race. In addition to effective listening skills, decision makers should understand African American culture (norms, expected behaviors, history, values) enough to effectively communicate their concerns, perspectives, and positions on a policy issue in a way that will be receptive to African Americans. Developing cultural competence skills (Cross, Bazron, Dennis, & Issacs, 1989; Mason, Benjamin, & Lewis, 1996) is as important in facilitating inclusive decision making as it is for studying higher education environments. The objective is not to get caught in a situation where everyone is saying the same thing but in different ways. In addition to a firm commitment to inclusive policy decisions, effective skills in field research are helpful in this process because research strategies involve collecting and analyzing data in the field, in this case rather rapidly. If the gathering of the new decision-making body (previous policy leaders plus African American leaders) is thought of as "the field," then the value of data collection techniques such as proxemics, kinesics, interviewing, and observation becomes apparent. The effective use of these skills can help the group move through the stages of group development (Tuckman & Jensen, 1978), especially the storming stage, so that consensus regarding higher education policy decisions can become a reality.

In addition to the effective use of field research strategies and strong communication skills, African American leaders need an additional asset in the policy process—a thick skin. Entering a new environment (policy process), it is natural to be rather sensitive and overwhelmed with uncertainty regarding the expected behaviors as a policymaker, the intent of those who are virtual strangers, and personal concern for the awesome responsibility of representing African Americans in higher education. African Americans entering the policy process should gain a confidence of their qualifications to contribute to the policy process and believe that their contributions to the process are valued. Being armed with valid and reliable data that can be generalized to a large group, understanding the implications of data, and, thus, supporting a position based on empirical evidence can contribute to developing a thick enough skin to maintain involvement in policy decisions.

Assessing Outcomes

Decision makers, even in higher education, do not operate without being held accountable to another body. For example, legislators are held accountable by their constituents. Higher education administrators are held accountable directly by their board of trustees and indirectly by students who elect to persist or leave institutions. Both experienced policy decision makers and new African American leaders who join that group are responsible for the decisions made by the group. Monitoring policy decisions as they move through each of the policy domains (development, implementation, and evaluation/assessment) is important to the survival of leaders in the policy process. Systematically monitoring each domain of the policy process can identify mistakes and point to rational options to correct those mistakes. Structured monitoring not only provides evidence for judgments to continue, modify, or abandon policy decisions but also requires policymakers to regularly pause and reflect on the extent to which policy decisions have resulted in desired outcomes or are moving toward achieving those outcomes.

CONCLUSION

An African proverb says "One hand can't tie a bundle" (McKnight, 1996, p. 108). These words indicate that some tasks require more than one hand, person, idea. The idea of inclusive collaborative efforts certainly applies to the higher education policy process. Fostering the meaningful involvement of African Americans in the higher education policy process would increase the chances of "tying policy bundles" that would benefit the higher education society as a whole without divesting a large segment of that society. Making this happen is not a quick fix and is likely to take considerable time and effort to become a reality. The real commitment of those currently holding the authority to make institutional policy decisions to function as change agents in order to facilitate the identification and recruitment of African American leaders to the policy process is a step in the right direction. However, since there are so few African Americans in institutional leadership positions and so few in, and completing, the educational pipeline leading to policymaking positions in higher education, this could be a yeoman's task. Still, with the investment of patience on the part of institutional policymakers, along with the investment of time and institutional resources, improving the involvement of African Americans in the decision-making process is more than possible; it is probable.

Enhancing African American involvement in the policy process is not the sole responsibility of those already christened with the authority to make decisions on behalf of large numbers of people. African Americans share this responsibility and should assertively seek opportunities to become involved. By actively studying policy issues and the policy process and by acquiring appropriate credentials to merit policy leadership roles, African Americans can make meaningful contributions to institutional policy decisions.

The strategy put forth here to foster African Americans' meaningful involvement in decisions regarding institutional policy, practice, and performance is complex and comprehensive. The shared responsibility model calls for behavior changes on the part of both those who are experienced policymakers and African Americans who strive to become future policymakers. Nonetheless, the idea of "shared responsibility" does not place responsibility or blame on anyone in particular for the underrepresentation of African Americans in the policy process. Rather, the strategy looks to the future by focusing on the importance of the collaborative efforts to foster inclusiveness in higher education decisions. The effective and efficient use of research methods, in both the quantitative and qualitative paradigms, provides a sound foundation for policy decisions at all levels (federal, system, and institutional) and in all domains of the policy process (development, implementation, and evaluation/assessment). More importantly, the skillful use of data and the effective realization of shared responsibility are invaluable tools for empowering African Americans to help tie bundles in higher education policy.

REFERENCES

Anderson, J. A. (1975). *Public policymaking,* (3rd ed.). New York: Holt, Rinehart & Winston.

Bardach, E. (1977). *The implementation game: What happens after a bill becomes a law?* Cambridge: The Massachusetts Institute of Technology.

Bell, J. C. (1995). *Famous Black quotations.* New York: Warner Books.

Bolman, L. G., & Deal, T. E. (1991). *Reframing organizations: Artistry, choice, and leadership.* San Francisco, CA: Jossey-Bass.

Boone, E. J. (Ed.) (1996). *Community leadership through community-based programming: The role of the community college.* Reprint ed. Raleigh: North Carolina State University.

Chen, H. T., & Rossi, P. H. (1983). Evaluating with sense: The theory-driven approach. *Evaluation Review, 7*(3), 383–302.

Cross, T. L., Bazron, B. J., Dennis, K. D., & Issacs, M. R. (1989). *Towards a culturally competent system of care: A monograph on effective services for minority children who are severely emotionally disturbed.* Washington, DC: CASSP Technical Assistance Center, Georgetown University Child Development Center.

Digest of Education Statistics 1995.

Jones, C. O. (1984). *An introduction to the study of public policy,* (3rd ed.). Belmont, CA: Wadsworth.

Mansfield, E. (1982). *Micro-economics: Theory and applications,* (4th ed.). New York: W. W. Norton.

Mason, J. L., Benjamin, M. P., & Lewis, S. A. (1996). The cultural competence model: Implications for child and family services. In C. A. Heflinger & C. T. Nixon (Eds.), *Families and the mental health system for children and adolescents: Policy, services, and research* (pp. 165–190). Thousand Oaks, CA: Sage.

McKnight, R. (1996). *Wisdom of the African world. The classic wisdom collection.* Novato: New World Library.

Nakamura, R. T. & Smallwood, F. (1980). *Policy implementation.* New York: St. Martin's Press.

The NEA 1994 Almanac of Higher Education.

Patton, M.Q. (1982). *Practical Evaluation.* Newbury Park, CA: Sage.

Roueche, J. E., Baker, G. A., III, & Rose, R. R. (1989). Shared vision: Transformational leadership in American community. Washington, DC: Community College Press.

Statistical Abstract of the United States 1994.

Stokey, E., & Zeckhauser, R. (1978). *A primer for policy analysis.* New York: W. W. Norton.

Tuckman, D. W., & Jensen, M. C. (1978). Stages of small group development revisited. *Group and Organization Studies, 2*(4), 419–426.

12

The Relationship between Evaluation Effort and Institutional Culture: Mixing Oil and Water?

Bruce Anthony Jones

Without question, assessment and evaluation have become critical components of any effort to understand the performance of institutions of higher education and of efforts to engage in higher education reform. From an internal standpoint, institutions of higher education need to know what factors are important for student success in higher education and what outcomes address or do not address this success. From an external standpoint, there is the "accountability" issue. Institutions of higher education expend tremendous amounts of public and private dollars. These institutions often employ a large workforce. In many localities, the institution of higher education is the single largest employer. In an age of corporate downsizing, shrinking government resources, and increased giving demands on the private philanthropic sector, institutions of higher education must be held accountable for how fiscal, human, and material resources are spent. Finally, in the context of evaluation effort there is the "diversity" issue. This issue is tied closely to both student performance and accountability concerns. Students on college campuses across the nation have become increasingly ethnically diverse. For example, the African American student presence on college campuses rose from 8.8% in 1984 to 10.1% in 1994. The percentage of Latino students rose from 4% in 1980 to 5.2% in 1989 (Nettles, 1995). While both of these percentage increases are small relative to the percentages of African Americans and Latino Americans in the population at large, they do represent an increase that has been generally upward since the 1960s. The growing ethnic diversity on the college campus is directly related to the growing ethnic diversity of the population of the United States and increased opportunities for representatives of previously disfranchised ethnic groups to attend colleges and universities.

With particular regard to the latter, this chapter focuses on the significance of institutional culture relative to the advancement of African American students and efforts to assess the performance of institutions of higher education. Institutional culture is concerned with political and social variables that relate to formal and informal policy practices and outcomes on the college or university campus. From a formal standpoint, institutional culture is concerned with the history and current practice of advancing ethnic diversity on campus through written policy. From an informal standpoint, institutional culture is concerned with how interrelationships within the academic community are advanced in ways that support ethnic diversity before and during student enrollment at the institution of higher education.

Historically, program assessment in higher education has not considered institutional culture except in some instances of assessment that have occurred through the accreditation process. Models and approaches to evaluation in higher education do not, in any explicit way, establish institutional culture as a key macro-variable to include toward institutional improvement. This chapter discusses program assessment and suggests an assessment approach that directly targets institutional culture as a key concern in evaluation.

THE CONTEXT FOR EVALUATION

In recent years, policymakers in higher education have begun to engage in what is known as *priority setting* in higher education. Performance funding is an example of state legislative action that has led to priority setting. According to Banta and Pike (1989), performance funding involves targeting additional resources as an incentive for institutions to illustrate program effectiveness through assessment. Priority setting via the flurry of program assessment activity has come about, in part, because of this performance funding concept. For example, at the University of Missouri-Columbia, academic units are engaged in program assessment then priority setting with the expectation of the creation of a "niche document." The niche document spells out program priorities that are in line with how fiscal, human, and material resources are to be spent under the rubric of program investment and disinvestment. According to Barak (1982), next to program improvement "resource allocation was the most frequently cited reason for conducting program reviews" (p. 39). Wilson (1985) reported that the growing significance of program review is directly related to the need to eliminate academic and nonacademic programs in tandem with shrinking fiscal resources.

EVALUATION IN HIGHER EDUCATION: COMMON FORMS

Evaluation entails the critical activity of determining the merit or worth of a particular perceived institutional program, or program need, or program direction. In general, there are two types, either summative or formative in nature. Summative evaluations are often implemented in the aftermath of a particular program direction or implementation. In this respect, these evaluations are retrospective in nature. Formative evaluations entail the collection of data while a program is in operation. Often, these data are fed back to the institution or program in a way to help the institution or program improve while in progress.

Numerous models of evaluation provide the vehicles to engage in the summative or formative type of institutional or program evaluation. Worthen and Sanders (1987) describe the most common forms:

Goals-Based Model

The goals-based model of evaluation is centered on developing an understanding of the extent to which the institution or program attains its preestablished goals and objectives.

Responsive-Based Model

The responsive-based model of evaluation is not concerned principally with preestablished goals and objectives of an institution or program. This model is more concerned with what Guba and Lincoln (1981) refer to as the search for outcomes, in particular, unintended outcomes that would not emerge in an evaluation grounded in a goals-based model approach.

Decision-Based (Management) Model

The decision-based (management) model of evaluation is centrally focused on meeting the informational needs of policy decision makers. This model of evaluation is to delineate, obtain, and provide useful information for judging decision alternatives. There is a heavy reliance on the use of survey methods in order to glean information about the nature of decisions and the characteristics and criteria used by decision makers.

Connoisseurship Model

The connoisseurship model of evaluation involves the identification and usage of an *expert* who will critique an institution or program and provide written analysis. The identified expert draws on his or her experience to develop this analysis.

Naturalistic or Participant Model

The naturalistic or participant model of evaluation is driven by stakeholder needs. Stakeholders are defined as those individuals and groups who are to be affected by the evaluation. These individuals are involved in the development, planning, and implementation of the evaluation.

Each of the preceding traditional approaches does not require, in a direct way, the need to consider variables that associate with institutional culture. The responsive, connoisseurship, and naturalistic models may lead toward an assessment of institutional features that associate with institutional culture but do not assure that this will occur. The goals-based model may lead toward an assessment of institutional culture only if it is considered a goal of the institution. Moreover, with each of the models often there is a heavy emphasis on the collection of data that are quantitative in nature. This is in line with the strong positivist tradition in evaluation (Hall, 1995). For example, with institutions of higher education there is an emphasis on linking institutional performance to student test scores, department rankings relative to other departments in the institution and other similar institutions, and numeric faculty performance rankings by students. The overemphasis on the need to collect numbers relative to institutional performance leaves out any opportunity to explain with rich qualitative data collection technique institutional culture as this relates to student achievement.

Finally, none of the models consider ethnic diversity as this relates to the evaluators themselves. The evaluation model proposed in this chapter centers on variables that associate with institutional culture, as well as ethnic diversity among those individuals or groups who conduct the evaluation. The model proposed dismisses the traditional idea that states evaluation is an objective and/or neutral enterprise. According to Burgard (1996), "[T]he plausibility of value-free evaluation has come under serious scrutiny. Most researchers, the critics as well as the positivists themselves, have accepted the impossibility of maintaining the observer/observed distinction when dealing with human subjects . . . evaluation is political . . . evaluations clearly can benefit some individuals at the expense of others" (p. 22). Given this, in any discussion about institutional culture it is just as critical a need to discuss ethnic diversity as it relates to those who engage in the analysis of this institutional culture. There is an urgent need to consider ethnic diversity particularly in this era of the growing ethnic diversity on the college campus coupled with institutional priority setting, retrenchment, and program reorganization.

SPECTRUM ANALYSIS AND INSTITUTIONAL CULTURE

Spectrum analysis is a method of evaluation that is essentially two-sided, with a focus on institutional culture relative to ethnic diversity and student achievement. On one side, there is a *direct* focus on understanding the cultural environment under which an institution or program operates relative to student achievement. These variables are not left to chance to emerge in importance, as might be the case under some other method of evaluation. On the other side, the mythical belief that evaluation is an absolutely neutral and objective enterprise is thrown out with spectrum analysis. Burgard (1996) writes that "every individual, including the evaluator, possesses a personal construction of the *truth* about an action that determines both her propensity to act and personal evaluation of the action" (p. 20). In this regard, there are not only a concern with the analysis of the program or academic unit being evaluated but also a concern with ensuring that *a wide spectrum of individuals who are ethnically diverse* are involved in evaluation planning, development, and implementation.

Three critical dimensions of African American student interaction with institutions of higher education are important to understand relative to institutional culture and spectrum analysis. These dimensions are the recruitment, selection, and retention processes, with a focus on what occurs within or during these processes.

Recruitment Dimension

The recruitment or preselection stage of African American students is concerned with policies and practices of institutions that encourage or discourage African American students to *consider* enrolling and addresses such issues as:

1. Providing fiscal and human resource allocations that enable the institution and academic units to seek out African American students (e.g., travel to and from locations where African American students can be recruited; personnel on hand to welcome African American students to campus);
2. Locating fiscal resources that enable African American students to visit college campuses as they make decisions about where to enroll;
3. Giving attention to, and learning from, locations where the institution actually recruits students and disseminates information about the campus.

Selection Dimension

Often recruitment effort is treated as synonymous with selection effort. However, for purposes of evaluation, recruitment and selection are distinguished as two separate activities, largely because it is possible for an institution of higher education to engage in a serious recruitment effort of African American students but actually never *select* African American students to enroll. This dimension is concerned with the assessment of the aftermath and actual outcome of recruitment effort and answers the following questions:

1. In the aftermath of a recruitment effort, how many African American students actually choose to enroll in the institution?
2. Why did the African American students choose to enroll?
3. What are the criteria for selection, and are the criteria fair?
4. Who establishes the criteria for selection, and are these individuals ethnically diverse?

Retention Dimension

The retention dimension is principally concerned with the assessment of the institution or academic unit effort to retain African American students through graduation. Retention is most directly related to the institutional climate. Nettles (1994) speaks to the importance of understanding institutional climate when he said that "student attitudes and experiences and institutional programs, practices and policies constitute institutional climate. Like student background characteristics, institutional climate contributes to both student and institutional outcomes. It accounts for much of the persistence, progress and academic achievement of college students" (p. 501).

Spectrum analysis and ethnic diversity concerns relative to *who* conducts, develops, and implements evaluation center on three multiple, constituency group strands. The first strand centers on those who are delegated or contracted to engage in the task of evaluation. These individuals or groups are accountable to ensure that the evaluation is conducted and completed. This may be an administrative team or an outside organization that has expertise in evaluation. The second strand includes policy decision makers and primary users. These individuals and groups exist within the institution or program under evaluative review. This may include students, faculty, and researchers at the institution or unit under review. Policy decision makers and secondary users constitute the third strand of individuals and groups who are external to the institution but are indirectly and importantly affected by the institution or program under review. This may include taxpayers, parents who pay tuition, legislators, and members of the indigenous surrounding community.

Spectrum analysis requires that members from each multiple constituency group are direct participants in the planning, development, and implementation of the assessment of the unit or program under evaluation. As important, this participation must be ethnically diverse. Ethnically diverse participants must be involved in crafting the assessment questions, data collection, and interpretation of the evaluative data.

With spectrum analysis and the focus on institutional culture and who conducts evaluation there is a central concern with policy and participation *impact*. Jones (1994) describes three possible types of impact in the policy arena that serve as a guide for data assessment under the rubric of spectrum analysis: *(1) Symbolic impact; (2) Retentive impact, and (3) Structural impact.* Symbolic impact describes policy processes and outcomes that are temporary and/or superficial in nature. For example, the analysis of retention efforts may reveal that the institution supports African American students only through parties and celebrations during Black History Month. Such events may be described as *feel-good* or *buttons and T-shirt* activity. This is symbolic because such activity does not represent fundamental change in the way the institution interacts with African American students. Symbolic impact may also occur on the level of participation of ethnic minorities on the evaluation team. In other words, it is possible to include, for example, African Americans on the evaluation team but not involve this group in any meaningful way on evaluative planning, development, and implementation. In common language, this is referred to as *tokenism* and is purely symbolic. Retentive impact describes *more of the same*. For example, over a period of time recruitment policymakers may determine the need to increase the number of mentoring programs on campus as a policy mechanism to attempt to attract more African American students. This type of determination does not represent new programming, and it does not necessarily, in a fundamental way, alter the way the institution recruits students. Efforts that are structural in nature do reveal policies and practices that fundamentally alter the institution in a way that is supportive of ethnic diversity. Structural impact is concerned with the physical development of programs that advance ethnic diversity in fundamental form, as well as changes in conceptual and attitudinal practices that undergird academic and nonacademic programming on the campus. Spectrum analysis takes into account all three impact *types* to highlight areas in campus institutional culture where substantial change actually occurs in comparison to areas where change may be more superficial.

CONCLUSION

The current political environment has placed an increased emphasis on the need for institutions of higher education to engage in ongoing evaluation at the broad institutional level and academic unit level. The outcomes of evaluation are being used to make policy decisions on what programs to cut, expand, or redirect. As campuses become more ethnically diverse with populations of students who have been historically excluded from engaging in higher education pursuits, institutional culture and its importance need to be advanced as a way to be more supportive of these students. Institutions that engage in traditional forms of evaluation may actually harm efforts or do little to advance ethnically diverse student populations unless they employ an evaluation model that incorporates ethnic diversity as a chief concern. Spectrum analysis is a form of institutional evaluation that attempts to meet this chief concern. In this way, there is the important recognition of the need to mix evaluation effort with the need to understand institutional culture.

REFERENCES

Banta, T. W., & Pike, G. R. (1989). Methods for comparing outcomes assessment instruments. *Research in Higher Education, 30*(5), 455–469.

Barak, R. J. (1982). *Program review in higher education.* Boulder, CO: National Center for Higher Education Management Systems.

Burgard, S. (1996). *Science meets society: Making evaluation useful and increasing its utilization.* Dayton, OH: Kettering Foundation.

Guba, E. G., & Lincoln, Y. S. (1981). *Effective evaluation: Improving the usefulness of evaluation results through responsive and naturalistic approaches.* San Francisco: Jossey-Bass.

Hall, P. M. (1995). The consequences of qualitative analysis for sociological theory: Beyond the microlevel. *The Sociological Quarterly, 36*(2), 397–423.

Jones, B. A. (1994). *Investing in U.S. schools: Directions for educational policy.* Norwood: Ablex.

Nettles, M. (1994). Assessing progress in minority access and achievement in American higher education. In J. Stark & A. Thomas (Eds.), *Assessment and program evaluation* (pp. 499–503). Washington, DC: Association for the Study of Higher Education, ASHE Reader Series.

Nettles, M. (1995). The emerging national policy agenda on higher education assessment: A wake-up call. *The Review of Higher Education, 18*(3), 243–263.

Wilson, R. (1985). *Academic program review: Institutional approaches, expectations, and Controversies.* Washington, DC: Association for the Study of Higher Education.

Worthen, B. R., & Sanders, J. R. (1987). *Educational evaluation: Alternative approaches and practical guidelines.* New York: Longman.

13

African Americans and College Choice: Cultural Considerations and Policy Implications

Kassie Freeman

Does it strike anyone else as odd that for at least the last 10 to 15 years multitudes of research have documented influences on African Americans and other ethnic groups' participation in higher education; yet the increase in African Americans choosing to participate in higher education continues to fluctuate between stagnation and decline with only a slight increase in 1995 (Carter & Wilson, 1993, 1994, 1995)? In other words, while there is a slight increase in African Americans participating in higher education, for all the research that has been conducted on this topic, the participation rate is nowhere near what it should be.

There is widespread agreement among researchers that when socioeconomic factors are held constant, African Americans tend to have higher postsecondary aspirations than other groups (Hearn, 1991; Orfield et al., 1984; St. John, 1991); and African American families perceive that a college degree is "very important" (Orfield, 1992). Given these realities, researchers and policymakers must begin to ask several questions: Why do not more African Americans choose to participate in higher education? What are the missing links between their aspirations to participate and their actual participation in higher education? How can policies be implemented to better address how African Americans can turn their aspirations into reality and to integrate more targeted, workable programs/models?

Closing this gap between aspirations and actual participation is particularly important since educators and economists are in agreement on the importance of increasing African American participation in higher education. Reports such as the Hudson Institute Workforce 2000 have indicated that by the twenty-first century, one out of every three jobs will require schooling beyond the secondary level. In his book *Faded Dreams,* Carnoy (1995) discusses, among other issues, the importance of African Americans increasing their educational opportunities. More specifically, Simms (1995) discusses the direct relationship between African American participation in higher education and African American participation in the economy.

The purpose of this chapter is threefold: to examine the literature as it relates to the factors that influence African Americans to participate in higher education; to examine the missing links between their aspirations and actual participation; and to assess intervention strategies for programs/models to increase African Americans' participation in higher education.

THE COLLEGE CHOICE PROCESS: INFLUENCES AND CONSIDERATIONS

While there is a great deal of literature on the college choice process as it relates to African Americans, the need for further exploration is merited. From the research addressing the factors that influence students as to whether or not to participate in higher education, there is generally uniform agreement on the factors that are the same for all students. While there is some research on how the process differs for African Americans specifically, this subject has not been exhausted.

Studies on the college choice process have indicated several areas where factors influencing all students are similar: the theories of cultural and social capital, economic/financial capital, and channeling (including quality of school attended). In understanding the gap between African American aspirations and actual participation, one would need to understand the ways in which their families impart values concerning higher education and the way economic expectations (i.e., the expectation of a job after completing higher education) influence these potential students.

Similarities of Influences in the College Choice Process for All Students

Unfortunately, most research focusing on how students in general choose to participate in postsecondary schooling has overlooked or has not included factors that are culture-specific (Alexander, D'Amico et al., 1978; Alwin & Otto, 1977; Anderson & Hearn, 1992; Boyle, 1966; Hossler & Gallagher, 1987; Mortenson, 1991; Stage & Hossler, 1989). While research certainly has focused on social and cultural capital, it usually has assessed these issues across all groups, not giving specific consideration to the culture of any particular group. Bourdieu and Passeron (1977), for example, tend to be the most widely cited on the topic of cultural capital; yet it is not clear what their specific experiences have been with different cultures within the United States. This is not to criticize previous research; the intent of this chapter is only to point out that, without question, while theories about how students choose to participate in college are applicable to all students (including African Americans), previous researchers, by their own admission, recognize the need to better understand the choice process for minority students (Hossler, Braxton, & Coopersmith, 1989; McDonough, Antonio, & Trent, 1995) as related to each groups differing culture.

Cultural and social capital. Discussions of aspirations and decision making about participating in higher education generally focus on cultural and social capital, economics and financial capital, or some combination of the two (Hossler et al., 1989). However, Orfield et al. (1984) conducted a comprehensive study of access and choice in higher education in Chicago that concluded that minorities are channeled into college based on defined geographic locations—where they live. While most choice theorists would include the concept of channeling—a concept that is greatly underexamined—under the cultural and social models of decision making, it was considered separately in the framework for this study.

In simplest terms, the concepts of cultural and social capital mean assets, in the form of behaviors, on which individuals or families can draw to meet a certain set of established values in a society. These societal values are generally established by majority groups in society and encompass behaviors such as the way individuals speak and the way they dress. The more individuals are able to meet these established standards, the more they are accepted by different institutions (e.g., schools) in society. Researchers such as DiMaggio and Mohr (1985) have suggested that cultural capital is typically a set of specialized social behaviors that makes one accepted at different levels of society. Other theorists (e.g., Coleman, 1990) have indicated that while social capital is related to cultural capital, social capital is more related to relations among persons. For example, Coleman (1988) explains social capital as the network that provides information, social norms, and achievement support.

There is no doubt, however, that the cultural and social capital that students bring to the secondary school classroom has tremendous implications as to how they will be accepted and treated, and whether they will be provided necessary information on which to choose to attend postsecondary schooling. According to Cicourel and Mehan (1985), students are provided different educational opportunities because students begin their schooling with different types of culture capital. It is generally accepted that African Americans do not bring the same kind of social and cultural capital to the classroom as Whites. This very underexplored phenomenon, perhaps, led Orfield et al. (1984) to indicate that some theorists had posited a theory that Blacks and Whites form aspirations in different ways and to say that "there has been little exploration of the social consequences of the huge gap between Black hopes and the reality of higher education for Blacks" (p. 16).

The sociological model of student choice (which is the umbrella model for cultural and social capital), at least as described by Hossler et al. (1989), focuses on the factors that influence aspirations. This model describes family socioeconomic level and student academic ability as predictors of student aspiration for college. It is important to note that in a study with socioeconomic status held constant, Blacks were more likely than Whites to begin some college education (Olivas, cited in Orfield et al., 1984, p. 34). Hossler et al. also indicate that expectations from others, such as parents, teachers, and friends, also influence student aspirations. According to Orfield et al. (1984), next to socioeconomic status, the secondary school attended is the primary structure that provides access to college. The school curriculum (academic versus technical-vocational), counseling (regarding college availability, preparation), and grading have a tremendous impact on whether or not students choose to participate in higher education.

However, if it is the case, as some theorists (Bourdieu & Passeron, 1977; Coleman, 1988, 1990; Collins, 1979) have suggested, that postsecondary aspiration and high school academic decision making grow out of the cultural and social capital of families, it seems logical, then, that aspiration and choice are culturally based and will not necessarily be based on societal (elite) values. It is ironic that models to increase aspiration have generally been based on society at large, completely ignoring the culture, in this case, of African Americans.

Econometric model and financial capital. In addition to cultural and social capital as one of the major rationales for how students choose college participation, the econometric model and financial capital have also been postulated as explanations in the decision-making process (Anderson & Hearn, 1992; Hossler et al. 1989; Orfield et al., 1984). In the econometric model, as these and economics of education theorists (e.g., Becker, 1975; Cohn, 1979; Johns, Morphet, & Alexander, 1983; Thurow, 1972) have suggested, expected costs and expected future earnings from attending college are the primary considerations for student perception of the value of higher education, even though economic status, race, and education of parents may have a bearing on future earning potential.

The notion of future earning potential has been a topic greatly underexplored as it relates to the participation of African American students in higher education. For example, Barnes (1992) completed a study on African American 12th-grade, male stay-ins (those who were persisting through high school), and as it related to those students' economic goals, she found the following: "It is interesting that 43.7 percent indicated they wanted to become wealthy or comfortable rather than identify an occupation" (p. 96).

Socioeconomic factors such as parental income level and occupation, educational level, and number of siblings, are also posited as indicators of the choice students make regarding college participation (Alwin & Otto, 1977; Anderson & Hearn, 1992; Boyle, 1966; Hossler & Gallagher, 1987). Parental income and educational levels have both a direct and an indirect effect on college choice. Indirectly, the lower the parental income and education levels, the less information parents will have available to assist their children with financial decision making. In direct ways, Orfield et al. (1984) stated it this way: "Family income is viewed as causing inequalities in educational access" (p. 30). As an example, "because family income is much lower for minority students than for White students, the former are three to four times more dependent on federal financial aid than the latter" (Morris, cited in Orfield et al., 1984, p. 25).

While research is replete with information about the impact that the lack of financial aid has on participation in higher education (Cross & Astin, 1981; Nettles, 1988), what is increasingly clear is that there is a void in understanding as to how different cultural groups interpret or perceive the expectations of future earnings in their decision-making process with regard to whether or not to participate in higher education.

Channeling. Aside from the influences inside the home, students are also channeled by forces outside the home in directions that impact their decision-making process concerning participation in higher education. The term "channeling" can be defined as the environmental forces (whether individuals, institutions, or circumstances) that influence the direction of student choice, whether to pursue or not to pursue college participation. Channeling, as it relates to college choice, of course, cuts across social and cultural capital and economic and financial capital. That is, the more capital an individual has, whether cultural or economic, the more likely he or she will be influenced by forces internal to the home. As further support of the importance of environmental influences on students choosing to participate in higher education, one of the most recent studies that specifically investigates underrepresented groups' choice process in higher education is a book written by Levine and Nidiffer (1996). In their book *Beating the Odds: How the Poor Get to College,* these authors interviewed twenty-four students, including African American students, from impoverished conditions. They found a common theme from all of their subjects in terms "of how they came to attend college" (p. 65). The common element, as reported by Levine and Nidiffer, "put simply was an individual who touched or changed the students' lives" (p. 65).

When used effectively, channeling can mediate social and cultural differences, can impact the financial aid process and students' economic outlook, and can influence the type of postsecondary school selected and subsequent college experiences. As Orfield et al. (1984) explained in discussing the concept of channeling, changes in the school situation can change outcomes (p. 28).

Influences on the College Choice Process of African Americans

In addition to what research indicates about the influences on all students, the ways in which African American families impart values concerning higher education differ from other ethnic groups (Freeman, in press; Wilson & Allen, 1987). Furthermore, while all students are influenced by economic expectations, African Americans are particularly influenced by the expectation of a job, or lack thereof, after higher education (St. John, 1991; Thomas, 1980). Another way in which African Americans differ in choosing to participate or not participate in higher education is in the gap between their aspirations and their actual participation (Hearn, 1991; St. John, 1991; and Thomas, 1980).

Although it might not always be evident to the larger society, education has always been valued by African American families. "The thirst for learning," according to Billingsley (1992), "like the thirst for family life, crossed the Atlantic with the African captives" (p. 174). What has not been adequately researched and understood is "the role of Black families in directing the educational achievement of their children" (Wilson & Allen, 1987, p. 64). According to Wilson and Allen, "Black families have been unfairly denigrated and accused of actually retarding the educational development of Black youngsters" (p. 64). In fact, African American families have promoted educational attainment at all levels (Billingsley, 1992). In terms of college choice, how the African American family participates in the decision process bears greater understanding (e.g., what role various family members play in the process and how motivation and aspiration get instilled in their children).

Because many African Americans are first-generation college goers, their decision to participate in higher education is influenced the greatest from three sources: (1) their mother's significant role, (2) their extended family's participation in higher education, as well as their own desire to go beyond the family's level of schooling, and (3) job market expectations following participation in higher education.

Role of the mother. While researchers, particularly economics of education theorists (Becker, 1979; Cohen, 1979; Shultz, 1961), generally agree that, while the education and occupation of the father have an influential role in whether or not his children choose to participate in higher education, the mother in the African American family is also very significant in influencing her children. In support of this position, Wilson and Allen (1987) have stated: "The educational attainment of the Black mother is significantly related to the educational attainment of her offspring" (p. 74).

Role of extended family. In cases where members of the immediate family (mother or father) are not in a position to influence the decision process, the role of the extended family in influencing African American students' choices to participant in higher education is particularly noteworthy. In the Levine and Nidiffer (1996) study, the students who participated listed "other family member" as the person most influential in their decision to participate in higher education. Even when there are no family members educated beyond secondary school, there still tends to be a strong desire for African American students to "go beyond the family's level of schooling" (Freeman, in press). African American students describe the feeling of carrying the "hopes and dreams" of the entire family (Freeman, in press).

Economic expectation. Economic expectation (job market opportunities) is another way in which African American students differ in their consideration of higher education participation. From an ethnographic study, Ogbu (1978) describes how economic expectations might impact students' interest in schooling. He argues that members of a social group facing a job ceiling recognize that they face it, and this knowledge shapes their children's academic behavior. In a recently completed study, Freeman (in press) found that the "poor" expectation of getting a job after the completion of higher education was among the top perceived barriers by African American students to their participation in higher education. The students who participated in that study indicated that African American students perceived that they would either not get a job following higher education or not get a job commensurate with their level of schooling. These findings have been widely supported by researchers such as St. John (1991), Thomas (1980), and Wilson and Allen (1987). Since many African Americans generally hold jobs not commensurate with their level of schooling, even after higher education, this understandably influences their perceptions in their consideration of higher education. As Wilson and Allen indicated, despite the higher educational attainment of the African American students in their sample, "a majority of these young adults were concentrated in either lower-level white collar jobs or blue collar jobs" (p. 69).

Do aspirations translate into participation? The most puzzling aspect of how African Americans differ in choosing whether or not to participate in higher education is the gap between their aspirations and their actual participation. Research literature abounds with what Mickelson (1990) calls the "paradox of consistently positive attitudes toward education, coupled with frequently poor academic achievement" (p. 44) among African Americans. The same paradox holds in terms of African Americans' stated aspirations to attend higher education and their actual participation. In order to further the understanding of this paradox, Chapman (1981) offers a workable definition of aspirations. He defines aspirations as "wishes or desires expressing an individual's hopes about the future" (p. 494). Many college choice theorists have written about this paradox as it relates to African Americans without explaining why such is the case (Hearn, 1991; St. John, 1991; Thomas, 1980). St. John explained that, while having high aspirations improves the chances of Blacks attending higher education, having high aspirations alone does not guarantee attendance.

Mickelson (1990) offers the best description of forces that might prevent African American students from acting on their aspirations. She divides the attitudes toward schooling into two categories: "abstract attitudes, [which] embody the Protestant ethic's promise of schooling as a vehicle for success and upward mobility; and concrete attitudes, [which] reflect the diverse empirical realities that people experience with respect to returns on education from the opportunity structure" (p. 45). According to Mickelson, students' realities vary according to their perceptions and understanding of how adults who are significant in their lives receive more equitable or less equitable wages, jobs, and promotions relative to their educational credentials. The notion that students are influenced by their perceptions, which inevitably shape their realities, sheds light on how African American students can aspire to participate in higher education but can also believe that actually participating in higher education might not be economically viable.

While it could be argued that the "who" and/or "what" that influences whether or not students participate in higher are similar with all cultures, the depth and meaning (the perception of reality) each culture attaches to these influences differ. For example, as pointed out, African Americans are greatly influenced by their mothers, extended family members, and job market expectations. While they place a high value on the benefits of higher education, their aspirations likely do not translate into higher education participation. Before workable policies can be developed to increase African Americans' participation in higher education, it would be instructive to better understand their realities. What this research demonstrates is the importance of considering culture when trying to better link African Americans' aspirations to actual participation. As the findings from the study by Thomas (1980) revealed, there are some important differences among groups regarding the college entry process.

THE MISSING LINKS BETWEEN AFRICAN AMERICANS' ASPIRATIONS AND ACTUAL PARTICIPATION: CULTURAL CONSIDERATIONS

Assessing what is missing between African Americans' aspirations and actual participation in higher education (i.e., the steps or pieces in the decision-making process that create the void between beliefs and actuality) is paramount both to bridging the gap in research and to developing workable programs or models that go beyond "this is just the way it is." This is particularly important if, as Mickelson (1990) and Ogbu (1978) have indicated, individuals act on what they perceive and not necessarily on what research says is reality.

While research has not dealt with this void in any appreciable way, what can be pieced together is that the missing links between African American students' aspirations and their actual participation can be broadly categorized into three factors: (1) the school factors—the academic curriculum (including the absence of courses that validate students' culture) and teachers and counselors as channelers; (2) the individual or psychological factors—missing voices and perceived barriers; and (3) structural or societal factors—financial aid.

School Factors—the Academic Curriculum and Teachers/Counselors as Channelers

Since many African American students are first-generation collegegoers, they look to the school for guidance. It is ironic, then, that the very system they look to often fails them, particularly with respect to the curriculum. Building on Mickelson's (1990) notion that individuals' realities are based on the experiences of people like themselves, the absence of validation of students' culture, in this case that of African Americans, in the curriculum surely influences students' decision making as to possibilities about actual higher education participation. This would be consistent with Ogbu's (1978) findings that members of a social group recognize the limitations that their group members face and that this information shapes their academic behavior.

Typically, studies have assessed the relationship between high school course taking and college attendance. For example, Pelavin and Kane (1990) examined students taking certain high school courses (i.e., mathematics, laboratory sciences, and foreign languages) and the relationship of these courses to college participation. They found that students enrolled in these courses in high school were more likely to attend college. It is noteworthy that African American students are often not in the general high school track but in the vocational track, which prevents them from taking the college preparatory courses (Pelavin & Kane, 1990). Aside from the studies that examine course taking and college attendance, rarely have studies focused on the absence of the cultures of ethnic group in the curriculum and how this absence impacts the students' decision concerning whether or not to participate in higher education. African American students have expressed that their culture is not appreciated and not seriously included in curriculum on either the high school level or college level (Freeman, in press).

Internal to the school, high school teachers and counselors exert a tremendous influence on whether African American students translate their aspirations into higher education participation. As Thomas (1980) indicated, exclusive of background, Black students more often than White students perceive school officials as having a positive influence on their plans to participate in higher education. Similarly, Wilson and Allen (1987) found that counselor helpfulness at the high school level was a major source of influence in the determination of years of schooling.

Outside the home, high school teachers and counselors are among those with the most influence in channelling students toward college participation (Barnes, 1992; Morrison, 1989; Orfield et al., 1984). In fact, Chapman (1981) listed counselors and teachers in the top five as being most helpful to students with college choice decisions. Teachers and counselors take on even greater importance for African Americans. As to the need for committed teachers, according to Barnes (1992), 47.5% of the African American 12th-grade, male stay-ins in her study reported that "assignment to excellent teachers helped keep them in school" (p. 106). She further stated, "It seems clear that one way to hold African-American males' attention and keep them interested in their school work is to assign them the best teachers in school. These teachers will hold their interest, educate them, and help them graduate" (p. 106). According to Morrison (1989), Counselors play an equally important function. For example, Morrison (1989) stated, "An opportunity for minority students and their parents to engage in programs that provide current institution information, a visual campus overview, interaction with faculty and alumni, and questions and answers can be of considerable benefit" (pp. 13–14). Typically, counselors help facilitate this process for high school students.

The quality of the high school understandably also has implications for the type of contact and services students receive from teachers and counselors (Alexander et al., 1978; Anderson & Hearn, 1992; Boyle, 1966). For example, students at the top of their class in an urban high school are less likely than their counterparts at a suburban high school to have access to college recruiters, are more likely not to have visited a college campus, and are frequently missing even the basic information necessary to participate in the higher education process. More significant than the location of the school itself is the services provided by those schools (e.g., teachers and counselors). "Schools in affluent suburbs encourage college attendance and channel their students into college preparatory curricula; schools in poor or working class neighborhoods tend to prepare students for jobs not requiring college training" (Jencks, cited in Orfield et al., 1984, p. 28).

Individual or Psychological Factors

Perceived psychological barriers and absent voices present the greatest challenge to closing the gap between aspirations and participation in higher education. These psychological barriers perceived by African Americans have to be better understood and examined in greater detail. In fact, African American high school students in response to questions about these perceived psychological barriers regarding participation in higher education, as well as about economic barriers, stated psychological barriers such as "loss of hope," "college never an option," and the "intimidation factor" (Freeman, in press). In order to better understand the depth of the meaning of these barriers to African American students, their voices surely have to be heard and better understood. The study by Freeman found not only that it is important for researchers to include African American individuals as subjects in their studies, but that it is equally important to include their voices in the development of solutions to their problems. Otherwise, these individuals might not buy into participation in programs. The college choice process has typically been evaluated in quantitative terms. Rarely, if ever, have studies assessed what the quantitative findings mean from the perspectives of different groups. There will always be a missing step between perception and reality if individuals of each group do not have a say in the definition of their reality.

Financial Aid

In order to close the gap between aspirations and participation, another need by African Americans, according to Levine and Nidiffer, is access to information about financial aid, as well as the aid itself. Research on the importance of African Americans receiving financial aid in order to choose to participate in higher education is interesting. For example, Levine and Nidiffer (1996) indicated that financial aid is "a necessary but insufficient condition for college attendance by the poor" (p. 156). In other words, while *financial* aid is an essential factor in African Americans choosing to participate in higher education, financial aid alone will not necessarily influence an African American to choose higher education participation. They need access to the information about financial aid. Just because it is out there does not mean that they know it is there and how to get it. Although the role of financial aid in the college choice process might be inconsistent, the need for, and information about, financial aid among African Americans take on huge proportions. Regarding the need for financial aid, according to Orfield (1992), "Among Blacks, 84 percent said that they would need help" (p. 339). In his findings, St. John (1991) indicated that "it appears that student aid is an important factor in promoting minority student access" (p. 155). Other theorists, such as Nettles (1988), have also suggested the need for more information on financial aid for African American students.

A better understanding of what prevents African American students from acting on their wishes and desires to participate in higher education holds great importance, particularly from a policy-making perspective.

POLICY-MAKING IMPLICATIONS: PROGRAMS OR MODELS THAT ARE CULTURE-SPECIFIC

While educators and policymakers generally want to avoid different programs for different groups, indicating cost-effectiveness as a reason, logically the costs are much higher for programs that are ineffective. A number of programs or models have been developed, with varying degrees of success, to increase the participation of underrepresented groups, including African Americans, in higher education. Levine and Nidiffer (1996), summarize the programs into three types: (1) transition programs, which attempt to bridge the gap between secondary school and higher education (e.g., Upward Bound); (2) early intervention programs established with the belief that students need to be reached in childhood, such as A Better Chance (ABC); and (3) comprehensive programs, which are inclusive of aspects of the other two but also provide local activities and plans for individual and financial aid. Obviously, they conclude that the comprehensive approach is the most effective.

Each of these programs, being in existence for some time—in some cases since the 1970s—has increased pockets of African Americans choosing to participate in higher education. However, generally, educators and researchers would agree that, for the resources spent on these programs and for the length of time the programs have been operational, the increase in African Americans choosing to participate in higher education should be considerably higher. This is particularly the case given the aspirations of African Americans and the value African American families place on higher education.

The exploration of the literature in this chapter points out, at least as a beginning, that students' realities are culturally based (i.e., students look to people like themselves on whom to base their academic behavior [Mickelson, 1990; and Ogbu, 1978]). African Americans' economic expectations after higher education are based on their perceptions of job opportunities of other African Americans. Therefore, before workable programs can be developed, this is an area that bears much greater understanding.

Also, according to this research, two additional phenomena as they relate to whether or not African Americans participate in higher education have to be further examined. First, for policies to be successful, researchers need to know why there exists such a gap between African Americans' aspirations and actual participation in higher education. Although this research suggests that, following Mickelson's (1990) line of reasoning, students divide their attitudes about schooling into abstract attitudes and concrete attitudes, understanding the dichotomy between these two attitudes might shed new light on the development of African Americans' realities and make for better programming.

The second phenomenon that needs greater understanding is African Americans' psychological barriers. There is already a great deal of research on school factors and financial aid and how they affect the college choice process. However, if it is the case that individuals act on what they perceive and not necessarily what research suggests, before models can be developed that will appreciably increase African Americans' participation in higher education, or other academic programs for that matter, how students feel has to be taken into account. Also, hearing African American students' interpretations of their realities is critical. That is, programs, in the long run, will not be successful if subjects have no voice or stake in the direction of their own lives.

Overall, research has indicated, and continues to indicate, that there are missing links between what the data tell us and what African Americans do, particularly in relation to whether or not to participate in higher education. In order to continue to increase African Americans' participation in higher education, programs must be culture-specific. As Ogbu (1988) has indicated, the historical and structural aspects of a culture have to be considered. Each culture has a different frame of reference; therefore, understanding how different groups give meaning to their realities is crucial to the success of any program development.

REFERENCES

Alexander, K., D'Amico, R., Fennessey, J., & McDill, E. (1978). *Status composition and educational goals: An attempt at clarification.* Report 244. Baltimore: Johns Hopkins University Center for Social Organizations of Schools.

Alwin, D. F., & Otto, L. B. (1977, October). High school context effects on aspiration. *Sociology of Education, 50,* 259–273.

Anderson, M., & Hearn, J., (1992). Equity issues in higher education outcomes. In W. E. Becker & D. R. Lewis (Eds.), *The economics of American higher education* (pp. 301–334). Norwell, MA: Kluwer Academic.

Barnes, A. S. (1992). *Retention of African American males in high school.* New York: University Press of America.

Becker, G. S. (1975). *Human capital* (2nd ed.). New York: Columbia University Press.

Billingsley, A. (1992). *Climbing Jacob's ladder: The enduring legacy of African-American families.* New York: Simon & Schuster.

Bourdieu, P., & Passeron, P. (1977). *Reproduction in education, society and culture.* London: Sage.

Boyle, R. (1966). The effect of the high school on students' aspirations. *The American Journal of Sociology, 6,* 628–639.

Carnoy, M. (1995). *Faded dreams: The politics and economics of race in America.* New York: University of Cambridge Press.

Carter, D., & Wilson, R. (Eds.). (1993). *Status on minorities in higher education.* Washington, DC: American Council on Education.

Carter, D., & Wilson, R. (Eds.). (1994). *Status on minorities in higher education.* Washington, DC: American Council on Education.

Carter, D., & Wilson, R. (Eds.). (1995). *Status on minorities in higher education.* Washington, DC: American Council on Education.

Chapman, D. W. (1981). A model of student college choice. *Journal of Higher Education, 52*(5), 490–505.

Cicourel, A. V., & Mehan, H. (1985). Universal development, stratifying practices, and status attainment. *Research in Social Stratification and Mobility, 4*(5), 728–734.

Cohn, E. (1979). *The economics of education.* Cambridge: Harper & Row.

Coleman, J. S. (1988). Social capital in the creation of human capital. *American Journal of Sociology, 94,* 95–120.

Coleman, J. S. (1990). *Foundations of social theory.* Cambridge: Belknap Press of Harvard University.

Collins, R. (1979). *The credential society: An historical sociology of education and stratification.* San Diego: Academic Press.

Cross, P., & Astin, H. (1981). Factors affecting Black students' persistence in college. In G. Thomas (Ed.), *Black students in higher education* (pp. 76–90). Westport, CT: Greenwood Press.

DiMaggio, P., & Mohr, J. (1985). Cultural capital, educational attainment, and marital selection. *American Journal of Sociology, 90*(6), 1231–1261.

Freeman, K. (in press). Increasing African Americans' participation in higher education: African American high school students' perspective. *The Journal of Higher Education.*

Hearn, J. C. (1991). Academic and nonacademic influences on the college destinations of 1980 high school graduates. *Sociology of Education, 64,* 158–171.

Hossier, D., & Vesper, N. (1993). *Consistency and change in college matriculation decisions: An analysis of the factors which influence the college selection decisions of students.* Paper presented at the meeting of the American Educational Research Association, Atlanta, GA.

Hossler, D., Braxton, J., & Coopersmith, G. (1989). Understanding student college choice. In J. C. Smart (Ed.), *Higher education: Handbook of theory and research* (Vol. 5, pp. 231–288). New York: Agathon Press.

Hossler, D., & Gallagher, K. (1987). Studying student college choice: A three-phase model and the implications for policymakers. *College University, 62*(3), 207–221.

Johns, R. L., Morphet, E. L., & Alexander, K. (1983). *The economics and financing of education* (4th ed.). Englewood Cliffs, NJ: Prentice-Hall.

Levine, A., & Nidiffer, J. (1996). *Beating the odds: How the poor get to college.* San Francisco: Jossey-Bass.

Litten, L., Sullivan, D., & Brodigan, D. (1983). *Applying market research in college admissions.* New York: The College Board.

McDonough, P. (1994, July/August). Buying and selling higher education: The social construction of the college applicant. *The Journal of Higher Education, 65*(4), 427–446.

McDonough, P., Antonio, A., & Trent, J. (1995). *Black students, Black colleges: An African American college choice model.* Paper presented at the meeting of the American Educational Research Association, San Francisco.

Mickelson, R. A. (1990). The attitude-achievement paradox among Black adolescents. *Sociology of Education, 63,* 44–61.

Morrison, L. (1989). The Lubin House experience: A model for the recruitment and retention of urban minority students. In J. C. Elam (Ed.), *Blacks in higher education: Overcoming the odds* (pp. 11–27). New York: University Press of America.

Mortenson, T. (1991). *Equity of higher educational opportunity for women, Black, Hispanic, and low income students.* American College Testing Program.

Nettles, M. (1988). *Financial aid and minority participation in graduate education.* Princeton, NJ: Minority Graduate Education Project for Educational Testing Service.

Ogbu, J. U. (1978). *Minority education and caste.* New York: Academic Press.

Ogbu, J. U. (1988). Cultural diversity and human development. In T. Slaughter (Ed.), *Black children and poverty: A developmental perspective* (pp. 11–27). San Francisco: Jossey-Bass.

Orfield, G. (1992). Money, equity, and college access. *Harvard Educational Review, 62*(3), 337–371.

Orfield, G., Mitzel, H., Austin, T., Bentley, R., Bice, D., Dwyer, M., Gidlow, L., Herschensohn, J., Hibino, B., Kelly, T., Kuhns, A., Lee, M., Rabinowitz, C., Spoerl, J., Vosnos, A., & Wolf, J. (1984). *The Chicago study of access and choice in higher education* (Report prepared for the Illinois Senate Committee on Higher Education). Chicago: Illinois Senate Committee.

Pelavin, S. H., & Kane, M. (1990). *Changing the odds: Factors increasing access to college.* New York: College Entrance Examination Board.

Schultz, T. W. (1961). Investment in human capital. *American Economic Review, 51,* 1–17.

Simms, M. (1995, July). The place to be: Washington. *Black Enterprise,* 24.

Stage, F., & Hossler, D. (1989). Differences in family influences on college attendance plans for male and female ninth graders. *Research in Higher Education, 30*(3), 301–315.

St. John, E. P. (1991). What really influences minority attendance?: Sequential analyses of the high school and beyond sophomore cohort. *Research in Higher Education, 32*(2), 141–158.

Thomas, G. E. (1980). Race and Sex differences and similarities in the process of college entry. *Higher Education, 9,* 179–202.

Thurow, L. C. (1972). Education and economic equality. *Public Interest, 28,* 66–81.

Wilson, K. R., & Allen, W. R. (1987). Explaining the educational attainment of young Black adults: Critical familial and extra-familial influences. *Journal of Negro Education, 56*(1), 64–76.

14

Higher Education and Teacher Preparation: Meeting the Challenges and Demands for Academic Success of Urban Youth

Clancie M. Wilson

Neither teacher preparation nor parental support is a panacea that will solve all the problems plaguing the school performance of economically disadvantaged urban youth. Research has indicated many factors influencing student success in school, for example, economic and social changes (Wilson, 1987); medical care, prior teaching, cultural differences, and environmental circumstances (Davies, 1989); lack of human resources (Slaughter, 1988); and racism and discrimination (Spencer, 1990). Yet, in most instances, policymakers and the public assign responsibility for student academic performance to teachers and parents. Davies (1991) reports that schools and families alone cannot solve the problem of educating the poor. He suggests that education should be a joint effort between schools, families, and the community. The importance of collaboration between home, school, and family also prevails in Dryfoos' (1994) account of familial needs. She contends that many children enter school with social, emotional, and health handicaps that impede school success.

Since teachers and parents, in essence, are viewed as the primary educational providers, this chapter examines several issues related to teacher preparation and the academic success of African American students. First, this chapter focuses on isolation as an environmental condition in the lives of urban youth, particularly African Americans. Second, youth in their social context are discussed in terms of Bronfenbrenner's (1979) ecological model. Third, implications of the educational needs of urban youth are addressed. Finally, successful educational models for urban youth will be specified.

The purpose of this chapter is not to lay blame or to infer that the problems confronting urban youth rest solely with higher education programs for teacher preparation for grades K-12. However, encouraging the examination by teachers of the students in their everyday environmental context could heighten their life chances as these students progress through school. This approach is particularly relevant and viable in light of numerous school reform failures for this population. Repeatedly, traditional methods used by schools to heighten academic performance for at-risk urban youth have failed. Consider Dryfoos' (1994) enlightening remarks that closely resemble previously held positions of "separate and unequal schools." She posits that some school systems hold dual expectations for academic attainment by their student population. For example, students living in more affluent, stable communities have access to more resources, and teachers' expectations are higher, while disadvantaged students in less stable communities are provided fewer opportunities to succeed, and teachers' expectations are lower.

Research has repeatedly revealed that a high percentage of teachers are white, middle-class females (Irvine, 1990; Stroddart, 1993; Zeichner, 1992). Stroddart (1993) posits that "these teachers are more likely to teach as they were taught and expect students to learn as they learned" (p. 30). Almost two decades of research have shown that students from cultural backgrounds similar to their teachers tend to perform better academically. The high performance of these students could be due to cultural experiences in the home that tend to mirror those of teachers (Bourdieu, 1977a, 1977b; Bourdieu & Passeron, 1977). In addition, Lareau (1987) alleges that students from middle-class families (regardless of race) advance more readily in public schools. Three decades ago, Deutsch (1967) discussed the economic advantages of school success and the role of culture on disadvantaged youth. He suggests that the school should provide some continuity between the school's culture, which typically mirrors middle-class standards, and the student's differing cultures.

It is highly unlikely that the economic status of urban parents will change in the near future. Consequently, the responsibility of ensuring that economically deprived students are linked, in a manner similar to economically advantaged students, to the culture of the school weighs heavily on teacher preparation programs. How do schools bolster student performance in spite of the fact that teachers and students do not share similar cultural and social backgrounds? Research indicates that the result of differing teaching strategies of schools and of parents will lead to conflict between the two environments (Bronfenbrenner, 1986; Holiday, 1985; Ogbu, 1988). Spencer, Blumenthal, and Richards (1995) suggest that "without specialized training, teachers and child care workers are unlikely to be sensitive to culturally linked learning styles . . . without cultural sensitivity children's behavior will be subjected to misinterpretation" (p. 151). Further, Bronfenbrenner (1986) asserts that conflict in differing teaching styles could inherently interfere with parents augmenting similar interpretations and understandings of school strategies.

ENVIRONMENTAL CONDITIONS: LIVING

Child development is characterized by change. Lerner (1986) defines development as systematic and organized change over time. For many students, particularly disadvantaged urban youth, change can be unsystematic, chaotic, and disorganized. Contributing factors hampering "continuous and organized" development are economic status, parent education level, racism, neighborhood safety, isolation, and lack of resources, to name a few. The literature depicts environmental conditions as a primary deterrent to optimal development of youth (Chase-Lansdale, Wakschlag, & Brooks-Gunn, 1995; Clark, 1983; Dryfoos, 1994; Garbarino, 1982; Ogbu, 1985; Spencer et al., 1995; Wilson, 1987, 1996).

The environmental conditions of disadvantaged youth, exacerbated by unchanged school policies, will most likely impede academic success. Consider Ogbu's (1988) description of cultural formulas for predicting cultural outcomes. He asserts that cultural outcomes—communicative, cognitive, and social-emotional—are culturally approved formulas one needs to perform cultural tasks. For example, he posits that "White middle-class parents stimulate their children to develop the attributes for their high-level, high-paying occupations and other social positions" (p. 17). But he fails to explain how parents living in impoverished conditions, a situation that Wilson (1996) argues has worsened, stimulate the development of their children.

The dearth of empirical research on child-rearing practices of African American families, coupled with Ogbu's (1988) omission of such practices, is disturbing. This lack of divergent research on child-rearing practices suggests that higher education institutions and policymakers adhere only to the practices based on the paradigms of White, middle-class formulas. Teaching students based only on one population's culturally approved formulas will cause teachers to view other cultures as defective (Brice-Heath, 1988). Given the increase of impoverished youth entering school (Chase-Lansdale et al., 1995; Wilson, 1996), higher education institutions must equip teachers with teaching strategies that bring about a more level playing field for all students by providing prospective teachers with techniques that maximize optimum learning for all students. This is not an easy task when considering social, cultural, and economic changes that have further polarized and isolated communities (Wilson, 1996).

Clearly, Ogbu's (1988) explanation provides one reason for the social and psychological adaptation conflicts of impoverished students with standards and values historically embedded in public schools of higher education. Middle-class families, particularly White, middle-class families, are less apt to encounter discontinuous learning than their counterparts from lower socioeconomic families, who must spend an inordinate amount of energy and time trying to subsist on limited funds and resources and must also, in light of other hardships, provide their children with coping mechanisms to persevere in a stressful environment (Slaughter, 1988). In addition, at-risk urban youth must contend with multiple stressful events in their broader community context, such as unemployment, low-wage jobs, economic stress, and isolation. Although these events may only indirectly impact young children, they nonetheless have grave consequences on their life chances. For instance, parents' behavior at home might be related to a job or to being unemployed, which could induce stress as well as influence the parents' network of friends. Other external influences on the developing person might be defined by activities set forth by the school board or other policy-making institutions that allocates resources or laws that impact the well-being of families and children on a daily basis.

Multiple stressful events without mediation are harmful. As pointed out by Rutter (1979), a single stressful event will rarely cause any long-term disorder; however, multiple, chronic stressful events will most likely cause long-term damage for disadvantaged families. Therefore, to extrapolate that environmental conditions are the only hindering factor to children's life chances would be misleading. Nevertheless, the broad effects of environmental conditions, especially isolation (whether self- or circumstantially imposed through policy), are viewed by both previous and contemporary researchers as hampering children's chances. For instance, Cooley (cited in Hartup, 1991) over 100 years ago stated:

> Human nature is not something existing separately in the individual, but a group nature of primary phase of society. It is the nature which is developed and expressed in those simple, face-to-face groups of the family, the playground, and the neighborhood. In the essential similarity of these is to be found the basis, in experience, for similar ideas and sentiments in the human mind. In these, everywhere, human nature comes into existence. Man does not have it at birth; he cannot acquire it except through fellowship, and it decays in isolation. (p. 2)

Isolation is particularly detrimental to families with children in environments characterized by (perceived) aberrant behavior because it limits the pool of role models to individuals within the confines of the cultural milieu. Children need a variety of role models, especially upwardly mobile role models, in order to offset basic, unhealthy, coercive models (Bronfenbrenner, 1979). If children are exposed only to persons modeling unsuccessful characteristics, then, as Wilson (1996) contends, aberrant cultural traits and behavior are more apt to crystallize.

Therefore, having systems in place that would compensate for differences in cultural child-rearing styles from the broader society is vital (Bronfenbrenner, 1979). This is particularly necessary since the academic prowess of children is compared to the standards of White, middle-class children, whose environment is less chaotic and more organized. Further, Bernard (1972) states of earlier teacher practices that "appropriately prepared teachers are first concerned with their pupils' habits of adjustment and then with the acquisition of academic skills" (p. 27). He recognizes that some students cannot or will not learn until inhibiting emotions, social development, and health concerns have been reduced. Thus, family support that can assist in preparing students to better negotiate between, the culture of home and the culture of school is necessary in order to improve their life chances within, as well as between differing cultures and environments.

How do urban parents solicit essential resources or garner necessary support outside their own cultural environment if they are isolated from the broader society? Isolation extends into public school systems in which disadvantaged youth are placed in an environment with little variation among social class. Keep in mind that isolation is not always looked upon negatively. In many urban neighborhoods, isolation is consciously embraced by parents as a protective device against the ill effects of unsafe neighborhoods (Wilson, 1996). However, isolation, for whatever reasons, inhibits bidirectional relationships among differing cultural and class groups.

YOUTH IN SOCIAL CONTEXT

Bronfenbrenner's (1979) human development model provides a systematic account of the importance of a bidirectional relationship. His integrative model depicts a child's development in the immediate environment and the bi-directional relationships among cultures. Additionally, Bronfenbrenner's (1979) ecology of human development model embodies shared responsibilities and influences by each institution in the ecology in order to promote optimum growth and development for children. The ecological model also emphasizes interdependence. Bronfenbrenner (1979) states that "the ecological environment is conceived as a set of nested structures, each inside the next, like a set of Russian dolls. At the innermost level is the immediate setting containing the developing person" (p. 3). One should keep in mind that the development of the child and the nested concept are a scaffolding concept explained in Bronfenbrenner's analyses of the microsystem, mesosystem, exosystem, and macrosystem—often referred to as levels or settings. Transition from one level or setting to another is paramount. It is important to keep in mind that the transition from one setting to another, in many ways, dictates continuous successes in the developing person's life course.

The first level, the immediate inner level for the child, is referred to as the microsystem. This level, although initially limited to the developing child and to the child's well-being, continues to expand into other arenas as the child develops. The onset of this transition, as pointed out by Bronfenbrenner (1979), begins with the child's relationship with the immediate family and extends later to the school, peer group, and religious organization (if applicable). Surveying children in context embodies them in their everyday environment and necessitates that teacher education programs more readily prepare teachers to help students negotiate from their culture to the culture of the broader society—a necessary transition if the perpetuation of middle-class values and standards continues to be the yardstick used to measure students' success. Successful navigation for students from their home cultural context to the cultural context of schools requires bidirectional understanding of both cultures (Delpit, 1995; Holiday, 1985; Ladson-Billings, 1994; Ogbu, 1988).

Garbarino (1982) points out that the macrosystem (encompassing the micro-, meso-, and ecosystems) is the essence of the ecology of human development. The context of parental practices and teaching styles is derived from emulating observed cultural practices. That is, earlier stages of teaching the developing person are based on acquired cultural practices learned by the parent. The ecology of the human development model is a multiperson system of interaction and is not committed to a single setting but rather requires that one take into account aspects of the environment beyond the immediate situation surrounding the person. Consequently, isolation makes it difficult for one to take into account aspects of the environment beyond the immediate situation. Then isolation not only inhibits bidirectional relationships but also obstructs parents in their efforts to identify, ascertain, and utilize available child-rearing resources in similar ways to the broader society. Clearly, children living in isolation coupled with deteriorating social environments enter school laden with additional "baggage." Yet children entering school with these additional constraints are expected to learn in a manner similar to children growing up in a relatively stress-free environment. Spencer (1988) posits that teachers often evaluate student success based on standards that are more predictive for students reared in White, middle-class families, who typically live in a more stress-free environment. Furthermore, Holiday (1985) contends that teaching paradigms typically focus on educating students more homogeneously, often dismissing the students' home and community context.

IMPLICATION OF STUDENT NEEDS: URBAN YOUTH AND LEARNING

Students in urban settings must contend on the primary level with teachers who often would rather not teach in their schools (Zeichner, 1992). They must also contend, upon entering school, with a strange environment that characterizes their language as deficient (Brice-Heath, 1988). These differences between students entering school and teachers who must instruct them often lead to conflict. Conflict between home and school, as Bronfenbrenner (1986) asserts, evokes turmoil in the child's world if there is no alignment with the school world (e.g., language, standards, and values).

Given the differences between the world of the student and the world of the teacher, teacher preparation should incorporate instructional change that prepares teachers to deal more effectively with students from low resource environments. Diversity, although a broad term, has been presented by a preponderance of researchers as a leading factor promoting change in teacher preparation (Cochran-Smith, 1996; Irvine, 1990; Ladson-Billings, 1994; Zeichner, 1992). Furthermore, Spiker (1991) suggests that "training for diversity in the twenty-first century will require graduate training of administrators and teachers to assure that their students have the capacity of inquiry, and the ability to infer from, and probe constructively in, knowledge domains beyond their own specialty areas" (p. 272).

The ineffectiveness of America's schools at all levels has been examined for over 30 years, particularly as it relates to students from low-income families (Clark, 1983; Coleman et al., 1966; Deutsch, 1967; Glasgow, 1980). Deutsch (1967) reports that there is little difference in language and intelligence between Black and White students in 1st grade, but the gap widens in the later grades. Regrettably, little has changed educationally, using traditional school models, for inner-city students. The failure of public schools to provide adequate education for students received its most unflattering remarks during the 1980s. In 1983, the National Commission on Excellence in Education discussed the imperiled state of America's school system. That report, *A Nation at Risk: The Imperative for Education* (1983), warns that "if an unfriendly foreign power had attempted to impose on America the mediocre educational performance that exists today, we might well have viewed it as an act of war" (p. 5).

The deplorable state of America's schools is further conveyed in Wilson's (1987) book *The Truly Disadvantaged.* He states that of 39,500 9th-grade students enrolled in Chicago schools, upon graduation only 6,000 students could read at or above the 12th-grade level, and less than 50% (18,500) completed high school. Of 25,000 students enrolled in predominantly African American or Hispanic low-resource community schools in Chicago, only 2,000 (8%) could read at or above the national average, and 63% of this population did not graduate from high school. The problems of inner-city school failure are not limited to Chicago. Reports show that the school reform movement has been irrelevant to a large number of African Americans and Hispanics in large urban schools (Carnegie Foundation for the Advancement of Teaching, 1988). This report further states that "the failure to educate adequately urban youth is a shortcoming of such magnitude that many people have simply written off city schools as little more than human storehouses to keep young people off the streets" (p. xi).

Again, three decades of writing have pointed out the educational inequalities existing between the middle class and the poor. Yet even with policymakers' aggressively promoting school reform as a corrective device that would benefit all students and provide them with comparable skills, inequality still exists. Schools, in response to identified public school inequities, introduced changes in their day-to-day operations (e.g., teacher testing, student testing, teaching models, and competency testing). However, these changes have had little impact on improving the school performance of inner-city youth. More recently, full-service school programs that attend to the needs of parents and their children more holistically have generated a lot of enthusiasm as a means for improving school performance of disadvantage urban youth (Coleman, 1991; Dryfoos, 1994; Levin, 1988).

SUCCESSFUL EDUCATIONAL MODELS FOR URBAN YOUTH

Customarily, teacher preparation programs prepare teachers to more effectively enhance the academic success of students if they are (1) healthy when entering school, (2) from secure neighborhoods where parents have adequate resources, and (3) youth who usually receive developmental stimulation in the home (see Dryfoos, 1994; Holiday, 1995; Lansdale & Brooks-Gunn 1995; Ogbu, 1988; Spencer, 1990). At-risk youth, in contrast, come from environments that are often dangerous, have fewer resources, and have lower levels of social support. Yet when high-resource and low-resource students enter school, these environmental conditions are discounted and used to label or condemn rather than used to develop individual plans for low-resource students that would enhance their learning experiences so they would be enabled to reach and sustain a learning threshold congruent with that of high-resource students.

Because of the enormous issues impeding the development of urban youth, teacher preparation programs that fail to provide a link between the home and community will not provide adequate learning opportunities. More explicitly, Coleman (1991) notes that social support will provide strength for parents and children to draw upon during difficult times, such as when encountering emotional or financial hardship or problems with schoolwork, teachers, or peers. Social support has also been proposed by Spencer (1990) to be a useful community intervention strategy for African American and Hispanic American youth living in poverty. For example, Comer's (1988) "reach out model," which emphasizes a team approach, encompassing teachers, specialists, parents, and community, has been reported as successful in improving inner-city youths' school performance. Another reportedly successful model linked to improving inner-city student school performance is Levin's (1988) "accelerated model." The intent of this model is to hasten at-risk children's learning prior to leaving elementary school. This model also advocates involving parents, teachers, and the community in the child's learning. Moreover, Dryfoos (1994) points out that full-service programs are able to provide services that will enhance at-risk children's life chances and reduce stressful events in the lives of disadvantaged families.

Dalin (1993) concluded that teaching that excludes linkages between the home and community will not provide adequate learning. In turn, Delpit (1988) more forcefully asserts that creating good teaching models that do not take into account the students' context is an impossibility. Without preparing teachers to put "self" aside in assessing students' needs in context, regardless of the number of successful academic models proposed, urban youth will still be at risk. Ultimately, the teachers are left with the task of observing each student without making judgments through the filters of their own culture. Kohl (1994) fittingly argues: "Central to what you see in someone is what you are looking for. If you want to find a child's weaknesses, failures, personal problems, or inadequacies, you'll discover them. If you look at a child and make judgments through the filters of your own cultural, gender and racial biases, you'll find characteristics you expect." (p. 44)

CONCLUSIONS AND IMPLICATIONS

Teachers, after leaving higher learning institutions, must make decisions that impact the lives of their students. Ultimately, their preconceived beliefs drive the way they interact with their students. It is imperative that teacher preparation programs prepare teachers to teach more effectively in multicultural situations, that is, to examine their students in the nested settings described by Bronfenbrenner. Since, as previously pointed out, students enter school from different environmental settings, a plethora of teaching styles is required in order to meet the emotional, cognitive, and social needs of diverse students.

Improving the life chances of students entering schools from more stressful neighborhoods is more complex, and rightly so, as these students enter school with additional baggage. However, that does not mean that they are incapable of learning; some successful urban school programs have discouraged such thinking. Providing continuous learning for this population means understanding how to make appropriate, abrupt pedagogy shifts that promote viable, sustained learning.

Over the past years, policymakers and practitioners have acknowledged the deterioration of America's public schools, especially inner-city schools in indigent neighborhoods. However, seeking viable solutions that would benefit all students has been difficult, even in the past, when conditions were less complex for students. Yet under the most depressed school situations, some program models have succeeded in improving school performance of urban students. Generally, program models that emphasize a collaborative approach that integrates the services of parents, community, and teachers report more sustained school success for urban youth.

Finally, higher education institutions must prepare prospective teachers to better utilize parents, family, and community support services. This merger is paramount in view of the economic and social changes confronting teachers today. Not only will community supporters serve as a buffer for stressful life events, but they could be relied on to mediate differences between the teachers' and their students' cultures. Moreover, such supporters, if they understand the cultural environment of urban youth as well as the culture of the schools, can be critical in helping teachers create learning strategies for students based on the everyday context of their lives.

REFERENCES

Bernard, H. W. (1972). *Psychology of learning and teaching* (3rd ed.). New York: McGraw-Hill.

Bourdieu, P. (1977a). Cultural reproduction and social reproduction. In J. Karabel & A. H. Halsey (Eds.), *Power and ideology in education* (pp. 487–511). London: Routledge and Kegan Paul.

Bourdieu, P. (1977b). *Outline of a theory of practice.* New York: Oxford University Press.

Bourdieu, P., & Passeron, J. C. (1977). *Reproduction in education, society and culture.* Beverly Hills, CA: Sage.

Brice-Heath, S. (1988). Language socialization. In D. T. Slaughter (Ed.), *Black children and poverty: A developmental perspective* (pp. 29–58). San Francisco: Jossey-Bass.

Bronfenbrenner, U. (1979). *The ecology of human development.* Cambridge, MA: Harvard University Press.

Bronfenbrenner, U. (1986). Alienation: And the four worlds of childhood. *Phi Delta Kappan, 67,* 430–435.

Carnegie Foundation for the Advancement of Teaching. (1988). *An imperiled generation: Saving urban schools.* Princeton: Author.

Chase-Lansdale, P. L., Wakschlag, L. S., & Brooks-Gunn, J. (Eds.). (1995). *Escape from poverty: What makes a difference for children.* New York: Cambridge University Press.

Clark, R. (1983). *Family life and school achievement: Why poor Black children succeed or fail.* Chicago: The University of Chicago Press.

Cochran-Smith, M. (in press). Teaching for social change. In A. Hargreaves, A. Lieberman, M. Fullan, & D. Hopkins (Eds.), *The international handbook of educational change.* Amsterdam, Netherlands: Kluwer.

Coleman, J. S. (1991). *Policy perspectives: Parental involvement in education.* Washington, DC: U.S. Government Printing Office.

Coleman, J. S., Campbell, E. Q., Hobson, C. J., McPartland, I., Mood, A. M., Weinfeld, F. D., & York, R. L. (1966). *Equality of educational opportunity.* Washington, DC: U.S. Government Printing Office.

Comer, J. (1988). Educating poor minority children. *Scientific American, 259*(5), 42–48.

Cooley, C. H. (1909). *Social organization.* New York: Scribner's.

Dalin, P. (1993). *Changing the school culture.* Cassell: Imtec Foundation.

Davies, D. (1989). *Poor parents, teachers, and the schools: Comments about practice, policy, and research.* San Francisco: America Educational Research Association. (ERIC Document Reproduction Service No. Ed 308 574)

Davis, D. (1991). School reaching out: Family, school, and community partnerships for student success. *Phi Delta Kappan, 72*(3), 376–382.

Delpit, L. D. (1988). The silenced dialogue: Power and pedagogy in educating other people's children. *Harvard Educational Review, 58*(3), 280–298.

Delpit, L. D. (1995). *Other people's children.* New York: New Press.

Deutsch, M. (Ed). (1967). *The disadvantaged child and the learning process.* New York: Basic Books.

Dryfoos, J. (1994). *Full-service schools: A revolution in health and social service of children, youth and families.* San Francisco: Jossey-Bass.

Garbarino, J. (1982). *Children and families in the social environment.* New York: Aldine.

Glasgow, D. G. (1980). *The Black underclass: Poverty, unemployment, and entrapment of ghetto youth.* San Francisco: Jossey-Bass.

Hartup, W. W. (1991). Social development and social psychology: Perspectives on interpersonal relationships. In J. H. Cantor, C. C. Spiker, & L. P. Lipsitt (Eds.), *Child behavior and development: Training for diversity* (pp. 1–33). Norwood, NJ: Ablex.

Holiday, B. G. (1985). Towards a model of teacher-transactional processes affecting Black children's academic achievement. In B. Spencer, G. K. Brookins, & W. R. Allen (Eds.), *Beginnings: The social and affective development of Black children* (pp. 117–130). Hillsdale, NJ: Erlbaum.

Irvine, J. J. (1990). *A cultural responsiveness in teacher education curriculum.* Paper presented at the National Symposium of the American Association of Colleges of Teacher Education. Tampa, FL.

Kohl, H. (1994). *I won't learn from you.* New York: New Press.

Ladson-Billings, G. (1994). *The dreamkeepers: Successful teachers of African American children.* San Francisco: Jossey-Bass.

Lareau, A. (1987, April). The importance of cultural capital. *Journal of Sociology of Education, 60,* 73–85.

Lerner, R. M. (1986). *Concepts and theories of human development.* (2nd ed.). New York: McGraw-Hill.

Levin, H. M. (1988). *Structuring schools for greater effectiveness with educationally disadvantaged or at-risk students.* New Orleans: LA. Paper presented at the Annual Meeting of the American Educational Research Association. ERIC Document Reproduction Service No. ED 300 923.

National Commission on Excellence in Education. (1983). *Nation at risk: The imperative for educational reform.* Washington, DC: U.S. Department of Education.

Ogbu, J. U. (1985). A cultural ecology of competence among inner-city Blacks. In M. B. Spencer, G. K. Brookins, & W. R. Allen (Eds.), *Beginnings: The social and affective development of Black children* (pp. 45–66). Hillsdale, NJ: Erlbaum.

Ogbu, J. U. (1988). Cultural diversity and human development. In T. Slaughter (Ed.), *Black children and poverty: A developmental perspective* (pp. 11–27). San Francisco: Jossey-Bass.

Rutter, M. (1979). Maternal deprivation, 1972–1978: New findings, new concepts, new approaches. *Child Development, 50,* 283–305.

Slaughter, D. (1988). Black children schooling, and educational interventions. In T. Slaughter (Ed.), *Black children and poverty: A developmental perspective* (pp. 109–116). San Francisco: Jossey-Bass.

Spencer, M. B. (1988). Self-concept development. In T. Slaughter (Ed.), *Black children and poverty: A developmental perspective* (pp. 59–72). San Francisco: Jossey-Bass.

Spencer, M. B. (1990). Parental value transmission: Implications for Black child development. In J. B. Stewart & H. Cheatham (Eds.), *Interdisciplinary perspectives on Black families* (pp. 111–130). Atlanta: Transaction.

Spencer, M. B., Blumenthal, J. B., & Richards, E. (1995). Child care and children of color. In P. L. Chase-Lansdale & J. Brooks-Gunn (Eds.), *Escape from poverty: What makes a difference for children* (pp. 138–156). New York: Cambridge University Press.

Spiker, C. C. (1991). Designing a graduate training curriculum to meet the challenges of a nonacademic career. In J. H. Cantor, C. C. Spiker, & L. P. Lipsitt (Eds.), *Child behavior and development: Training for diversity* (pp. 73–113). Norwood, NJ: Ablex.

Stoddart, T. (1993). Who is prepared to teach in urban schools? *Education and Urban Society, 26*(1), 29–48.

Wilson, W. J. (1987). *The truly disadvantaged: The inner city, the under class, and policy.* Chicago: University of Chicago Press.

Wilson, W. J. (1996). *When work disappears: The world of the new urban poor.* New York: Alfred A. Knopf.

Zeichner, K. M. (1992). *Educating teachers for cultural diversity.* East Lansing: Michigan State University, College of Education, National Center for Research on Teacher Learning.

Higher Education Policies and Professional Education in American Black Colleges

Beverly Lindsay

When I was a doctoral student about 20 years ago, I closely examined the phenomenon of progressive education in American Black colleges and published one of my first refereed articles entitled, "Progressive Education and The Black College" (Lindsay & Harris, 1977). Since that time, in the mid-1970s, I have continued to examine the particular roles and contributions of American historically Black colleges and universities (HBCUs), which were largely creations after the conclusion of the American Civil War in the 1860s. Although a few HBCUs such as Lincoln University in Pennsylvania trace their origins prior to the 1860s, most began as secondary schools or teacher training institutions to provide education for former slaves. With few exceptions, the approximately 100 HBCUs are situated in the southern states ranging from border states such as Maryland and Kentucky, to those along the Atlantic seaboard, to the Gulf of Mexico, reaching Texas. Located in the geographical areas where over one-half of African Americans reside, the doors of HBCUs have constantly been open to all demographic groups.

This chapter focuses on the critical interactive linkages between higher education policies and the preparation of educators at specific American HBCUs. What I articulate are pivotal phenomena that portray the contemporary unique contributions of HBCUs to American higher education, while simultaneously responding to comprehensive state and national postsecondary policies and standards. These external policies influence internal institutional policies, which, in turn, impact external policies. In short, illuminating interactive nexuses is the conceptual underpinning of this chapter. Integral to my concluding discussion is the increasing importance of international matters.

DEFINITIONS AND CONCEPTUAL PERSPECTIVES OF POLICIES

Kearney (1996), Bond (1996), and Ginsburg and Lindsay (1995) explore the multiple levels of analyses in viewing public and educational policies that affect the preparation of professional educators. Concentration on macro-, intermediate, and microlevel policies is central to the comprehension of the dynamic interactions between external entities and higher education institutions. Macrolevel policies essentially focus on international, national, and state-level matters. Such policies may be in the form of laws, court decisions, official documents, executive orders, and the like. That is, comprehensive executive, legislative, and judicial actions—de jure or formal decisions—often serve as the foundation for public policies that are often influenced by economic and fiscal considerations (Klein, 1987; Lindsay, 1994). While policies at the macrolevel may originally refer to one set of principles, they uphold and affect principles at other levels.

Intermediate-level policies (Lindsay, in press) may be in effect at the state or regional level with specific applicability to particular institutions or types of situations. They are often the transitional connection or coupling between broad principles or directives and what should occur in a specific institutional or educational setting. For example, a major unit within a board of trustees or regents may develop lenient policies (and subsequent programs) to ensure that higher admission criteria are used throughout public universities within the state. Policies may be formal de jure or informal de facto ones, although the latter can have the effect of formal pronouncements. Microlevel policies are based on *individual* systems interests. The salience of local cultural ethos and norms is evident in microlevel de facto policies that are deemed beneficial to local institutions (Ginsburg & Lindsay, 1995).

While there is an interactive relationship among macro-, intermediate, and microlevel policies, there are also contradictions and tensions among the levels. Ensuring a comprehensive global or macroperspective may be perceived as being at odds with microlevel policies, which are grounded in local communities and their cultures. What appears to be democratic and equitable at the macrolevel may be viewed as imposing control at the microlevel. Yet, an increasing emphasis is being placed presently on international education policy and how it is a vital component of domestic higher educational policy. In the past, the focus of national differences made devoid the science of education from the multitude of voices from within countries. Comparative research could now focus on cultural diversity and pluralism rather than individual differentiation and on social integration rather than primarily political and economic homogenization (McGinn, 1996, p. 342). Here the association between global, macro-, intermediate, and microlevel policies becomes apparent. As stated in Lindsay (1989): "The atmosphere for mutual understanding, desired by all audiences, can be created through open and probing discussions of common educational and cultural problems in the United States and other nations" (p. 436).

These issues are national in scope, as universities are changing to meet new demands of the emerging era of technology and knowledge transfer within a shrinking global economy. Lewis and Altbach (1996) discuss the changes: "There is a near universal trend toward more emphasis on teaching, demands that faculty members account for their activities with assessment as a means of measuring the effectiveness of academic effort, and a growing societal unease with traditional ideas of university autonomy" (p. 258). Policymakers are regarding academic institutions as large undertakings needing newer forms of management being applied to other economic sectors.

With this background in mind, I now turn to some descriptive statistical information regarding the earning of degrees by African Americans and the missions and purposes of American HBCUs.

THE PORTRAITS AND SOCIOCULTURAL TRENDS

From an historical period to the contemporary era, African Americans have consistently earned more degrees in education than in any other profession. Prior to the 1960s, earning degrees in teaching and other education professions afforded one of the few viable professional opportunities for African Americans during formal segregation. Only in the 1954 Supreme Court decision *Brown v. the Board of Education* (347 U.S. 483, 74 S.Ct. 686, 98 l.Ed. 873 [1954]) did segregation begin to crumble in schools and other institutions. Moreover, the overwhelming majority of all baccalaureate degrees earned by Blacks were earned in HBCUs. As recently as 1981, these tertiary institutions produced about 48% of the Black teachers in the United States. While they represent about 8% of the nation's colleges and universities and their enrollments have declined, they have been credited with furnishing about two-thirds of Black teachers (Garibaldi, 1989). In the fall of 1993, approximately 217,462 full-time students were enrolled in HBCUs, which produced about 31,937 bachelor's, master's, doctoral, and first professional degrees (NCES, 1995a).

Although African American enrollments have shifted to predominantly White universities (PWIs) and students have the opportunity to major in a myriad of fields, education was the third highest area where baccalaureate degrees were earned in 1992–93 (the last year when comprehensive national data were available). Of the 77,872 degrees awarded in 1992–93: 19,187 were granted in business, 9,964 in social sciences and history, and 5,590 in education. Approximately 34% (26,140) of the baccalaureate degrees were awarded at HBCUs, where African Americans usually constitute over 90% of the matriculates. These same patterns no longer prevailed at the master's level, where 19,780 degrees were earned: 6,725 in education, 4,474 in business administration, and 2,271 in public administration and the sciences. Of the master's degrees earned, about 23% (or 4,612) were awarded at HBCUs. At the doctoral level, of the 1,352 earned by Blacks, the largest number was also in education for a total of 552, compared to 134 in psychology, 91 in social sciences and history, and 66 in health professions and the sciences. Since only a handful of Black universities offered the doctorate degree, only 16% (219) were earned at HBCUs (National Center for Educational Statistics, 1994, 1995a).

Given the shifting enrollments in HBCUs, particularly at the postbaccalaureate level, where often over 50% of the enrollees are European Americans, and the presence of judicial policies requiring the elimination of segregated institutions, a critical challenge for many HBCUs is to determine and articulate their fundamental missions. Underlying this challenge is the desire to maintain and enhance their cultural ethos, which has focused on Americans of African descent, yet be responsive to demographic and political trends emerging in the local, state, regional, national, and international arenas. In essence, the question is: What macro-, intermediate, and microlevel policy formulation and subsequent program implementation need to emerge, as well as continue, especially with reference to the preparation of professional educators?

A succinct explication of national, state, and institutional sociopolitical, economic, and demographic trends is warranted. In the early 1980s, with the advent of the presidential administration of Ronald Reagan, a series of contemporary national educational reforms began that would permeate much of the formal primary and secondary and tertiary education system. Perhaps the best known of these was the work of the president's National Commission on Excellence in Education, which produced the document *A Nation at Risk* (U.S. Department of Education, 1983). A rising tide of mediocrity that ostensibly threatened America as a nation was a central contention. In the mid-1980s, the Holmes Group was organized by education deans at major research universities. Preparing teachers, public schools, and colleges and schools of education for the twenty-first century was an overarching concern of several reports issued by the Holmes Group, which was headquartered at Michigan State University. While the federal government and higher education institutions were focusing on educational matters, corporate leaders and state governors and legislators were turning their attention to education, most often because the need for a well-prepared workforce pervaded their actions regarding education at various levels (Garibaldi, 1989). While an intense focus on education was not a new phenomenon, the shifting political currents evinced in the post-Cold War era and fluctuating national and international economic relations among nations accentuated the role of education in the social and political development of nations.

Simultaneous to the aforementioned were the tremendous demographic changes witnessed by migrations to the United States of people of color from Latin America, Asia, the Caribbean, and Africa and the increasing number of young people of color, including indigenous Native Americans and African Americans, who are under the age of 30. Of special concern to some public policy-makers and legislators was the reality that in 1994, slightly less than two-thirds of elementary and high school enrollment comprised White, non-Hispanic students, compared to slightly more than three-fourths 20 years earlier. Between 1974 and 1994, Black students rose from 14.4% to 16.3% of all elementary and high school enrollment, and students of other races from 1.6% to 5.2%. Hispanic students rose from 6.3% to 13.0% of all elementary and high school students. Total minority enrollment (persons other than White, non-Hispanic) rose from 22.3% to 34.5% of all students (Bruno & Curry 1996, p. x). More than one-third of students were Hispanic in California, New Mexico, and Texas; while over half of the students were Black, non-Hispanic in the District of Columbia and Mississippi. Additionally, White, non-Hispanic students constitute less than one-half of the student population in six states (NCES, 1995b, p. 3). This increase in the percentage of minority students represents who will be the largest entrants to the workforce at the dawn of the twenty-first century. For educators, increasingly different demographic patterns require the integral inclusion of teaching styles, curriculum, evaluation, assessment, and accountability in the educational structure.

In light of the historical missions of HBCUs and contemporary social trends, I perceived the necessity to examine closely the interactive nexuses among higher education policies, the preparation of educators, and the roles of HBCUs.

THE METHODOLOGY

To ascertain the relationship among policies and the preparation of educators (most often in-service or preservice teachers) in HBCUs, I undertook qualitative research with four HBCUs. The institutions were selected in light of the following criteria. Geographical locations included one in a border state; a second located in the "New South" (an area deemed to be more progressive than other regions of the South); a third situated in what is termed the "Deep South," which is still relatively entrenched in conservative, sociopolitical, and cultural millieux; and the fourth, a historically significant site located in a northeastern area. The institutions were also selected on the basis of public and private, coeducational and single-sex. One institution focuses exclusively on undergraduate education; another is a comprehensive university offering baccalaureate, and post-baccalaureate study at the master's level and other special programs; a third is a comprehensive doctoral university; while the fourth is a state institution offering programs in multiple off-campus sites. In the selection process, it was also discovered that the comprehensive private university operates a professional laboratory school that focuses on early childhood and elementary education.

To ensure anonymity, the four institutions are given the fictional names of Chapel University (with a professional education faculty that is approximately 80% African American and 20% European American), Bridge College (whose education faculty is all African American), Adams University (whose faculty is about 84% African American, 13% European Americans, and 3% other demographic groups), and Original University (with a faculty that is 80% European American and 20% African American).[1] I spent extensive periods ranging from several days per visit to several months at Bridge College, Original University, and Chapel University. Thus, a series of in-depth participant observations occurred at these institutions, including classroom observations; interactions in meetings and other formal settings with faculty, students, administrators; and interviews with faculty, vice presidents, and presidents. Although I did not visit Adams University, I knew various professionals at the institution via their administrative roles, involvement with professional associations, and scholarly reputations and, therefore, was able to interview them, which aided me in the collection of necessary data.

In order to examine comparable issues among the four institutions, semistructured interviews were held with the deans or heads of the professional education preparation unit, whether a school or department. The dean of liberal arts and education and the department head of education were interviewed at Chapel University. The dean of the College of Education and the director of professional field services were interviewed at Adams University. At Bridge College and Original University, the department of education chairs were interviewed. The interview questions included the following:

1. What is the institutional mission statement? What is unique about this mission at your institution?
2. What are your institutional goals? What is unique about these as an HBCU?
3. What particular higher education policies influence your professional education programs (institutional level, state level, regional level, national level, international level)?
4. What do you identify as continuing policy issues?
5. What do you identify as emerging policy issues?
6. Does your education program have particular goals or missions pertaining to school reform via your professional preparation programs? What are they? How are they evaluated?
7. Do preservice and in-service educators have direct involvement in community activities, other than those associated with professional education preparation?
8. Are there specific methods that your institution initiates to help educators address social inequities that educators will encounter in schools and classrooms?
9. Are the resources (e.g., fiscal/human/other) adequate to meet your program and institutional goals?
10. What are the most critical features in your preservice programs?
11. What are the most critical features in your in-service programs?
12. What percentage of your education students were African American in 1990 and again in 1995?
13. What percentage of students were of other ethnically diverse groups in 1990 and again in 1995?
14. What is the demographic profile of your education faculty?
15. What was the number of students in 1990 and 1995 who graduated with bachelor's, master's, and doctoral degrees?
16. What percent of your graduates passed:
    State Examinations in 1990—1st time, 2nd time, 3rd time
    State Examinations in 1995—1st time, 2nd time, 3rd time
    National Examinations in 1990—1st time, 2nd time, 3d time
    National Examinations in 1995—1st time, 2nd time, 3d time
17. Are there initial criteria that students must meet before entering professional preparation programs at undergraduate, master's, and/or doctoral levels?

18. Are there other comments or remarks that you wish to make?

In addition to the aforementioned methodologies, information regarding policies, goals, and missions was collected from each institution's catalog and strategic plan.

THE THEMATIC MOTIFS

Institutional Missions and Goal

An examination of the formal mission statement of Chapel University, a select private comprehensive university, as articulated in the strategic plan and catalogs and often voiced by the president and other executives, asserts that Chapel is dedicated to the:

> promotion of learning, the building of character, and preparation of promising students for *professional positions of leadership and service* [italics added]. Its curricular emphasis is scientific and professional with a strong liberal arts under-girding. An historically Black institution, the University is also committed to multiculturalism. Chapel serves students from diverse nations, cultural, educational, and economic backgrounds. From its beginnings to the present, the institution has enrolled students from five continents. . . . Placing its students at the center of its planning, the University provides a holistic educational environment. Learning is facilitated by a range of educational offerings . . . multiple leadership and service opportunities, along with the development of character which values respect, dignity, integrity, and decency. Research and public service are integral parts of the University's mission.

While viewing itself as a contemporary, preeminent academic institution, there is also the recognition that there is a historical and current mission of service "to uplift our people" and give back to the community via concrete programs and activities. "As we had strong tall shoulders to stand on, we must also provide strong shoulders for the community and future African Americans." The words of Booker T. Washington were often evoked in faculty and administrative meetings and in numerous student settings.

University-wide policies reflect the mission statement and the traditions of Booker T. Washington and the first president of the institution. Articulating and disseminating the mission statement and eight vision statements—ranging from an interdisciplinary and multicultural curriculum, to active research by faculty and students, to adhering to a code of conduct, to administering efficiently and effectively all business services and enrollment management, to strengthening technological capabilities—were designed to produce unique institutional goals at an HBCU.

Expanding the definition of multiculturalism to include international components, Chapel University has, from its beginning, enrolled students from five continents and from diverse nations such as Cherokee and Sioux nations; Gabon, Kenya, and Ghana; Japan and the People's Republic of China; Armenia, England, and Russia.

At Bridge College, a private HBCU for women, the mission is to strive for academic excellence in liberal education and to encourage students to think critically, logically, and creatively so they are prepared for graduate and professional study and entry into the workforce by developing the total person via an academic and social environment that enables women to become self-confident and culturally and spiritually enriched. An appreciation for the multicultural communities of the world is part of the cultural enrichment. Expounding the mission occurs via 14 goals largely centered around intellectual development, preparation for graduate or professional school and the workforce, and personal development. Dedicating itself to the development of Black women makes this institution one of a handful of such colleges. As a historically Black college for women, Bridge attempts to create an environment that produces an appreciation in its students for the multicultural communities of the world in which they find themselves, as well as instill a sense of responsibility for bringing about positive changes in that world.

Although founded as a private seminary "for the moral, religious and intellectual improvement of Christian leaders of the colored people of [the particular state] and the neighboring states," Adams University's mission no longer emphasizes religious dimensions, especially since it is a public university funded by the state. It quotes its current mission in its 1995–96 catalog as:

> to develop persons who can and will assume prominent roles in the dynamics of societal growth and change. For this purpose, resources of the University are applied to the discovery, transmittal, and preservation of knowledge. The University is pledged to the *advancement of a free society and the continued progress of democracy* [italics added]. The major task . . . is to guide students in acquiring the knowledge and developing the skills, understandings, appreciations, and attitudes which are essential to general, liberal, and professional education . . . to initiate careers, and to contribute to the social, cultural, and economic development of the state, nation and world.

Since Adams University is located in a metropolitan area with comprehensive programs at the undergraduate, master's, and doctoral levels, a key feature of its mission is to address urban sociocultural, economic, and educational problems. Moreover, the designation by the legislature and the board of trustees as the urban university of the state further guides the development of goals to address complex urban problems and to propose solutions. Its historical origins as a Black institution and the predominant presence of African Americans and other minorities in the metropolitan area connote an ongoing concern with multiple demographic concerns emerging from racial, ethnic, economic, and social matters. Adams proposes to enable students to contribute to the social, cultural, and economic development of the state, nation, and the world.

Founded in 1854, in the midst of slavery, as stated in its 1993–94 catalog, Original University's motto is: "If the son shall make you free, ye shall be free indeed." It recognizes three distinct, historically placed purposes: (1) to teach honestly without fear of censure what has painfully and persistently been learned regarding the environment and its people; (2) to preserve the knowledge for future generations; and (3) to increase and add to this wealth of knowledge. Original seeks to prepare its students for the demands of the twenty-first century by providing a liberal arts education with a specialized field of study. This curricular approach is combined with experience with technological skills as well as interpersonal skills such as adaptability to change, achievement motivation, and exploration of values in order to benefit society. From these premises, Original University is dedicated to achieving the following in each of its students:

1. Cultivate the inquiring and critical mind capable of discerning the emotional, logical, and quantitative implications of persuasive discourse and of pursuing truth and meaning as a capstone of the human experience.
2. Develop appreciation of the scientific methods and of the significance of science and technology in modern society.
3. Nourish sensitivity to the artistic and philosophical values of the humanities.
4. Promote an understanding of contemporary societies and cultures which is rooted in an appreciation of the past and which inspires a vision of the future.
5. Qualify the student for successful graduate or professional study.
6. Develop a healthy and balanced perspective on personal as well as professional relationships, and on the value of leisure as well as work.

The professionals interviewed at Original University stated that *Blueprint 2000,* outlines the strategies that will help to accomplish several university-wide goals. These include (1) increasing student enrollment in math and science majors to one-third of the total population of students, (2) having 33% of the population proficient in a second language with a long-range goal of 75%, (3) increasing opportunity and involvement in study-abroad programs, with an institutional goal of 50% of the population actually studying abroad, (4) providing clear demonstration of computer literacy in respective fields of study, and (5) providing leadership to encourage global involvement in business, as well as entrepreneurships.

The international mission statement of Original University, as stated in its catalog, explicitly declares: "[T]he University endeavors to . . . promote an understanding of contemporary societies and cultures which is rooted in an appreciation of the past and which inspires a vision of the future." Original presently sponsors several international programs, including Language House, study-abroad programs, Crossroads Africa, and overseas internships.

The underlying themes of leadership, service, and commitment to multicultural phenomena in the local, regional, national, and international arenas appear to permeate the missions of the four institutions. Hence, their historical and contemporary missions appear congruous: *they wish to enhance democracy at the macro-, intermediate, and microlevels.*

The Interplay between External and Internal Policies for Preparing Educators

All four universities immediately emphasized the salience of external national, regional, and state accreditation agencies in adequately preparing their students for roles as professional educators. Meeting the requirements of the National Council for the Accreditation of Teacher Education (NCATE) was the overarching accrediting concern. Without the NCATE stamp of approval, state and some regional bodies would not recognize an institution's education program or its graduates. The Southern Association for Colleges and Schools (SACS) is the regional accrediting body for Chapel, Adams, and Bridge, while the Middle States Association of Colleges and Schools (MSACS) sets the criteria for Original. Continuing and emerging policy issues arising from accrediting agencies, particularly from NCATE, were of paramount concern. In some instances, the deans and other executives working in professional education preparation were involved in national and state or regional matters pertaining to education. Thus, they believed that their input enabled them to influence external policies affecting their education units. In other instances, there was relatively little involvement, especially for one professional who had recently assumed her role.

Student performance on standardized examinations, such as the National Teacher Examination, was a continuing policy concern at Adams, the public university, since the results help determine funding and resource allocations for the education unit. While this has been an ongoing concern, Adams students, in fact, have performed quite well on state and national examinations. In 1995 and 1990, about 90% of the students passed the state entrance examination for those entering the teaching profession. Another 5% passed on the second attempt, and an additional 4% passed by the third attempt. Thus, virtually all graduates from the programs have successfully completed the state examination. At Bridge College, about 99% of the students passed on the first attempt, while others passed the second time. The state where Chapel University is located does not require a state examination. Notable improvements occurred on the pass rates between 1990 and 1995 on national examinations. At Adams University, about 60% passed the first time in 1990; by 1995 about 83% passed the first time. By the second try, in both 1990 and 1995, a total 90% had passed if they obtained assistance such as tutoring or examination review. At Chapel University about 80% passed national examinations on the first attempt in 1990; this percentage increased to 97% by 1995. Also at Chapel, an additional 15% passed on the second attempt in 1990, ensuring the pass rates evinced in 1995 in a continuous programmatic thrust, which reflects state and national macrolevel policies. The professionals interviewed at Original University reported that the education students are proud to declare "a perfect record" regarding both the state and national examinations in 1995. Original students benefit immensely from a course entitled Survival in the Testing World, designed to prepare them for the test.

Adams, a public university, is located in a state where two major judicial decisions helped determine the foci of the institution. The *Adams* decision required the elimination of dual systems of public higher education and the *Ayers v. Fordice* (111 F.3d 1183 [5th Cir. 1997]) case, filed by a Black farmer, requested that inequitable funding and facilities be eliminated between HBCUs and PWIs. In the early 1990s, the judge in the *Adams* case essentially stated that many vestiges of segregation had been eliminated in the states with dual systems of higher education; thus, the public universities were no longer mandated to design programs and options to eliminate segregation. The *Ayers* case is continuous, so Adams and other HBCUs are still trying to ensure they maintain their status as comprehensive universities with equitable conditions in financing, facilities, and resources, while maintaining their ethos as Black institutions and simultaneously addressing the multiple needs of diverse populations and metropolitan matters.

Continuing to upgrade professional preparation often means the elimination of the undergraduate education major, as was the case in the state where Chapel University is situated. Incorporating substantive preparation into academic disciplines for elementary and secondary majors is another option. While upgrading the academic content of the program as required by external accrediting bodies and state legislators is central, the incorporation of multicultural curriculum and related matters is an overwhelming priority of the institutions. Multiculturalism is a priority that may or may not be fully appreciated by regional and state accrediting bodies, yet national accrediting bodies regularly include multicultural requirements as part of their accreditation. In essence, tensions or contradictions may exist or emerge between macrolevel policies of the national level with intermediate policies of regional or state bodies. This tension is sometimes further exacerbated because intermediate-level policies are to be the linkages between macro- and microlevel entities. Charting the balance between the two levels is necessitated in microlevel institutional policies because HBCUs are responsive to the macro- and intermediate-level policies.

While the aforementioned policy matters were often referred to, only one of the respondents seemed to comprehend and articulate the multiple dimensions of the equations. In identifying emerging policy issues, for example, one dean stated that while some national, state, and regional bodies are advocating and sponsoring more nontraditional routes for entry into the teaching profession, often these nontraditional approaches are less rigorous than the current traditional approaches, which have been severely criticized by external macrolevel policy agencies. Yet these same agencies advocate nontraditional approaches. Another emerging policy concern encompasses the infusion of significant funds into the sciences and technological fields at the postsecondary level, including Chapel University. Yet, the quality of instruction in primary and secondary education in the sciences often does not appear adequate due to insufficient funding. According to this respondent, where the nation will invest its funds is the fundamental question. Certainly, the continuous movement in some quarters to privatize school services and provide vouchers for students to attend magnet public or private schools could be seen as a chief feature of funding policies.

Components of Professional Preparation

While the literature (Clinchy, 1991; Dilworth, 1992; Garibaldi, 1989; Mirel, 1994; Strike, 1993; Tyack and Tobin, 1994; Vinovskis, 1996) and professional education associations advocate various dimensions of primary and secondary school reform, the real challenge is to ascertain how this becomes operationalized microlevel policies that become operant in programs of preparation. At the four HBCUs, several common program configurations emerged. One feature involved the placement of preservice teachers and some in-service teachers in what was termed reforming environment (i.e., sites where teachers and administrators were involved in, or trying to engage in, reform of school practices). Critical to this reform are the proactive responses to changing social conditions, multicultural student bodies, and various styles of teaching and learning. Other features included sites with shared governance, school-university partnerships, HBCUs agency partnerships, and corporate school partnerships. Original's mission regarding school reform involves mobilizing the new teacher to be responsive to multicultural issues in the coming century. Its mission includes (1) enabling students to understand the relationship between the State Department and the underfunded (i.e., inferior inner-city education) and to recognize that these issues are not "just a Black thing," since the Latino population is rapidly increasing; and (2) addressing the need for more teaching modules from a multicultural perspective. In short, sharing and coopera-tion characterize reforming environments. At this time, however, many of the HBCUs indicate that systematic evaluations are not in place to ascertain the success of their endeavors in reforming the environment in urban milieux.

Since leadership and service are emphasized in the missions and goals of the four HBCUs, it seemed important to discern if students have actually engaged in direct community activities. For the most part, the education administrators interviewed consistently stated that students have volunteered in boys' and girls' clubs, Young Men's Christian Association (YMCA), mental retardation centers, church and community tutorials, and hospital settings, including work with AIDS patients. Such volunteer activities could be incorporated into their portfolio, demonstrating a range of professional competencies. As part of some of the formal preservice clinical experiences and often in the in-service preparation, community service activities have occurred. However, in many instances they have not appeared to be any more extensive than some of the volunteer activities. At Bridge College, service requirements are being built into the overall baccalaureate degree requirement, ensuring that students begin service activities that will continue throughout their lives, part of the rationale for Bridge's service requirement.

All respondents stated that addressing social inequities that educators encounter in schools and classrooms is critical to their programs. Whether within student teaching seminars, early clinical experiences, evaluation and assessment courses, or other formal courses, uniform themes included issues pertaining to diversity, minority students' socioeconomic background, dialects, language usage, and the like. Special historical concern focusing on young Black males has been a continuing area of consideration concurrent with different and increased manifestation of violence as evolving policy and programmatic matters. One site also included the future educator's self-esteem as part of that complicated solution, explaining that they need to be "better" than other teachers and give time to allow the students to cope with their own possible feelings of inferiority. When asked how these concerns were unique at HBCUs, all respondents indicated that the constant addressing of these problems in concrete, institutionalized fashions distinguished them from various PWIs, where rhetoric was often the reality.

The infusion of technology into the curriculum and related education preparation components was viewed as an area requiring additional fiscal and physical resources by all four universities. The inability to prepare educators for a range of technological uses in their educational environments causes a lag between what primary and secondary students are often accustomed to (frequently via extracurricular settings) and what professional educators are able to deliver. Both funding and professional development for those who prepare education personnel would be needed to lessen the lag.

FUTURE POLICY IMPLICATIONS

I have discussed succinct explications and analyses of the historical and contemporary roles of American HBCUs via their mission statements and degree offerings to a vast percentage of African Americans. In addressing their missions and purposes, the interplay between macro- (including international and national dimensions), intermediate, and microlevel policies was a paramount concern. While policy issues will continue to dominate the persistent character of HBCUs, it will be helpful to elucidate some evolving and future policy issues. Selected salient illustrations encompass the following.

As current demographic patterns continue, how will HBCUs, especially those in urban areas, assume proactive positions regarding the roles of groups other than African Americans? If African Americans no longer remain the dominant "minority" group, how will they and HBCUs effectively interact with other people of color? For instance, as revealed in this chapter, by the year 2000, the Latino population will increase, thus making them the largest minority group in the United States. This population, however, contains multiple ethnic and racial groups within its configuration, such as Puerto Ricans, Chicanos, Cubans, Mexicans, Colombians,

Costa Ricans, Salvadorians, Peruvians, and others (Gimenez, 1993). This demands a complex view of multiculturalism and global communities.

In a civic meeting convened at Chapel University among various demographic groups of the city, one European American voiced his concerns. He asserted, "I feel very uncomfortable as a white person in this city. . . . I will be a minority in a few years; and that makes me uncomfortable. How will I be treated?" Perhaps the voicing of this realization will help European Americans begin to work in genuine fashion to achieve humanistic understandings and cooperative relations among all people. This reality may help contribute to an underlying basis of understanding forming between people of color and others. Colleges of education will need to reassess their philosophical statements regarding multiculturalism to address this changing phenomenon, as well as redesign their curricula to meet these changing demands within school environments.

Since many current immigrants to the United States arrive from developing nations, what does this portend for the curriculum and structure of HBCUs, which have often focused on people of color who have resided in America for decades or even centuries? Multiculturalism has new dimensions even for HBCUs. Depending on the geographical locations of HBCUs, recent immigrants will provide a natural field setting for preservice and in-service teacher education programs, since Vietnamese, Chicanos, Haitians, African Americans, and European Americans are in the same classrooms and schools. Colleges will need to address these community changes through implementation of varied research, new policy, and curriculum changes focused on how schools, teaching, and learning will be influenced.

Ensuring that mutations on affirmative actions and educational equity do not adversely impact HBCUs and the preparation of educators is critical so that such institutions and programs do not cease to exist. In advocating educational equity, the equity should be ensured via policies that are fair to all colleges and universities. In short, there should not be a disproportionate impact on HBCUs, as some policies and plans have pronounced. Through the placement of graduate and professional programs in education policy, research on these issues can be carried out. These programs can be magnets for research and policy recommendations.

Finally, HBCUs, like other American institutions, will have to ascertain continually their roles in international matters, whether exchanging professional personnel or students, establishing cooperative linkages, or engaging in cross-national research to contribute to both national and international development. Mutually interactive relations on generic and cross-national concerns establish the foundation, while democracy embracing diversity acts as the fuel of the movement (McGinn, 1996, p. 355).

Properly blending policies at the macro-, intermediate, and microlevels so that we can envision paradigms that do not exist can embody potential benefits for all. "The great experiment . . . is to learn how to use all kinds of education to build a society that honors all people and where all work together in the pursuit of the good of all" (McGinn, 1996, p. 357). These new ideals and pursuits in education will lead to a redefinition of the roles of HBCUs based on globalization and new forms of democracy.

NOTES

This chapter is a revised version of a keynote plenary international address presented at the Annual Conference of the New South Wales Teacher Education Council in Sydney, New South Wales, Australia, in June 1996. The research and travel were sponsored, in part, via the Public Australian Universities Senior Professor Grant for International University Research and Development. The author also expresses appreciation to her doctoral assistants, Michael Cross and Monica deMello Patterson for their research assistance.

1. In order to protect the anonymity of the interviewees, I have used the fictitious names of Chapel University, Adams University, Bridge College, and Original University throughout the body of this chapter in citations where quotations were taken from the strategic plans, mission statements, or college catalogs of these institutions. These sources of valuable information have not been included in the list of references due to this ethical research issue.

REFERENCES

Adams v. Ayers v. Fordice, 111 F.3d 1183 (5th Cir. 1997).

Bond, S. L. (1996). The experience of feminine leadership in the academy. In M. L. Kearney & A. H. Ronnig (Eds.), *Women and the university curriculum: Toward equality, democracy, and peace.* (p.p. 35–52). London and Paris: Jessica Kingsley and UNESCO.

Brown v. Board of Education, 347 U.S. 483, 74 S.Ct. 686, 98 L.Ed.2d 873 (1954).

Bruno, R. R., & Curry, A. (1996). *School Enrollment: Social and economic characteristics of students: October 1994.* Washington, DC: U.S. Bureau of the Census. Current Population Reports. U.S. Government Printing Office, P20/487.

Clinchy, E. (1991). America 2000: Reform, revolution, or just more smoke and mirrors? *Phi Delta Kappon, 73*(3), 210–218.

Dilworth, M. E. (1992). *Diversity in teacher education: New expectations.* San Francisco: Jossey-Bass.

Garibaldi, A. M. (1989). *The revitalization of teacher education programs at historically Black colleges: Four case studies.* Atlanta: Southern Education Foundation.

Gimenez, M. E. (1993). Latinos/Hispanics . . . what next! Some reflections on the politics of identity in the U.S. *Heresies: A Feminist Publication on Art and Politics, 7*(3/27), 38–42.

Kearney, M. L. (1996). Women, higher education, and development. In M. L. Kearney & A. H. Ronnig (Eds.), *Women and the university curriculum: Toward equality, democracy, and peace.* (pp. 1–33). London and Paris: Jessica Kingsley and UNESCO.

Klein, S. S. (1987). *The role of public policy in the education of girls and women.* Paper presented at the annual conference of the American Educational Research Association, Washington, DC.

Lewis, L. S., & Altbach, P. G. (1996). Faculty versus administration: A universal problem. *Higher Education Policy, 9*(3), 255–258.

Lindsay, B. (1989). Integrating international education and public diplomacy: Creative partnerships or ingenious propaganda? *Comparative Education Review, 33*(4), 423–436.

Lindsay, B. (1994). Legislation and minority rights in higher education: American and Kenyan case studies. In W. Tulasiewicz & G. Strowbridge (Eds.), *Education and the law: International perspectives* (pp. 3–28). New York: Routledge.

Lindsay, B. (in press). Review of the state and the school: An international perspective. In J. D. Turner (Ed.), *Comparative education.*

Lindsay, B., & Ginsburg, M. B. (1995). Transforming teacher education, schooling, and society: Lessons learned and political commitments. In M. B. Ginsburg, & B. Lindsay (Eds.), *The political dimension in teacher education: Comparative perspectives on policy formation, socialization and society* (pp. 265–276). Washington, DC: The Falmer Press.

Lindsay, B., & Harris J. J., III. (1977). Progressive education and the Black college. *The Journal of Black Studies, 7*(2), 341–357.

McGinn, N. F. (1996). Education, democratization, and globalization: A challenge for comparative education. *Comparative Education Review, 40*(4), 341–357.

Mirel, J. (1994). School reform unplugged: The Bensonville new American school project. *American Educational Research Journal, 31*(3), 481–518.

National Center for Education Statistics (1994). *Findings from the condition of education 1994: The educational progress of Black students.* Wasington, DC: U.S. Department of Education, Office of Educational Research and Improvement, NCES 95–765.

National Center for Education Statistics. (1995a). *Digest of education statistics 1995.* Washington, DC: U.S. Department of Education, Office of Educational Research and Improvement, NCES 95–029.

National Center for Education Statistics. (1995b). *Statistics in brief: Overview of public elementary and secondary schools and districts: School year 1993–1994.* Washington, DC: U.S. Department of Education, Office of Educational Research and Improvement, NCES 95–799.

National Council for Accreditation of Teacher Education. (1995). *Standards, procedures, and policies for the accreditation of professional education units.* Washington, DC: National Council for Accreditation of Teacher Education.

Strike, K. A. (1993). Professionalism, democracy, and discursive communities: Normative reflections on restructuring. *American Educational Research Journal, 30*(2), 255–275.

Tyack, D., & Tobin, W. (1994). The "grammar" of schooling: Why has it been so hard to change? *American Educational Research Journal, 31*(3), 453–479.

U.S. Department of Education. (1983). *A nation at risk: The imperative for educational reform.* Washington DC: U.S. Government Printing Office.

Vinovskis, M. A. (1996). An analysis of the concept and uses of systemic educational reform. *American Educational Research Journal, 33*(1), 53–85.

Concluding Thoughts

Kassie Freeman

Researchers and policymakers alike will acknowledge that different paradigms are needed for research and policy making as they relate to African Americans' participation in higher education. After more than 30 years since the passing of the Civil Rights Act and 50 years since *Brown v. Board of Education* (347 U.S. 483, 74 S.Ct. 686, 98 L.Ed. 873 [1954]), African Americans' participation in higher education is nowhere near what it could or should be, particularly with the increased needs for higher skill levels. Persistent problems such as poor retention of African American students and faculty in higher education institutions are still far too commonplace. One important beginning would be having more African American researchers and scholars involved in research and policymaking related to the African American culture.

As the chapters in this book point out, African American researchers can bring a perspective unlike that of others. A prevalent theme throughout these chapters is that, while African Americans hold varying views, most share common frames of reference.

Someone once asked me, "Are you saying non-African Americans cannot or should not research African Americans?" That is not what I am saying, nor is any author of this book. However, individuals who research groups outside their own must provide a cultural context to their writing—these researchers must have an understanding of the other cultures as a whole system: the history, language, frame of reference, and customs. This cannot be done by merely coresearching with an African American, having African Americans as friends, or having one or two interview sessions with an African American individual or group. As Winbush and Alexander-Snow, among others, suggest, it means understanding the history of the African American people even before the beginning of slavery.

This book just touches the surface of pressing higher education research issues related to African Americans. Certainly, many more issues could be considered.

While we in higher education are still addressing twentieth-century problems as they relate to African Americans, we are now faced with twenty-first century dilemmas. Examples of issues that bear greater understanding include a better articulation between K-12 and higher education that is inclusive of an appreciation of an African American historical perspective, which writers like Jerome Morris at the University of Georgia and Carter Savage at Vanderbilt University are researching; dilemmas that threaten the survival of HBCUs; gender and gender orientation topics among African Americans in the higher education pipeline; African Americans' transition from higher education to work and workplace differences, such as salary and upward mobility differentials; as well as African American participation in the global dialogue at HBCUs and PWIs as it relates to African descendants everywhere.

As the policy writers in this book indicate, logically and intuitively, an African American cultural context has to be included in researching and developing policies that will affect the outcomes of the lives of African Americans. Otherwise, higher education researchers and policymakers are likely to look back another 50 years from now and wonder why the theories and programs they developed are inappropriate or ineffective. The answer then will be as it is today—missing cultural context.

Index

academic self-concept, 37-40; and
  empowerment, 37-38; and
  faculty support, 38; and
  measurement of, 35-36; and
  peer support, 38-39
Achebe, Chinua, and storytelling, 1
activism, over time, 135
administrative positions, and
  African American faculty, 137
affirmative action, 51-53;
  challenges to, 52-53; history
  of, 52
African American culture: current,
  29-31; and group connectedness, 34-35; and HBCUs,
  144; and public policy, 168.
  See also African culture
African American education,
  history of, 34
African American faculty: need
  for, 133-42; at Yale, 140-41
African American self-concept;
  and group identity, 34, 35; and
  HBCUs, 36-37; independent
  vs. communal, 35; and racial
  identity, 36; and students,
  34-41. *See also* academic self-
  concept
African American students:
  diversity among, 93-115; at

HBCUs, 81; at PWIs, 80-81;
  as self-segregating, 124-25
African culture: current,
  29-31; preslavery, 23-25;
  slavery experience, 25-29. *See
  also* African American culture
African philosophy, defined, 30-31
African value system: group
  identity, 25; one with nature,
  23-24, 28; religion, 23-24, 28;
  vs. European value system,
  26-27
Afrocentricity, *vs.* Eurocentricity,
  15-16
Afrocentric psychology, 19
Afrocentric research, 15-16,
  19-21; history of, 19; and
  natural science, 20
Akbar, N., on Afrocentric
  psychology, 19
Allen, W.: racial attitudes study,
  64-73; on self-segregation, 126
An American Dilemma, as
  negrocentric research, 18-19
aspiration/participation gap, and
  college choice, 181, 187-90
assessment of higher education,
  173-79
Astin, A.: conceptual framework
  for student learning, 76; on
  self-concept, 36

Atlanta University, and cultural
    capital, 149
attainment levels, for African
    Americans, 48
attendance. *See* participation in
    higher education

Banks, J.: on research perspective,
    2; on self-concept, 36
Banta, T. et al., and evaluation of
    higher education, 174
Barak, R., and evaluation of higher
    education, 174
Barnett, M., on Black
    organizations, 126
*Beating the Odds: How the Poor
    Get to College,* 185
The Bell Curve, as racist, 17, 19
Bennet, L., on storytelling, 29
Bernard, H., on teachers, 198
Billingsley, A., and college choice,
    185
Black church, influence of, 68, 70
Black community, 110-13
*Black Consciousness, Identity and
    Achievement,* 113
Black faculty, need for, 133-42
Black identity, 95, 107-10
Black organizations: on campus,
    94, 106-7; participation in,
    125; on PWIs, 114-15
Black racial identity models, 114
Black Rage, as negrocentric
    research, 19
Black Self-Concept, 36
Black separatism, and self-
    segregation, 124-27
Black students. *See* African
    American students
Board of Education, Brown v., 48,
    51, 62, 128, 209, 223
Boone, E., on public policy, 164
Bourdieu, P., on cultural capital,
    75, 148
Bronfenbrenner, U.: ecological
    model of development, 199; on
    teachers, 196
Brown, I., on culture, 2

Brown v. Board of Education, 48,
    51, 62, 128, 209, 223
Burgard, S., and evaluation of
    higher education, 176

Carnoy, M., participation in higher
    education, 181
channeling, and college choice,
    183, 184-85, 188-189
Chapman, D.: on channeling
    students, 189; and college
    aspirations, 187
Chicago schools, as urban example,
    201
child development: ecological
    model, 199-200; of urban
    youth, 196-97
*The Chronicle of Higher
    Education,* 130
Cicourel, A. et al., and college
    choice, 183
civil rights: effect on HBCUs, 49;
    and mass protests, 52; and
    participation in higher
    education, 10
Civil Rights Act of 1964: and
    HBCUs, 49; and segregation,
    122
civil rights legislation, 44
Civil War, African American
    education during, 145
class differences, and racial
    attitudes, 72
Coleman, J.: on social capital, 183;
    on urban youth, 202
collective commitment, defined,
    62-63. *See also* racial attitudes
collective memory, and self-
    segregation, 125-27
college access: and college
    preparatory courses, 45-46;
    and K-12 teachers, 45; and test
    scores, 46
The College-Bred Negro, 146
The College-Bred Negro American,
    146
college choice, 181-92; aspirations
    vs. participation, 181, 187-90

college preparation courses, and college choice, 45-46, 188-89

Comer, J., on urban youth, 202

community, Black, 110-13

community-based programming, and public policy, 164

compensatory and remediation model, and HBCUs, 147

connoisseurship evaluation, and higher education, 175

Cooley, C., on isolation, 198

The Crisis of the Negro Intellectual, 133

Cruse, H., on African American faculty, 134-35, 141

cultural capital: and college choice, 182-84; defined, 75; HBCUs as, 148-50; Scholastic Aptitude Test (SAT) as, 79

cultural preservation, and self-segregation, 126

culture: African, 23-29; African American, 29-31, 34-35, 144, 168; as context, 1-4; defined, 2, 23; and environment, 27; institutional, 173-74, 176-79

Dalin, P., on urban youth, 202

dance, ring: as African culture, 28-29; as religious metaphor, 24

Davies, D., on participation in higher education, 195

Davis, R., on HBCUs, 81

decision-based evaluation, and higher education, 175

Delpit, L., on urban youth, 202

desegregation: cases, 10; defined, 122; of K-12, 51

Deutsch, M., on urban youth, 196

development of education policy, 158-59

DiMaggio, P. et al., on cultural capital, 183

diversity: and evaluation of higher education, 173; and teacher preparation, 200

dominance, White, 60, 123-24

Dryfoos, J.: on participation in higher education, 195-96; on urban youth, 202

Drylongso: A Self-Portrait of Black America, on minority education, 60-61

D'Souza, D., on racism, 17

DuBois, W.E.B.: early studies, 146; on HBCUs, 50; on minority education, 61

Duster, T., on self-segregation, 130

ecological model, and child development, 199-200

econometric model, and college choice, 184-85

economic conditions. *See* financial issues

education, degree in, 209-10

educational models, for urban youth, 201-2

empowerment, and academic self-concept, 37-38

The End of Racism, as racist, 17, 19

enrollment: African American in higher education, 162t. *See also* participation in higher education

environment: and culture, 27; and public policy, 165-66; and student learning, 79-80, 81-83; of urban youth, 196-98

environmental support model, and HBCUs, 148

equality: defined, 123; history of, 44

Erikson, E., on self-concept, 38

Eurocentricity, *vs.* Afrocentricity, 15-16

European value system, and slavery, 26

evaluation models, 175

evaluation of higher education, 173-79

evaluation of policy, 160-61, 169

Even the Rat Was White, as racist book, 20

exchange programs, and student
learning, 89
extended family, and college
choice, 186

faculty, postsecondary: and
academic self-concept, 38;
African American, 133-42; and
college choice, 188-89;
student evaluation of, 87-88;
and student learning, 84
Faded Dreams, 181
family: and college choice, 185-86;
parent education levels, 79, 89,
184; and urban youth, 197-99
Feagin, J. et al., on self-
segregation, 126
Ferguson, Plessy v., and equality,
44, 49-50, 145
financial aid, and college choice,
190
financial capital, and college
choice, 184-85
financial issues: and attainment
levels, 48; and college choice,
184, 186; and participation in
higher education, 9; and racial
attitudes, 68-70, 69t, 71; and
student learning, 78; wages,
147
Fleming, J., student evaluation of
faculty, 87-88
Frederick D. Patterson Research
Institute, 46-47, 53 n.2
future earning potential, and
college choice, 184

Garbarino, J., on child
development, 199-200
geometry, for college preparation,
46
Gilligan, C., on women, 34-35
goal-based evaluation, and higher
education, 175
graduate school attendance, and
HBCUs, 147
graduation rates for African
Americans, 48

group identity: and African
American culture, 34-35; and
African American self-concept,
34, 35; and African value
system, 25
groupthink, and self-segregation,
128
Gurin, P. et al.: on Black identity,
113; racial attitudes study,
62-65, 66t-67t
Gwaltney, J., on minority
education, 60-61

HBCUs (historically Black colleges
and universities): African
American students at, 47, 62,
81, 143-44; characteristics of,
150-51, 207, 209; civil rights
affect on, 49; as cultural
capital, 148-50; and culture,
144; and effectiveness, 147-48;
history of, 8, 49, 144-46, 207;
as multicultural, 220; policy
and preparation study, 211-18;
and public funding, 49-51;
racial attitudes, 63-64; role of,
8-9, 146-48; and self-concept,
36-37; student profile, 9; *vs.*
PWIs, student learning, 77-88
Hernstein, R. et al., on racism, 17
history, K-12 teaching of, 46-47
Holloway, J.: on ring dance, 28; on
slave occupations, 27-28, 28t
Holmes Group, and teachers of
future, 210
Hopwood v. State of Texas, 123
Hossler, D. et al., and college
choice, 183
Hudson Institute Workforce 2000
Report, 181
Hurtado, S., on self-segregation,
123
Hurtado, S. et al., on self-
segregation, 124-25, 127

identity, Black, 107-10
impact types, and spectrum
analysis, 178

implementation of policy, 159–60
institutional culture, and evaluation
    of higher education, 173–74,
    176–79
integration: defined, 123; in higher
    education, 124; at PWIs,
    128–30
isolation, and urban youth, 197–98

Jackson, Jesse, and public policy,
    167

K-12 education: and cultural
    capital, 183; desegregation, 51;
    and participation in higher
    education, 11, 188–89;
    teaching of history, 46–47
King, Dr. Martin Luther: on public
    policy, 161; on segregation,
    128
kinship: on plantation, 29; and
    survival of tribe, 25
Kochman, T., on cultural
    preservation, 126, 127, 130
Kohl, H., on urban youth, 202
K-12 teachers: and college access,
    45; and college choice, 188–89;
    and preparation, 200–201, 218,
    219; and student expections,
    196; and urban youth, 195–96,
    198, 200–202
Kuhn, T., on scientific advances,
    15

Lareau, A., on urban youth, 196
Latino population: as minority,
    210–11; and minority policy,
    219
leadership, in public policy,
    166–67
learning, study of student, 75–90
Lee, S. et al., on cultural capital,
    149
Lefkowitz, M., on Afrocentricity,
    15
legislation: civil rights, 44; civil
    rights challenges, 52–53

Lerner, R., on child development,
    196–97
Levin, H., on urban youth, 202
Levine, A. et al.: on college choice,
    185; on education models, 191;
    on financial aid, 190
Lewis, L. et al., on public policy,
    209
Lincoln, Abraham, on equality, 44
Lindsay, B.: HBCUs policy and
    preparation study, 211–18; on
    public policy, 208

MacKay, K. et al., on student
    learning, 79
Madhere, S., on self-concept, 36
Maltz, E., on civil rights, 44
Marcus, J., on segregation, 123
marriage rates, and HBCUs, 147
Mbiti, J., on African philosophy,
    30–31
McEwen, M. et al., on racial
    identity, 108, 114
McLaurin v. Oklahoma State
    Regents for Higher Education,
    122
media strategy, and African
    American faculty, 138–39
Mickelson, R.: and college
    aspirations, 187; and college
    choice, 188–89
minority students (general),
    210–11, 219–20
The Mis-Education of the Negro,
    and HBCUs, 50
Montgomery bus boycott, 121–22
Morrill Act of 1890, 145–46
Morris, J., on future issues, 224
Morrison, L., on channeling
    students, 189
mother, role of, and college choice,
    186
multicultural perspective, 210–11,
    218–20

A Nation at Risk: The Imperative
    for Education, 201, 210

National Assessment of
   Educational Progress (NAEP),
   on test scores, 46
National Center for Education
   Statistics (NCES), 45, 47-48,
   53 n.1
National Commission on
   Excellence in Education,
   200-201, 210
national organizations, and African
   American faculty, 139
National Post Secondary Aid
   Study, 1990, and HBCUs, 147
naturalistic or participant
   evaluation, and higher
   education, 175
nature, in African value system,
   23-24, 28
Negrocentricity, 18-19
Nettles, M.: on financial aid, 190;
   on institutional climate, 177
Nobles W.: on African philosophy,
   30-31; on self-concept, 40

occupational preference, for slaves,
   27-28, 28t
Ogbu, J.: on African American
   culture, 2, 192, 197; and
   college choice, 188-89; on
   minority education, 60
Oklahoma State Regents for
   Higher Education, McLaurin
   v., 122
Orfield, G.: and college choice,
   184; on financial aid, 190

Pace, C., conceptual framework for
   student learning, 76
Page, C., on integration, 128
parent education levels, and student
   learning, 79, 89
parent income, and college choice,
   184
Parham, T. et al., racial identity
   attitude test, 108
Parks, Rosa, 121
participation in higher education,
   7-13, 47-48; and aspiration,
181; current status, 10-11; and
   decline of civil rights, 10; and
   desegregation cases, 10;
   enrollment levels, 7, 162t;
   financial issues, 9; and
   HBCUs, 47; history of, 7-10,
   47; infant mortality, 10; and K-
   12 education, 11; and life
   expectancy, 10; and poverty,
   10; and unemployment, 10.
   See also college choice
peer group: and academic self-
   concept, 38-39; and self-
   segregation, 126-27
performance funding, and
   evaluation of higher education,
   174
Person, D., on Black organizations,
   125
Pitts, J., on racial attitudes, 63
Plessy v. Ferguson, 44, 49-50, 145
policy, defined, 157
policy process, the, 157-61
politics, and racism, 44-45
Powell, G., on self-concept, 37
preslavery African culture, 23-25
priority setting, and evaluation of
   higher education, 174
program evaluation in higher
   education, 173-79
public funding, and HBCUs, 49-51
public policy: and college choice,
   191-92; decision making,
   161-70; and future, 219-20;
   multi-level analysis, 208-9; and
   student gains, 89
PWIs (predominantly White
   institutions): African American
   students at, 9-10, 62, 65,
   80-81; and black organizations,
   114-15; and integration, 126,
   128-30; negative effects of, 62;
   racial attitudes, 62-65; self-
   segregation in, 124-25; vs.
   HBCUs, student learning,
   77-88

race consciousness, defined, 62.
    See also racial attitudes
racial attitudes, 59‑73; and campus
    race, 68‑70, 69t; class
    differences, 72; financial
    issues, 68‑70, 69t, 71;
    measurement tool, 72‑73;
    research on, 63‑64; sex
    differences, 65‑68, 66t‑67t,
    68‑70, 69t; time trends,
    66t‑67t, 71
racial attitudes study: by Allen, W.,
    65‑73; by Gurin, P. et al.,
    63‑65, 66t‑67t
racial identity: and African
    American self-concept, 36;
    attitude test, 108
racialized space, and self-
    segregation, 126‑27
racism: in academy, 16‑17;
    institutional, 44‑45; as
    political, 44‑45
Reagan/Bush administration, 10
Reconstruction period, and African
    American education, 145‑46
recruitment dimension, and
    spectrum analysis, 177
Reed, A., on Negrocentricity, 18
religion, and African value system,
    23‑24, 28
research: of higher education, 3‑4;
    by non-African Americans, 2‑3
research, Afrocentric, 15‑16,
    19‑21
responsive-based evaluation, and
    higher education, 175
retention selection dimension, and
    spectrum analysis, 177
Rooney, G., on Black
    organizations, 94
Roueche, J. et al., on public policy,
    163
Rutter, M., on stress, 198

Savage, C., on future issues, 224
Schenrich, J. et al., on racism,
    16‑17

scholar/activist, African American
    faculty as, 133‑34, 140‑42
Scholastic Aptitude Test (SAT), as
    cultural capital, 79
science, and Afrocentric research,
    20‑21
secondary school. *See* K-12
    education; K-12 teachers: and
    college choice, 188‑89
segregation: defined, 122; de facto
    defined, 122‑23; de jure defined,
    122; White flight as, 127
selection dimension, and spectrum
    analysis, 177
self-concept. *See* academic self-
    concept; African American self-
    concept
self-esteem, and teacher
    preparation, 219
self-segregation, 121‑30; by
    African American students,
    124; and black separatism,
    124‑27; in PWIs, 124‑25
Senegambians, as field workers, 27
sex differences, and racial
    attitudes, 65‑68, 66t‑67t,
    68‑70, 69t
shared responsibility model, and
    public policy, 164‑66, 170
slavery: economics of, 26‑27;
    history of, 25‑26; impact on
    African culture, 25‑29;
    occupations, 27‑28, 28t
slave ships, 26
social capital. *See* cultural capital
Soul on Ice, as negrocentric
    research, 19
spectrum analysis, and evaluation
    of higher education, 176‑79
Spencer, M.: on teachers, 200; on
    urban youth, 202
Spiker, C., on diversity, 200
St. John, E.: and college
    aspirations, 187; on financial
    aid, 190
State of Texas, Hopwood v., 123
storytelling, and African culture, 29
stress, and urban youth, 197‑98

Stroddart, T., on teachers, 196
Stuckey, S., on ring dance, 24
student learning: conceptual
    framework, 76-77; HBCUs *vs.*
    PWIs, 77-88
student organizations, and African
    American faculty, 138
survival of the tribe, 25-26; as
    African culture, 25, 28; on
    plantation, 29

teacher. *See* faculty, postsecondary;
    K-12 teachers
technology, and teacher
    preparation, 219
tenure, and African American
    faculty, 136
Terman, L., as racist psychologist,
    20
territorial imperative, and self-
    segregation, 126
test scores: and college access, 46;
    NAEP history, 46; NAEP
    math, 46
Thomas, G.: on channeling
    students, 189; on college
    choice, 187
transformational leaders, and
    policy formation, 163
tribe, survival of, 25-26, 28-29
The Truly Disadvantaged, 201

urban youth: and educational
    models, 201-2; and
    environment, 196-200; and
    teacher preparation, 200-201

volunteer activities, as teacher
    preparation, 218

wages, and HBCUs, 147
Watkins, W., on racism, 44-45
Watson, L. et al., student learning
    study, 75-90
White, L.: on Black organizations,
    125; Black student diversity
    study, 93-115
White flight, and segregation, 127
White students, as self-segregating,
    124-25
White supremacy, in higher
    education, 17-18
Williams, J., on HBCUs, 51
Willie, C. et al., on Black
    separatism, 126
Wilson, K. et al.: on channeling
    students, 189; and college
    choice, 185
Wilson, R., and evaluation of
    higher education, 174
Wilson, W., on Chicago schools,
    201
Wolofs, as house servants, 27
Woodson, C.: on HBCUs, 51;
    importance of culture, 1-2; on
    minority education, 61
Worthen, B. et al., and evaluation
    of higher education, 175
Wright, B., on victim analysis, 17

Yale, and African American
    faculty, 140-41

About the Editor and Contributors

KASSIE FREEMAN is Assistant Professor of Higher Education in the Department of Educational Leadership at Peabody College of Vanderbilt University. Her research interests include cultural considerations related to African Americans and college choice and comparative/international issues related to higher education and the labor market. Her research publications have appeared in such journals as *The Journal of Higher Education* and the *Journal of Education Policy*. She is currently writing a book entitled *African Americans and College Choice*. She has twice been the recipient of the Pro Renovanda Cultura Hungariae Foundation Award to be a visiting professor and scholar at the Budapest University of Economic Sciences, and she was the recipient of a Spencer Postdoctoral Fellowship. She currently serves on the Board of Directors of the Comparative and International Education Society and on the President's Board of Advisors on Historically Black Colleges and Universities (HBCUs) and chairs the Publications Committee of the Association for the Study of Higher Education.

MIA D. ALEXANDER-SNOW is presently in the Department of Educational Leadership at Peabody College of Vanderbilt University. She was selected as the Vanderbilt University Department of Education Leadership representative to participate in the Graduate Student Policy Seminar, Division J, of the American Educational Research Association. She has spent several years teaching at independent schools, including the Harpeth Hall School and Cushing Academy. Her research focuses on independent/boarding school students' transition to, and retention in, higher education.

WALTER R. ALLEN is currently Professor of Sociology at the University of California–Los Angeles. His research and teaching focus on family patterns, socialization and personality development, race and ethnic relations, African American males, health inequality, and higher education. His more than 50 publications appear in such publications as the *Harvard Educational Review, Journal of Negro Education,* and *Research in Higher Education.* He has coedited numerous books, including *College in Black and White: African American Students in Predominantly White and in Historically Black Public Universities.* He has received innumerous awards for his research, including Distinguished Scholar Award, American Educational Research Association (1987, 1993) and Distinguished Career Award, Association of Black Sociologists (1995).

SYBRIL M. BENNETT is presently in the Department of Educational Leadership at Peabody College of Vanderbilt University. Her research interests include the experiences of Black students on predominantly White campuses and Black student identity development, culture, intergroup relations, and academic persistence. She was selected as departmental representative to participate in the Graduate Student Policy Seminar of the Association for the Study of higher Education, on the Black Caucus of the American Association of Higher Education's Graduate Student Panel, and in the Summer Research/Teaching Fellowship Program at Washington State University in Pullman, Washington.

JAMES EARL DAVIS is Associate Professor in the Department of Educational Studies at the University of Delaware. His main fields of research interest are the sociology of higher education, race and gender issues in education, and evaluation research. His most recent publications are on evaluating multicultural curriculum in higher education and school contextual influences on the experience of Black males in college.

WILLIAM B. HARVEY is Dean of the School of Education at the University of Wisconsin–Milwaukee. He has held faculty and administrative appointments at North Carolina State University, the State University of New York at Stony Brook, the University of Pennsylvania, Richard Stockton College, Earlham College, and Brookdale Community College. His research and scholarly activity has focused on the cultural and social factors that affect African American populations, with particular emphasis on college and university settings. He is coauthor of *Affirmative Rhetoric, Negative Action,* and coeditor of *New Directions for Community Colleges: Recruiting and Retaining Minority Faculty.* He has also published in a variety of journals and popular publications, including the *Journal of Negro Education,* the *Journal of Black Studies,* and *Education and Urban Society.* He is a member of the Editorial Board of the Review of Higher Education and the Negro Education Review and a consulting editor for *Change: The Magazine for Higher Learning.*

TAMELA M. HEATH is Associate Dean for Institional Research at Trinity College in Washington, D.C. She was previously a research associate at the Higher

Education Research Institute and the Center for the Study of Evaluation at the University of California–Los Angeles. Her research interests include psychosocial development as well as research methods for studying minority students.

BRUCE ANTHONY JONES is Associate Professor and Director of the Center for Educational Policy Analysis at the University of Missouri–Columbia. His primary areas of research and teaching are evaluation and policy analysis in elementary, secondary, and higher education. His secondary research focus is cross-cultural and institutional collaboration. He is coauthor of *Investing in U.S. Schools: Directions for Educational Policy* and has recently published "School-Community Based Collaboratives: Differentiating between Different Types" in *Educational Research Quarterly*. In addition to the National Association of Partners in Education, he serves on the Board of Directors of Family Services America, Inc.

WYNETTA Y. LEE is the Assistant Director for Evaluation with the ACCLAIM project and is Assistant Professor in the Department of Community College Education at North Carolina State University. In addition to 10 years of experience in program assessment/evaluation, she has extensive experience in program development and implementation in both higher education and nonprofit organizations. Her research interests include the impact of higher education policy and programs on special student populations (minorities, transfer students, women, and nontraditional students).

BEVERLY LINDSAY is Dean of International Programs and Professor of higher Education and Education Policy Studies at Pennsylvania State University, where she addresses all university-wide academic, research, and public service international matters for the university system. Her research, focusing on public and educational policies in cross-national settings, planning, and social issues, has been presented at national conferences and via invited addresses in Europe, Australia, Africa, South America, and the Caribbean. Her work appears in over 60 articles, chapters, and essays in academic publications and in her three books (*The Political Dimension in Teacher Education*, with Mark B. Ginsburg; *African Migration and National Development*; and *Comparative Perspectives of Third World Women*). She is listed in various editions of *Who's Who* in the United States and in Great Britain.

CAROLYN J. THOMPSON is Assistant Professor in the Department of Educational Organization, Administration and Policy at the State University of New York at Buffalo. Previously she worked on state-level policy reform issues at the Education Commission of the States. She has been a secondary school teacher and Director of the Youth Leadership Training Program at Charles Drew Medical School. Her research interests include the socialization of African Americans in and through higher education institutions and attempts to identify and understand their resilience. Aspects of her research focus on college student leadership and development, African-American faculty stress and satisfaction, and higher education policy issues. She is a member of the SUNY Press Editorial Board and the Advisory Board of the ASHE-ERIC Higher Education Reports.

LEMUEL W. WATSON is Assistant Professor of Higher Education and Student Affairs in the Department of Educational Administration and Foundations at Illinois State University.

LORI S. WHITE is Assistant Vice Provost for Education and Director of Undergraduate Advising at Stanford University, as well as a Lecturer in the Stanford School of Education. Her research interests focus on the experiences and identity development of Black students in higher education. She previously served as the Director of the Cross Cultural Center at the University of California–Irvine and the Director of Student Programs at Georgetown University. Additionally, her work in higher education has included serving as a consultant to the California State Legislature's Committee on Higher Education and as a Special Assistant to the University of California, Office of the President. She is currently editing a book on the role of higher education in school reform.

CLANCIE M. WILSON is presently in the Developmental and Educational Psychology Department at Boston College. Her research interests include the impact of social support and parental involvement on inner-city youths' achievement, the effects of direct and indirect support groups on parent satisfaction, and inner-city youths' achievement. In her over 20 years of experience as a public school teacher, she received a grant to develop strategies for dealing with high-risk children, was selected to participate in the school district's leadership and mentoring programs, and participated in a diversity workshop for prospective teachers at University of Colorado in Colorado Springs. Her teaching experiences include teaching in West Africa as a Peace Corps volunteer.

REGINALD WILSON is currently Senior Scholar of the American Council on Education, in Washington, D.C. He originally joined the council as its Director of the Office of Minority Concerns. Previously, he was President of Wayne County Community College, in Detroit. He has coauthored and edited writings on the issues of the urban community, civil liberties, and racial equality in higher education. Among his many publications, he is coauthor of *Minorities in Higher Education, Race and Equity in Higher Education,* and *Human Development in the Urban Community*. He is author of *Civil Liberties and the U.S.* He serves on the editorial board of *The American Journal of Education, The Urban Review,* and *About Campus*. He received the Anthony Wayne Award, the Distinguished Service Medal from the City of Detroit, and the Harold Delaney Exemplary Leadership Award from the American Association of Higher Education. The American Council on Education's *Annual Status Report on Minorities in Higher Education,* which he began in 1982 and currently coauthors, is widely cited as the authority on the position of underrepresented groups in higher education.

RAYMOND A. WINBUSH is the Benjamin Lawson Hooks Professor of Social Justice at Fisk University and Director of the University's Race Relations Institute. He is the former Assistant Provost and Director of the Johnson Black Cultural Center at Vanderbilt University. His research interests include infusing African American studies into school curricula, African American adolescent development, Black male and female relationships, and the influence of hip-hop on contemporary African American Culture. He is a specialist in Afrocentric education. He is currently authoring a book entitled *Cinque's Children: Raising Healthy Black Men in a Racist Society*. His consultations are numerous, including the National Research Council and the Ford Foundation. He is a member of the Executive Board of the National Council for Black Studies.

ISBN 0-275-95844-2

EAN

9 780275 958442

HARDCOVER BAR CODE